THE EARLIEST SEMITIC PANTHEON

THE EARLIEST SEMITIC PANTHEON

A Study of the Semitic Deities Attested in Mesopotamia before Ur III

By

J. J. M. Roberts

THE JOHNS HOPKINS UNIVERSITY PRESS
Baltimore and London

Manufactured in the United States of America

The Johns Hopkins University Press, Baltimore, Maryland 21218
The Johns Hopkins University Press, Ltd., London

Library of Congress Catalog Card Number 70-186515
ISBN 0-8018-1388-3

To

Genie,

Kay, Amy, Susan,

and now Nathan

PREFACE

The present study is a thoroughly revised and much expanded form of the writer's dissertation which was written under Professor Thorkild Jacobsen's direction and submitted to Harvard University in 1969 in partial fulfillment of the requirements for the degree of Doctor of Philosophy. Like most books originating as dissertations, it owes much to the dissertation director. The writer's indebtedness to Professor Jacobsen, however, is far more than ordinary. Without his interest, his stimulating suggestions, and his helpful criticism the book could never have been written. For his kindness, patience, and, above all, his friendship, the writer is deeply grateful.

The writer is also indebted to his other teachers at Harvard for their help and encouragement. He would especially like to thank Professor William L. Moran, who read an earlier draft of the study and made numerous suggestions and corrections, and Professor Frank M. Cross, both for his specific suggestions on the West Semitic material and for his more general interest in the work and its author.

Obviously the book is also dependent on the work of many other scholars as will be evident from the text. One should specifically mention I. J. Gelb, however, for without his pioneering work on Old Akkadian grammar and lexicography such a study as this would have been unthinkable. The author's debt to him should be obvious on almost every page.

The writer is also deeply grateful to Professor Hans Goedicke for his persistent encouragement and to the Near Eastern Department of the Johns Hopkins University, which provided a generous stipend to prepare the manuscript for publication. Finally, a special note of thanks goes to Mrs. Joy Pankoff, who performed the unenviable task of typing the final manuscript.

Baltimore

J. J. M. Roberts

TABLE OF CONTENTS

ABBREVIATIONS

The abbreviations used in this work follow those given in R. Borger, Handbuch der Keilschriftliteratur I (Berlin: Walter de Gruyter & Co., 1967), pp. 661-672, with the following additions or exceptions:

ABRT — James A. Craig, Assyrian and Babylonian Religious Texts, AB XIII/2 (2 vols., Leipzig: J. C. Hinrichs, 1895-1897).

ADS — Sabatino Moscati (ed.), Le antiche divinità semitiche, Studi Semitici I (Rome: Centro di Studi Semitici, 1958).

AHw — Wolfram von Soden, Akkadisches Handwörterbuch, unter Benutzung des lexikalischen Nachlasses von Bruno Meissner (1868-1947) (Wiesbaden: Otto Harrassowitz, 1959-).

AMT — R. C. Thompson, Assyrian Medical Texts From the Originals in the British Museum (London: Oxford University Press, 1923).

ANG — J. J. Stamm, Die akkadische Namengebung, MVAG XLIV (Leipzig: J. C. Hinrich, 1939).

APNMT — H. B. Huffmon, Amorite Personal Names in the Mari Texts: A Structural and Lexical Study (Baltimore: The Johns Hopkins Press, 1965).

AT — T. G. Pinches, The Amherst Tablets Part I: Texts of the Period Extending to and Including the Reign of Bûr-Sin (London, 1908).

Atra-ḫasīs — W. G. Lambert and A. R. Millard, Atra-ḫasīs: The Babylonian Story of the Flood (Oxford: Clarendon Press, 1969).

AUP — Giorgio Buccellati, The Amorites of the Ur III Period (Naples: Instituto Orientale di Napoli, 1966).

BANE — G. E. Wright (ed.), The Bible and the Ancient Near East: Essays in Honor of William Foxwell Albright (Garden City: Doubleday & Co., 1961).

BBR	H. Zimmern, *Beiträge zur Kenntnis der babylonischen Religion*, AB XII (Leipzig: J. C. Hinrich, 1896-1901).
BDB	F. Brown, S. R. Driver, and C. A. Briggs, *A Hebrew and English Lexicon of the Old Testament* (Oxford: Clarendon Press, [1953]).
Bezold Cat.	Karl Bezold, *Catalogue of the Cuneiform Tablets in the Kouyunjik Collection* (5 vols., London: British Museum, 1889-1899).
BK	Martin Noth (ed.), *Biblischer Kommentar Altes Testament* (Neukirchen: Neukirchener Verlag, 1961-).
BMS	L. W. King, *Babylonian Magic and Sorcery* (London: Luzac & Co., 1896).
BWL	W. G. Lambert, *Babylonian Wisdom Literature* (Oxford: Clarendon Press, 1960).
CH	E. Bergmann, Codex Hammurabi, *textus primigenius*, Scripta Pontificii Instituti Biblici (Rome: Pontificium Institutum Biblicum, 1953[3]).
Coll. de Clerq	M. de Clercq, *Collection de Clercq par De Clercq avec la collaboration de J. Menant* (7 vols., Paris: E. Leroux, 1888-1911).
CST	Thomas Fish, *Catalogue of Sumerian Tablets in the John Rylands Library* (Manchester: John Rylands Library, 1932).
CTC	Thorkild Jacobsen, *Cuneiform Texts in the National Museum, Copenhagen* (Leiden: Brill, 1939).
De Sarzec DC	Ernest de Sarzec et al., *Découvertes en Chaldée* (2 vols., Paris: E. Leroux, 1884-1912).
DN	Divine name
DP	F.-M. Allotte de la Fuÿe, *Documents présargoniques* (3 vols., Paris: P. Leroux, 1908-1920).
Dream Book	A. L. Oppenheim, *The Interpretation of Dreams in the Ancient Near East With a Translation of an Assyrian Dream-Book*, Transactions of the American Philosophical Society NS XLVI/3 (Philadelphia: The American Philosophical Society, 1956).

EBPN	Hermann Ranke, Early Babylonian Personal Names, BE Res. III (Philadelphia: University of Pennsylvania, 1905).
EDSA	C. J. Gadd, The Early Dynasties of Sumer and Akkad (London: Luzac & Co., 1921).
EK	S. Langdon et al., Excavations at Kish (3 vols., Paris: Libraire Orientaliste Paul Geuthner, 1924-1934).
En.el.	W. G. Lambert and Simon B. Parker, Enuma Eliš: The Babylonian Epic of Creation, The Cuneiform Text (Oxford: Clarendon Press, 1966).
Finet L'Accadien	André Finet, L'Accadien des lettres de Mari, Académie royale de Belgique, classe des lettres et des sciences morales et politiques, Mémoires (Brussels: Palais des Académies, 1956).
FM	I. J. Gelb, Old Akkadian Inscriptions in Chicago Natural History Museum, Fieldiana: Anthropology XLIV/2 (Chicago: Chicago Natural History Museum, 1955).
GAG	W. von Soden, Grundriss der akkadischen Grammatik, AnOr 33 (Rome: Pontificium Institutum Biblicum, 1952).
Gelb, "Lingua"	I. J. Gelb, "La lingua degli Amoriti," Atti della Academia Nazionale dei Lincei, Rendiconti della Classe de Scienze morali, storiche e filologiche, Serie 8, Vol. XIII (1958), 143-164.
GVGSS	Carl Brockelmann, Grundriss der vergleichenden Grammatik der semitischen Sprachen (2 vols., Berlin: Reuther, 1908-1913).
Heb.	Hebrew
HEI	George C. Cameron, History of Early Iran (Chicago: University of Chicago Press, 1936).
HSAO	D. O. Edzard (ed.), Heidelberger Studien zum Alten Orient, Adam Falkenstein zum 17. September 1966 (Wiesbaden: Otto Harrassowitz, 1967).
HWB	Friedrich Delitzsch, Assyrisches Handwörterbuch (Leipzig: J. C. Hinrichs, 1896).

IDAG	J.-R. Kupper, L'iconographie du dieu Amurru dan la glyptique de la Ire dynastie babylonienne, Académie royale de Belgique, classe des lettres et des sciences morales et politiques, Mémoires LV/1 (Brussels: Palais des Academies, 1961).
IPN	Martin Noth, Die israelitischen Personennamen im Rahmen der gemeinsemitischen Namengebung (Stuttgart: Kohlhammer, 1928).
KAI	H. Donner and W. Röllig, Kanaanäische und Aramäische Inschriften mit einem Betrag von O. Rössler (3 vols., Wiesbaden: Otto Harrassowitz, 1962-1964).
KAR	Erich Ebeling, Keilschrifttexte aus Assur religiösen Inhalts, WVDOG XXVIII, XXXIV (2 vols., Leipzig: J. C. Hinrich, 1919-1923).
KAV	O. Schroeder, Keilschrifttexte aus Assur verschiedenen Inhalts, WVDOG XXXV (Leipzig: J. C. Hinrich, 1920).
Kich	H. de Genouillac, Premières recherches archéologiques à Kich (2 vols., Paris: Librairie ancienne Édouard Champion, 1925).
LNPSS	G. Ryckmans, Les noms propres sud-semitiques (3 vols., Louvain: Bureaux du Muséon, 1934).
MAD 4	I. J. Gelb, Sargonic Texts in the Louvre Museum, Materials for the Assyrian Dictionary No. 4 (Chicago: University of Chicago Press, 1970).
MAD 5	I. J. Gelb, Sargonic Texts in the Ashmolean Museum, Oxford, Materials for the Assyrian Dictionary No. 5 (Chicago: University of Chicago Press, 1970).
MAS	A. Ungnad, Materialien zur altakkadischen Sprache bis zum Ende der Ur-Dynastie, MVAG XX/2 (Leipzig: J. C. Hinrichs, 1916).
Min.	Minaean
MO	Maništušu Obelisk in Vincent Scheil, MDP II (Paris: E. Leroux, 1900), plates 1-10.
MSP	Jacques de Morgan, Mission scientifique en Perse (5 vols., Paris: E. Leroux, 1894-1905).

Nab.	Nabataean
Nik., Dok.	Michail V. Nikolsky, *Dokumenty chozjajstvennoj otčetnosti drevnej Chaldei iz sobranija N. P. Lichačeva* (2 vols., Moscow, 1908-1915).
NTSŠ	Ramon R. Jestin, *Nouvelles tablettes sumériennes de Šuruppak au Musée d'Istanbul*, Bibliotheque archéologique et historique de l'Institut français d'archéologie de d'Istanbul (Paris: A. Maisonneuve, 1957).
Orient.	Orientalia
PB	Anton Deimel, *Pantheon Babylonicum: Nomine deorum e textibus cuneiformibus excerpta et ordine alphabetico distributa* (Rome: Sumtibus Pontificii Instituti Biblici, 1914).
PD	Ernst F. Weidner, *Politische Dokumente aus Kleinasien: Die Staatsverträge in akkadischer Sprache aus dem Archiv von Boghazkoi*, BoSt VIII-IX (Leipzig: J. C. Hinrichs, 1923).
Phoen.	Phoenician
PNC	Ferris J. Stephens, *Personal Names from Cuneiform Inscriptions of Cappadocia*, YOS Res. XIII/1 (New Haven: Yale University Press, 1937).
PRU	*Palais royal d'Ugarit*, MRS (several vols., Paris, Imprimerie Nationale).
Pu.	Punic
Qat.	Qatabanian
REA	G. Wissowa (ed.), *Paulys Real-Encyclopädie der classischen Altertumswissenschaft* II (Stuttgart: J. B. Metzlerscher Verlag, 1896).
RTC	François Thureau-Dangin, *Recueil de tablettes chaldéennes* (Paris: E. Leroux, 1903).
Sab.	Sabaean
Saf.	Safaitic

SAHG	Adam Falkenstein and W. von Soden, *Sumerische und akkadische Hymnen und Gebete*, Die Bibliothek der Alten Welt (Zürich: Artemis-Verlag, 1953).
SAKI	François Thureau-Dangin, *Die sumerischen und akkadischen Konigsinschriften*, VAB I (Leipzig: J. C. Hinrichs, 1907).
SCWA	William H. Ward, *The Seal Cylinders of Western Asia* (Washington: Carnegie Institution of Washington, 1910).
SF	Anton Deimel, *Schultexte aus Fara, in Umschrift herausgegeben und bearbeitet*, WVDOG XLIII (Leipzig: J. C. Hinrichs, 1923).
SKL	Thorkild Jacobsen, *The Sumerian King List*, AS XI (Chicago: University of Chicago Press, 1939).
SLT	Edward Chiera, *Sumerian Lexical Texts from the Temple School of Nippur*, OIP XI (Chicago: University of Chicago Press, 1929).
SPAO	*Studies Presented to A. Leo Oppenheim, June 7, 1964* (Chicago: University of Chicago Press, 1964).
STT	O. R. Gurney et al., *The Sultantepe Tablets*, Occasional Publications of the British Institute of Archaeology at Ankara III, VII (2 vols., London: British Institute of Archaeology at Ankara, 1957-1964).
Šurpu	Erica Reiner, *Šurpu: A Collection of Sumerian and Akkadian Incantations*, AfO Beih. XI (Graz: E. Weidners Selbstverlag, 1958).
Tākultu	Rintje Frankena, *Tākultu: De sacrale maaltijd in het assyrische ritueel met een overzicht over de in Assur vereerde goden* (Leiden: E. J. Brill, 1954).
Tallqvist, Götter-epitheta	Knut L. Tallqvist, *Akkadische Götterepitheta, mit einem Gotter-verzeichnis und einer Liste der prädikativen Elemente der sumerischen Götternamen*, StOr VII (Helsinki: Societas Orientalis Fennica, 1938).
Tammuz	Thorkild Jacobsen, *Toward the Image of Tammuz and Other Essays*

on Mesopotamian History and Culture, edited by William L. Moran (Cambridge: Harvard University Press, 1970).

TCS — A. Leo Oppenheim (ed.), Texts from Cuneiform Sources (several vols., Locust Valley, N.Y.: J. J. Augustin, 1966-).

TDP — René Labat, Traité akkadien de diagnostics et pronostics médicaux (Leiden: E. J. Brill, 1951).

TH — A. W. Sjoberg and E. Bergmann, The Collection of the Sumerian Temple Hymns, TCS III (Locust Valley, N.Y.: J. J. Augustin, 1969).

TSA — H. de Genouillac, Tablettes sumériennes archaïques: Matériaux pour servir à l'histoire de la société sumérienne, publiées avec introduction, traduction et tables (Paris: P. Geuthner, 1909).

TSŠ — Raymon R. Jestin, Tablettes sumériennes de Šuruppak conservées au Musée de Stamboul, Mémoires de l'Institut français d'archéologie de Stamboul III (Paris, 1937).

TuL — Erich Ebeling, Tod und Leben nach den Vorstellungen der Babylonier, I: Texte (Berlin: Walter de Gruyter & Co., 1931).

Ug. — Ugaritic

UT — Cyrus H. Gordon, Ugaritic Textbook, AnOr XXXVIII (Rome: Pontificium Institutum Biblicum, 1965).

WF — Anton Deimel, Wirtschaftstexte aus Fara, in Umschrift herausgegeben und bearbeitet, WVDOG XLV (Leipzig: J. C. Hinrichs, 1924).

WM — H. W. Haussig (ed.), Wörterbuch der Mythologie I (Stuttgart, [1962]).

ZZB — D. O. Edzard, Die "zweite Zwischenzeit" Babyloniens (Wiesbaden: Otto Harrassowitz, 1957).

CHAPTER I

THE PROBLEM

The comparative, historical study of Semitic religions has suffered from a debilitating handicap since the introduction of the history of religions approach in the last century.[1] One has not been able to make full use of the oldest available evidence, the cuneiform material from Mesopotamia, because of the thorough interpenetration of Sumerian and Semitic elements in "Mesopotamian" religion.[2] There is a great need, then, for a study, or a series of studies, that will unravel this apparently seamless garment; that will decompose "Mesopotamian" religion into its component elements, and so make them available for analysis in isolation from one another. Such a task will not be easy, but it is essential if Semitists ever hope to produce an adequate treatment of the history of Semitic religion.

Recently Jean Bottéro has suggested an approach to the problem which holds some promise of at least partial success.[3] In his view a thorough diachronic study of the Semitic deities of Mesopotamia could provide a way of untying the syncretistic knot and so of clarifying the whole history of the Semitic religions and civilizations.[4] Because of the danger of historical distortion implicit in any diachronic study, however, it is advisable to begin the project with synchronic studies of the Semitic deities attested in each of the major periods of Mesopotamian history. The present study is dedicated to one aspect of this preliminary task. It will provide an annotated list of the Semitic deities worshipped in Mesopotamia during the period extending from the time of the earliest written sources through the so-called Gutian period.[5]

Even this preliminary task, however, is fraught with problems, stemming mainly from the character of the source material. Our knowledge of the Semitic deities of this period is derived almost exclusively from the Semitic theophoric names scattered through the early Old Akkadian and Sumerian documents.[6] This poses three very serious problems for the investigator: (1) How can one be sure that a personal name does in fact contain as its theophoric element a proper divine name? (2) How can one be sure that the proper divine name is Semitic rather than Sumerian, or even something else? (3) How can one say anything about the character of a deity from the rather meager and obviously stereotyped contents of the theophoric personal names?

Since the Old Semitic personal names sometimes use epithets as substitutes for proper divine names and often employ hypocoristic endings, which in some cases approximate certain divine names, one must beware of overpopulating the Old Semitic divine world with non-existent deities. To avoid this danger one must critically evaluate any element suspected of being a proper name. One can be absolutely sure that the suspected element is a proper divine name only if it occurs as an independent divine name elsewhere in the same period in an unambiguous context, e.g., in a curse formula. Obviously this is not often the case, or there would be no problem. One must usually settle for a similar occurrence in a later period. This is still good evidence, but it leaves open the possibility that one is dealing with an original epithet which only became an independent deity in the later period. In many cases, however, even this evidence is not available. Then one is thrown back on syntactical considerations. Two major principles come into play here: (1) If the suspected element consistently occurs in the syntactical positions occupied in other personal names by known deities,[7] one has good grounds for thinking that the element is a proper divine name. (2) If, on the other hand, the suspected element sometimes occurs in personal names as an epithet for a known deity, it is unlikely that it would appear in a different name as a proper divine name.[8]

After one has established with some degree of certainty that an element is in fact a divine name, he must then face the far more delicate issue whether it is a Semitic divine name. To prove that the deity is originally Semitic one should ideally be able to demonstrate a clear Semitic etymology for the name.

Where this is not possible, one may point to the occurrence of the same divine name in other Semitic languages as strong evidence for a Semitic origin. Of course the strength of this argument is dependent on the number of other Semitic languages in which the name occurs and their lack of proximity to the Mesopotamian sphere of influence. If the name only occurs in one other Semitic language and in an area subject to strong Mesopotamian influence, it may represent no more than secondary borrowing of the name from Akkadian.[9] One may also conclude that a deity is Semitic if its name consistently occurs in Akkadian sources while consistently absent from Sumerian sources.[10] This does not prove that the divine name is Semitic in origin, however. It leaves open the possibility that the Semites at a period anterior to our sources borrowed the name and perhaps the deity as well from the Sumerians or some other non-Semitic linguistic group. One should also note the helpful criterion provided by the normal Old Akkadian orthographic practice of omitting the determinative before Akkadian divine names when these are spelled syllabically.

Unfortunately, even when one has managed to isolate the Semitic deities occurring in the Old Semitic names, one is able to say very little about their character on the basis of these names alone. One can sometimes get a glimpse of elements of their original nature from the etymology of their names, and one can see certain aspects of the way in which they were regarded by their devotees by the verbal and nominal elements used with their names in the formation of theophoric personal names. Even in the best of cases, however, one recovers but a mere skeleton of the original deity and perhaps a highly deformed one at that. In some cases one must settle for these dry bones, for the historian of religion has not yet learned to reconstruct extinct gods as proficiently as the vertebrate paleontologist recreates extinct animals. Most of the Old Semitic deities do not die out until long after the Gutian period, however, and in these cases the later development of the deity can throw light on its earlier character. Of course there is always the danger that this use of the later tradition may anachronistically attribute late traits to the earlier form of the deity, for the gods like the men who worship them do undergo historical change. Nevertheless, there must be some continuity in the nature of the deity between its earlier and later phases, or it would hardly have maintained the identity implied by the continuity of the name. Thus while one must be cautious and sensitive to the dangers involved in such a process, he is still justified in using the later tradition to breathe some life into the dead bones of the Old Semitic deities.

The task of providing an annotated list of the Semitic deities worshipped in Mesopotamia before Ur III is not the sole purpose of this study, however. It will also attempt to put the list in proper perspective by examining the other theophoric elements in the Old Semitic names and Old Akkadian inscriptional material. In this way one may hope to gain some idea of the non-Semitic influences already at work during the Old Akkadian period which has made it difficult to distinguish between Sumerian and Semitic elements in Mesopotamian religion. After listing the divine names attested in the Old Semitic personal names,[11] the study will isolate and discuss the general character of the Semitic pantheon that can be drawn from those names, distinguishing as far as possible between Old Amorite and Old Akkadian elements. Then it will discuss the generic use of ilum in the personal names and the role of the personal god. Finally, it will conclude with a study of the imperial pantheon of the Sargonic dynasty and a discussion of the extent of Sumerian-Semitic syncretism in the pre-Ur III period.

Before turning to the divine names, however, one must consider a final preliminary question of a more technical nature. It is often difficult, if not impossible, to tell which of the elements in a nominal-sentence name is the subject and which is the predicate. But, since this distinction can sometimes be of crucial importance in deciding whether one is dealing with a proper divine name, it is methodologically important to establish the normal order in those names where the order can be controlled. For this purpose the Presargonic names will have to be omitted since one cannot be sure of the word order in them.[12] The Sargonic control names, moreover, must be divided into two groups for precise analysis.

A. In the first group are the nominal-sentence names which are composed of a noun and the stative:

1. Damiq/damqū

a. Damiq-ilum (SIG_5-i_3-lum; SIG_5-DINGIR)

b. Ilum-damiq (DINGIR-SIG_5)

c. Ilū-damqū (I_3-lu-dam-ku)

d. Su'en-damiq (^{d}EN.ZU-SIG_5)

2. Dān/dannat/dannū

a. Dān-ilī (Dan-i_3-li)

b. Dān-ma-LUM

c. Dān-Nūnu (Dan-Nu-nu)

d. Dān-Tibar (Dan-Ti-bar)

e. 'Ay(y)a-dān (E_2-a-dan)

f. Eštar-dān ($Eš_4$-dar-dan)

g. Eštar-dannat ($Eš_4$-dar-da-na-at)

h. Ilī-dān (I_3-li_2-dan)

i. Ilšu-dān (DINGIR-su-dan)

j. Ilum-dān (I_3-lum-dan; DINGIR-dan)

k. Ilū-dannū (I_3-lu-da-nu)

l. Su'en-dān (^{d}EN.ZU-dan)

3. Rabi/rabiat

a. Rabi-(i)lum (Ra-bi_2-(i_3)-lum; Ra-bi_2/GAL-DINGIR)

b. Ra-bi_2-PI-li-ir

c. 'Ay(y)a-rabi (E_2-a-ra-bi_2)

d. Eštar-rabi(at) ($Eš_4$-dar-ra-bi-at/GAL)

e. Ilšu-rabi (DINGIR-su-ra-bi_2)

f. Ilum-rabi (DINGIR-ra-bi_2)

g. Šamaš-rabi (^{d}UTU-ra-bi_2)

4. Ṭāb

a. Ṭāb-ilī (Tab-i$_3$-li$_2$)

b. 'Ay(y)a-ṭāb (E$_2$-a-DUG$_3$)

c. Ālī-ṭāb (A-li$_2$-DUG$_3$)

d. Ilšu-ṭāb (DINGIR-su-DUG$_3$)

e. Ilum-ṭāb (DINGIR-DUG$_3$)

5. Watar

a. Watar-ilī (Wa-dar-i$_3$-li)

b. 'Ay(y)a-watar (E$_2$-a-DIRIG)

c. Ilī-watar (I$_3$-li$_2$-DIRIG)

A careful study of this group of names shows that the stative can occur in either first or last position, with a slight preference for final position. One cannot relate the choice of word order to geographical areas, since it seems to be spread throughout the area covered by Old Akkadian. It is noteworthy, however, that the proper divine names normally appear in first position in these names.

B. In the second group are those names composed of two nouns, where one of the two is in the predicate state and thus must be considered the predicate:

1. Abum

a. Aba-ilum (A-ba-DINGIR)

b. Ilšu-aba (DINGIR-su-a-ba)

c. Ilum-aba (DINGIR-a-ba)

2. Aḫum

a. Ilšu-aḫa (DINGIR-su-a-ḫa)

b. Ilum-aḫa (DINGIR-a-ḫa)

3. Ammum

a. Amma-Su'en (A-ma-^{d}EN.ZU)

b. Ilum-amma (DINGIR-a-ma)

4. Bāni'um

a. 'Ay(y)a-bānī (E$_2$-a-ba-ni)

b. Ilī-bānī (I_3-li-ba-ni)

c. Ilum-bānī (DINGIR-ba-ni)

d. Su'en-bānī (^{d}EN.ZU-ba-ni)

5. Banûm

a. Ilum-banâ (DINGIR-ba-na)

6. Illatum

a. Eštar-illat ($Eš_4$-dar-il_3-la-at)

b. Ilī-illat (I_3-li_2-il-la-at)

c. Ilum-illat (DINGIR-il-la-at)

d. Šamaš-illat (^{d}UTU-il-la-at)

7. Kimtum

a. Ilum-kimat (DINGIR-gi-ma-at)

8. Lab'um

a. Laba-ilum (La-ba-DINGIR)

b. Eštar-laba ($Eš_4$-dar-la-ba)

c. Ilšu-laba (DINGIR-su-la-ba)

d. Ilum-laba (DINGIR-la-ba)

e. Inin-laba (I-nin-la-ba)

9. Lalā'um

a. Ilum-lalā (DINGIR-la-la)

10. Malkatum

a. Eštar-malkat ($Eš_4$-dar-ma-al-ga-at)

11. Mūda'um

a. 'Ay(y)a-mūda (E_2-a-mu-da)

b. Eštar-mūda ($Eš_4$-dar-mu-da)

c. Ilum-mūda (DINGIR-mu-da)

d. Su'en-mūda (^{d}EN.ZU-mu-da)

e. Šamaš-mūda (^{d}UTU-mu-da)

12. Nāṣirum

a. Ilum-nāṣir (DINGIR-na-zi-ir)

13. Qurādum

a. Ilum-qurād (I_3-lum-gur-ad)

14. Šarrum/šarratum

a. 'Ay(y)a-šar (E_2-a-sar)

b. Ilum-šar (I_3-lum/DINGIR-sar)

c. Mamma-šarrat (Ma-ma-sa-ra-at)

d. Su'en-šar (^{d}EN.ZU-sar)

15. Šūrum

a. Ilī-šūr (I_3-li_2-su-ur)

An examination of this group of names reveals that the noun which serves as the predicate is almost always put in final position. The only formally clear exceptions involve nouns ending in -a,[13] and even here the final position for the predicate predominates.

This analysis of the different types of nominal-sentence names indicates that the normal order in the Old Semitic names is subject + predicate. In the case of names where the predicate is a stative the order is relatively flexible, but, where it can be controlled, the order in a name composed of two nouns is fairly rigid.[14] Methodologically, therefore, one should expect this same rule to hold in the names where one cannot control the syntactical word order by morphological considerations. Nevertheless, one should beware of holding too rigidly to such formal rules. One must also pay attention to the criterion of meaning, for some names will not fit the mold and still make acceptable sense. E.g., according to the formal rule the name Dūr-il should be interpreted as predicating something about a certain wall or fortress, The-Wall/Fortress-Is-God/Divine(?), but such an interpretation is very awkward. In spite of the word order it is far more likely that the name intends to predicate something of the deity, Il-Is-A-Wall/Fortress.

[1]There were antecedents, of course, but the first serious, extensive application of this approach to Semitic religion began in the last century and found its most exhaustive early presentations in Wolf W. G. Baudissin's Studien zur semitischen Religionsgeschichte I-II (Leipzig, 1876-78), W. Robertson Smith's Lectures on the Religion of the Semites (New York, 1889), and M. J. Lagrange's Études sur les religions sémitiques (Paris, 1905).

[2]This led Smith to reject the Mesopotamian evidence as "the right point of departure for a general study of Semitic religion" (Religion of the Semites, p. 15) and while Lagrange roundly criticized Smith for neglecting the Mesopotamian material (Études, pp. ix, 66-67), he offers no real solution to the problem, partly because the knowledge of Sumerian was not advanced enough in his day for him to realize the full extent of the problem (ibid., pp. 55-56). More recent scholars have seen the problem more clearly, but they have not resolved it. For all practical purposes what Moortgat wrote in 1950 still stands: "An investigation which attempts to separate systematically the Sumerian and Akkadian elements in the religion of Mesopotamia still has not appeared." ("Geschichte Vorderasiens bis zum Hellenismus," in Ägypten und Vorderasien im Altertum, by Alexander Scharff and Anton Moortgat [Munich, 1950], p. 476).

[3]ADS, pp. 17-63.

[4]ADS, p. 63.

[5]Most of the Presargonic and Sargonic sources available for this study have been listed and briefly described by I. J. Gelb in the second edition of his grammar, MAD 2, but one must now add to his list T. Donald, "Old Akkadian Tablets in the Liverpool Museum," MCS 9/1 (1964), R. D. Biggs, "Semitic Names in the Fara Period," Orient. NS 36 (1967), pp. 55-66, A. Goetze, "Akkad Dynasty Inscriptions from Nippur," JAOS 88 (1968), pp. 54-59, and Gelb's two recent volumes, MAD 4-5.

[6]Gelb has included the vast majority of these names in his glossary of Old Akkadian, _MAD_ 3, but this should not obscure the fact that dialectical differences are discernible. Though a large majority of the names are undoubtedly Akkadian, enough West Semitic elements are present in the names to justify von Soden's attempt to distinguish between Old Amorite (the term Old Amorite is used in this study as a cover term for the dialect[s] represented by these West Semitic elements. Whether they may all be attributed to a single dialect or language, however, is a moot point) and Old Akkadian ("Zur Einteilung der semitischen Sprachen," _WZKM_ 56 [1960], pp. 177-191). For this reason this study will refer to the names en masse by the less prejudicial, if less specific, term Old Semitic.

[7]E.g., a proper divine name usually serves as the subject in a verbal-sentence name of the type Preterite + Subject and as the _nomen rectum_ in a genitive-construction name beginning with _Ur_-, _Šu_-, or _Puzur_-.

[8]Thus while the names _Itbe-laba_ and _Šu-labi_ (_MAD_ 3, p. 160) suggest that _laba_ be interpreted as a divine name, the occurrence of the same element as an epithet in _Eštar-laba_ (_MAD_ 3, p. 159) makes it more likely that one is dealing with a mere epithet which has occasionally replaced the proper divine name.

[9]E.g., the occurrence of Nikkal in Ugaritic proves only that Ugaritic or, more precisely, the speakers of Ugaritic assimilated a Sumerian deity because of strong Sumerian influence, not that Ningal was originally Semitic.

[10]One must check this argument against (1) the texts written in one language, (2) the bilinguals, and (3) the personal names. Only when there is a consistent distribution in each of these categories of texts can one really consider this argument decisive.

[11]In most cases the presence of clear Semitic elements in the syntactical construction of the Old Semitic personal names leaves no doubt about the classification of the names. In the case of names formed with such elements as _Puzur_ or _Ur_, which may be read as either Sumerian or Akkadian, the question is more difficult, and the method followed in this study has been to exclude such names

unless the theophoric element contained in them could be shown to be Semitic.

[12]Until the time of Eannatum of Lagash there was no rigid order for the writing of the signs. Some of the Presargonic names no doubt come from texts written after the introduction of this rigid order and thus could provide reliable evidence, but it seemed better to limit the investigation to those names where there could be no question about the order of writing.

[13]These nouns should perhaps be listed separately as examples of the predicate in -a for which Gelb has argued (MAD 2, pp. 146-153), but over against that one should note that the ending is restricted to words with less than three strong consonants apart from the single exception of the far from decisive ma-ḫi-ra.

[14]The difference in treatment may be explained by the need for clarity. When a stativ occurred in a nominal-sentence name, there was no difficulty in recognizing the predicate, but in names composed of two nouns a stricter word order was necessary to make the syntactical relation clear.

CHAPTER II

DIVINE NAMES ATTESTED IN THE OLD SEMITIC PERSONAL NAMES

Alphabetical List of Divine Names

1. *Ab(b)a*

Sargonic: *Ab(b)a-il* Ab(b)a-Is-God (*A-ba-DINGIR*, ITT, V, p. 39, 9450; *MDP* 14, 6, obv. 3), *Ab(b)a-kīn* Ab(b)a-Is-Faithful[1] (*A-ba-GI*, *HSS* X, several; *A-ba-GI$_4$*, *AT*, p. 15).[2]

The same orthography is also used in some names for the predicate state ending in -*a* of *abum*, "father," but in the names above it appears to be a proper divine name.[3] In the later period the writings *^{d}A-ba*, *A-ba*, *Ab(a)*, and *Ab-ba* are all attested, probably as simple orthographic variants for the same deity.[4] From the evidence collected by Gelb it would appear that Ab(b)a was feminine,[5] and while the etymology of the name is unknown, a late Old Babylonian seal inscription suggests that she was an Amorite deity.[6]

2. *Abiḫ*

Presargonic: *Abiḫ-il* Abiḫ-Is-God (*EN.TI-il*, *RA* 31, p. 143).

Sargonic: *EN.TI-ni-bi$_2$* (*ITT* II/2, 4362), *Ir'e-Abiḫ* Abiḫ-Shepherded (*Ir$_3$-e-^{d}EN.TI*, *HSS* X, 35:11), *Ur-Abiḫ* Man-Of-Abiḫ (*Ur-^{d}En.TI*, *PBS* 9, 9:7).

As Thureau-Dangin demonstrated, the ideogram *EN.TI* has the reading *A/Ebiḫ* as the name of a mountain,[7] the present day Hamrin range which stretches across Assyria into the Diyala region.[8] By analogy with the other deified place names in the Old Akkadian period,[9] it is probable that the god Abiḫ is merely the deified mountain,[10] and the Sumerian myth of Inanna and Abiḫ supports this interpretation.[11] The etymology of the name is unsure, but the West Semitic explanation suggested by Lewy, *(Y/W)āpiḫ*, "Blower," remains a possibility.[12]

3. *Ab/pra* (?)

Presargonic: *Ur-Ab/pra* Man-Of-Ab/pra (*Ur-Ab-ra*, *CT* 32, 7 iv).

Sargonic: *Ab/pra-il* Ab/pra-Is-God (*Ab-ra-il*, *MO* D 4:4; 5:4; *Ab-ra-il$_2$*,

TMH V, 1074), Ur-Ab/pra Man-Of-Ab/pra (Ur-Ab-ra, MO C 15:3; 18:6, 24).

The correct reading and derivation of Ab-ra is uncertain. Albright has discussed certain West Semitic names found in Egyptian texts which appear very similar to our Ab/pra-il,[13] but it is difficult to separate the first element in this name from the last element in Ur-Ab/pra, so neither of Albright's interpretations seems to explain Ab-ra. Perhaps it is a deified place name.[14]

4. (Adad)/Adda(?)/Ad(d)u/Anda

Presargonic: Il-Addu Addu-Is-God (DINGIR-Ad-du, WF, VAT 12511, 9:5--the reference in WF, p. 26, must be corrected; NTSŠ 276, obv.(?), 2:5).[15]

Sargonic: A-du-ba-na (BIN 8, 148:70; 152:75),[16] Ad(d)u-bānī Ad(d)u-Is-My-Creator (A-du-ba-ni, BIN 8, 95:2), Anda-išš-takal Trust-In-Anda (An-da-iš-da-gal, ITT II/2, p. 6, 2914), Addu/Anda-šar Addu/Anda-Is-King (^{d}IM-sar, MAD 5, 21:4; 36:2), Addu/Anda-šadu Addu/Anda-Is-A-Mountain ($^{\langle d \rangle}$IM-sa-tu, MAD 1, 163, iv 30), Ibbi-Anda Anda-Named[17] ([I]-bi$_{2}$-An-da, HSS X, 159, iii 10), Ibni-Addu/Anda Addu/Anda-Created (Ib-ni-^{d}IM, MDP 18, 33), Īṣi-Anda Anda-Went-Out (I-zi-An-da, HSS X, 169:7),[18] Meḫri-Addu/Anda Answer-Of-Addu/Anda(?)[19] (Me-eḫ-r[i$_{2}$-^{d}]IM, MAD 5, 68, iii 2), Pu-Addu/Anda Mouth-Of-Addu/Anda (Pu-$^{\langle d \rangle}$IM, MO B 3:13; Pu$_{3}$-An-da, HSS X, 29:24; 117:4), Puzur-Addu/Anda/Adda(?) Protection-Of-Addu/Anda/Adda(?) (PU$_{3}$.ŠA-^{d}IM, RTC 80, 11; MO D 12:6; PU$_{3}$.ŠA-An-da, CT 44, 48:23; PU$_{3}$.ŠA-Ad-da, HSS X, 145, iii 7; 154, v 12),[20] Rīs-Addu/Anda Joy-Of-Addu/Anda (Ri$_{2}$-is-^{d}IM, UET 1, 275 iii), Ša-Anda He(?)-Of-Anda (Ša-a-An-da, HSS X, 187, i 12),[21] Šu-Addu/Anda He-Of-Addu/Anda (Šu-^{d}IM, HSS X, 36, iii 1; MDP 14, 72 i).

Gelb read an-da as ^{d}DA,[22] but the dissimilation of -dd- to -nd- is well attested with the god Addu, at least in the West,[23] and it is hard to imagine the scribe using this orthography for any other Semitic god. A non-Semitic deity, moreover, would not be expected in such good Semitic name formations as DN-iš-takal, Ibbi-DN, and Īṣi-DN. It might be possible to interpret the ideogram ^{d}IM as standing for another Semitic storm god--a Sumerian reading is again unlikely in Semitic names--but Ad(d)u/Anda seems more probable. Adad is attested by syllabic spellings in Ur III,[24] but this vocalization is not attested and may not have been in use in the earlier period.

Addu/Anda also occurs in Ugaritic and Aramaic in the form *Haddu/Hadad*.[25] Etymologically the name is probably connected with Arabic *hadda*, "to break," *haddat*, "noise," and *hāddat*, "thunder."[26] He is only one of several Semitic storm gods attested in the Old Akkadian period.

5. *Admu*

Sargonic: *Šu-Admu* He-Of-Admu (*Šu-Ad-mu*, *MO* B 4:10).

Ad-mu could be read as Sumerian for *abī*, "my father," and the Ur III name *ᵈŠulgi-AD.MU* might support that reading,[27] but the name *Šu-abī* is otherwise unattested in the Sargonic period, and the later material from Mari leaves no doubt that there was a deity named Admu.[28] The nature of the deity, however, is disputed. Birot suggested that the name might refer to a "dieu-Enfant,"[29] since there is an Akkadian word *(w)atmu* = *māru*, "son."[30] Buccellati pointed to the Phoenician name *'dmy[tn]* and suggested Admu could be the deified form of Ugaritic *'adm*, "people," and Hebrew *'ādām*, "man."[31] The Ur III divine name *ᵈNin-admu*,[32] however, suggests that Admu may be a deified city name like Girsu in ᵈNin-girsu.[33] It may be identified with the city or village of this name attested as early as the Old Babylonian period near the northern rim of the great Mesopotamian plain.[34]

6. *Ay(y)a*

Presargonic: *Šumu-Ay(y)a* Name-Of-Ay(y)a (*Su-mu-ᵈA-a*, *DP* I, 2, i 13').[35]

Sargonic: *Puzur-Ay(y)a* Protection-Of-Ayya (*PU₃.ŠA-A-a*, *BIN* 8, 301:5; *RSO* 32, 87), *Šu-Ay(y)a* He-Of-Ay(y)a (*Šu-A-a*, *HSS* X, 71:3).[36]

The pronunciation of *A-a* is indicated, at least for the Old Babylonian period, by the variant writing *ᵈA-ya* in a context where there can be no doubt that *ᵈA-a* is meant.[37] Ay(y)a appears to be Akkadian since she occurs almost exclusively in Akkadian sources,[38] and her marriage relationship with Šamaš as well as her Sumerian equivalents make it probable that she was an astral deity.[39] The etymology of Ay(y)a, however, remains unsure.[40]

It is difficult to find an independent social character for Ay(y)a. Her most characteristic Akkadian epithets are *kallātum*, "bride,"[41] and *hīrtum*, "spouse," both of which express her relationship to Šamaš. Several of her names suggest a strong trace of sexuality,[42] but contrary to an earlier view,[43] the *nadītu*-women of Ay(y)a were not prostitutes, and her cloister was not a temple brothel.[44]

7. *Alim*

Sargonic: *Alim-ālī* Alim-Is-My-City (*A-lim-a-li*$_2$, *MAD* 1, 161, i 2; *MAD* 5, 67, ii 2),[45] *A-lim-ga-la* (*HSS* X, 187, iii 7), *A-lim-gu-ru-ud* (*MO* A 5:7).

A-lim in these names is probably to be interpreted as a title for Enlil, "bison."[46] The title came into Akkadian as a Sumerian loan word, and the Akkadians rendered it by the more general word *kabtum* or *šūpûm*, "of high rank, honored."[47]

8. *Ālum*

Presargonic: *Ālum-ṭāb* The-City-Is-Good (*A-lum-DUG*$_3$, *CT* 32, 7 iv), *Ālum-dūrum* The-City-Is-The-Wall (*A-lum-BAD*$_3$, *EK* IV, Pl. xlv, iv; *Orient*. NS 36, p. 64), *A-lum-BA* (*DP* 116, col. 6),[48] *Ālum-dān* The-City-Is-Strong (*A-lum-dan*, *DP* 116).

Sargonic: *Ālī-ṭāb* My-City-Is-Good (*A-li*$_2$*-DUG*$_3$, *MDP* 14, 72 iv), *Alšu-dād* His-City-Is-Beloved (*Al-su-da-ad*, *MDP* 14, 47 obv.),[49] *Qāssu-ālum* The-City-Is-His-Hand(?) (*Qa*$_2$*-su*$_2$*-a-lum*, *MO* A 5:4).

There are other names which possibly contain *ālum*, "city," as the theophoric element,[50] but these are the most sure, and even some of them may be questioned.[51] Enough remain to make it possible that *ālum* could be used as a theophoric element, but it is clear that *ālum* used in this way does not have the same status as a divine name like Erra. A proper divine name like Erra does not occur with a pronominal suffix as *ālum* does. Thus while *ālum* functions as a theophoric element, it does so on a secondary level.

9. *Amurru*

Sargonic: *Amurrûm* (*A-mur-ru-um*, *MAD* 5, 74:9; *A-mur-u[m]*, *MAD* 5, 103:2),[52] *Amurru-kīma-Il* Amurru-Is-Like-Il (*A-mur-ru-k[i?-m]a?-DINGIR*, *MAD* 5, 62:6),[53]

Ibri-Amurru Amurru-Inspected[54] (Ib-ri$_2$-^{d}MAR.TU, ZA 12, p. 336), Urrī-Amurru Amurru-Is-My-Light (Ur-ri$_2$-^{d}MAR.TU, ZA 12, p. 337).[55]

The character of the god Amurru is difficult to delineate sharply, because he appears to be a personification, not of a natural phenomenon, but of a social group--the Semitic nomads from the western steppe.[56] As such Amurru is probably a creation of the Babylonians and thus does not correspond to any specific West Semitic deity.[57] Even his storm god traits may derive from this background, for the Sumerian literature often compares the invasion of Semitic nomads to a storm.[58] As the god of these nomads, he was also associated with the steppe,[59] and since the steppe was thought of as the haunt of demons and other underworld types,[60] Amurru has some ties to the underworld.[61]

10. Annu(m)

Sargonic: Annu-bānīni Annu-Is-Our-Creator (An-nu-ba-ni-ni, MSP IV 161),[62] Anniš-tikal Trust-In-Annu (An-ni-iš-ti-gal, UET VIII/2, 14, iii 3), Šu-Annum He-Of-Annum (Šu-A-num, HSS X, 55:1; 209:3; Šu-A$_2$-nu-um, HSS X, 36, iii 8).[63]

Annu(m) is merely the Akkadianized version of An, the personified heaven and chief god of the Sumerian pantheon. This is clear from the Annu-bānīni inscription in which An-nu-um and An-tum occur in the curse formula yoked together as husband and wife.[64] The double-nn- in Annu(m) is suggested by the normal Old Babylonian orthography, which has the doubled -nn-,[65] and by the fact that Annu(m) can occur at the end of the line in Babylonian poetry where the next to the last syllable must be stressed and long.[66]

11. Apsû(m)

Sargonic: Ibbi-Apsû Apsû-Named (I-bi$_2$-Zu.AB, MO C 4:2), Ur-Apsû Man-Of-Apsû (Ur-ZU.AB, MO C 5:15).[67]

Apsû(m) is a Sumerian loan word in Akkadian.[68] It designates the fresh underground waters and is an old name for Enki.[69]

12. Ašar(?)

Sargonic: Ali-Ašar Where-Is-Ašar (A-li-A-sar, HSS X, 185, ii 6).[70]

Ašar occurs as a divine name in several Ur III personal names,[71] some

Akkadian names from Mari,[72] a few Amorite names,[73] and independently in a broken inscription from Ur.[74] It is possible, then, that Ašar in this Sargonic name is a divine name, but against this interpretation it must be noted that the name formation *Ali-DN* is otherwise unattested in the Old Semitic names.[75]

13. *Baba*

Sargonic: *Baba-elī* Baba-Is-My-God (*Ba-ba-e-li*$_2$, *MAD* 1, 41, rev. 2), *Baba-ilum* Baba-Is-The-God (*Ba-ba-DINGIR*, *HSS* X, 55:9; *Ba-ba-lum*, *MAD* 1, 243),[76] *Mut-Baba* Man-Of-Baba (*DAM-Ba-ba*, *MO* A 7:19; C 10:20),[77] *Šu-Baba* He-Of-Baba (*Šu-Ba-ba*, *RSO* 32, p. 91).

Ba-ba is probably to be taken as a variant orthography for the name of the Sumerian city goddess of Lagash which is normally written *^{d}Ba-ba*$_6$.[78] She is attested as early as the Fara period,[79] and was widely worshipped in the later periods.[80] Originally perhaps just a local mother goddess, Baba soon acquired the traits of a goddess of healing, and from the Old Babylonian period on she was identified with Gula-Nin'insina.[81]

14. *Balīḫ*

Sargonic: *Bēlī-Balīḫ* Balīḫ-Is-My-Lord (*Be-li*$_2$*-Ba-liḫ*$_3$, *MAD* 1, 317, iii 10; 324, ii 6), *Kurub-Balīḫ* Pray-To-Balīḫ (*Ku-ru-ub-Ba-liḫ*$_3$, *MAD* 3, p. 214), *Šumšu-Balīḫ* His-Name-Is-Balīḫ (*Šum-su-Ba-liḫ*$_3$, *RA* 9, p. 34, rev. ii 11).[82]

The element *ba-liḫ*$_3$*/luḫ* could be interpreted as the stative of *palāḫum*, "to fear," in the first and last names above: *Bēlī-paluḫ* My-Lord-Is-Awe-Inspiring, *Šumšu-paluḫ* His-Name-Is-Awe-Inspiring. This interpretation will not work in the second name, however, and all three names have parallels in which a proper divine name occupies the same position as *ba-liḫ*$_3$ does here.[83] It is probable, therefore, that one should interpret *ba-liḫ*$_3$ as a divine name and identify it with the river *Balīḫum*, located between the Ḫabur and the Euphrates.[84]

15. *Bītum*

Sargonic: *Paluḫ-Bītum* The-Temple-Is-Awe-Inspiring (*Ba-lu-uḫ*$_2$*-E*$_2$, *MDP* 14, 44; *Ba-luḫ-E*$_2$, *MDP* 14, 72 iv),[85] *Iddi(n)-Bītum* The-Temple-Gave (*I-ti-E*$_2$, *CT* 1, la),[86] Ur-Bītim Man-Of-The-Temple (Ur-E_2, MAD 3, p. 93).

Bītum in these names apparently means "temple," since none of the other meanings of bītum suits the predicate paluḫ, "awe-inspiring," as well. The names indicate that the temple was sometimes deified in the Old Akkadian period and thus could be used as a theophoric element just as in the later periods.[87]

16. D/Ṭaban

Sargonic: Pu-D/Ṭaban Word-Of-D/Ṭaban[88] (KA-Da-ba-an, MAD 1, 163, viii 40), [Ki]nnam-D/Ṭaban Establish-For-Me-O-D/Ṭaban ([Ki]-nam-Da-ba-an, MAD 1, 72 rev. 5).

D/Ṭaban is the name of a river lying south of the Diyala and probably to be identified with the modern Ab-i-Neft or Ab-i-Gangir.[89] It is also the name of a city,[90] but the parallel with Durul suggests that the theophoric element in these names is the deified river.[91]

17. Dagan

Sargonic: Dagan-ilšu Dagan-Is-His-God (Da-gan-DINGIR-su, RTC 127, rev. ii), Dagan-rē'īšu Dagan-Is-His-Shepherd (^{d}Da-gan-ri$_2$-i$_3$-su, MAD 1, several times), Iddi(n)-Dagan Dagan-Gave (I-ti-^{d}Da-gan, MO C 16:7; MAD 1, 335:8-11; 163, x 18-19; MAD 4, 16, rev. i 6), Ir'am-Dagan Dagan-Loved (Ir$_3$-am-^{d}Da-gan, MAD 1, 326, ii 8; Ir$_3$-ra-am-^{d}Da-gan, ITT II/2, p. 39, 4700), Ir'i-Dagan Dagan-Shepherded (Ir$_3$-ri$_2$-^{d}Da-gan, ZA 12, 334), Iškun-Dagan Dagan-Placed (Iš-ku-un-Da-gan, ITT I, 1167; Iš-ku-un-^{d}Da-gan, ITT I, 1316:2), Išma-Dagan Dagan-Heard (Iš-ma$_2$-^{d}Da-gan, Syria 21, p. 162), Īṣi-Dagan Dagan-Went-Out (I-zi-^{d}Da-gan, MDOG LIV, 23; cf. MAD 3, p. 70),[92] Man-balum-Dagan Who-Can-Be-Without-Dagan (Ma-an-ba-lum-^{d}Da-gan, Ma-ba-lum-^{d}Da-gan, MAD 3, p. 177), Pu-Dagan Mouth-Of-Dagan (Pu$_3$-^{d}Da-gan, MO A 5:8), Šu-Dagan He-Of-Dagan (Šu-^{d}Da-gan, MO A 11:15), Tūra-Dagan Return-To-Me-O-Dagan (Tu-ra-^{d}Da-gan, AFO 3, p. 112), Uwaššer-Dagan (?) Dagan-Released (U$_3$-a-še-er-Da-ga-an, ITT V, 6718),[93] Ubar-Dagan Foreign-Guest-Of-Dagan (U-bar-^{d}Da-gan, MCS 9/1, 243:10).[94]

Dagan is probably to be connected to the Semitic root dgn, "to be cloudy, rainy."[95] This interpretation of the name is based on an understanding of

Dagan's character as a storm god which is supported by his identification with Enlil,[96] the similarity in the name of his spouse Šalaš with Adad's wife Šala,[97] and his paternal ties with the storm god.[98] Dagan, like his Sumerian counterpart Enlil,[99] also has ties with the underworld. In both the Ugaritic and Mari material he is the recipient of sacrifices for the dead,[100] and in a new Mari text he is given the epithet *bēl pagrê*, "lord of the sacrifices for the dead."[101] Moreover, a long known text appears to have Dagan gathering the underworld deities and entrusting them to Allatum.[102] This link with the underworld probably grows out of the fructifying role of the rainstorm, since both Enlil[103] and Dagan[104] were thought of as the impregnating power which caused the earth to produce grain.[105]

18. *Durul*

Sargonic: *Šu-Durul* He-Of-Durul (*Šu-Dur-ul$_3$*, *MAD* 1, 219:12; *HSS* X, 143:10; *AS* 11, p. 115:9; *OIP* LXXII, no. 701; De Genouillac, *Kich* II, pl. 54, 9; Gadd, *EDSA*, pl. 3, *passim*), *I$_3$-me-Dur-ul$_3$* (*FM* 9:5).[106]

Durul occurs as a river name in Ur III and later periods.[107] The reading of the name as *Dur-ul$_3$* is not entirely certain,[108] but it seems clear that the name as a theophoric element is the deified river, probably to be identified with the Turnat.

19. *(Ea)/'Ay(y)a*

Presargonic: *Šu-'Ay(y)a* He-Of-'Ay(y)a (*Šu-E$_2$-a*, *OIP* 14, 23).

Sargonic: *'Ay(y)a-bānī* 'Ay(y)a-Is-My-Creator (*E$_2$-a-ba-ni*, *JAOS* 52, 113), *'Ay(y)a-bēlī* 'Ay(y)a-Is-My-Lord (*E$_2$-a-be-li$_2$*, *CT* 1, 1c), *'Ay(y)a-dān* 'Ay(y)a-Is-Strong (*E$_2$-a-dan*, *RTC* 127, obv. vi; *MAD* 5, 66, iii 7, rev. i 9; 68, i 4; 84:5), *'Ay(y)a-ilī* *'Ay(y)a-Is-My-God* (*E$_2$-a-i$_3$-li$_2$*, *FM* 1:7; *MAD* 5, 56, i 14), *'Ay(y)a-mūda* 'Ay(y)a-Is-Wise (*E$_2$-a-mu-da*, *BIN* 8, 160:20), *[E$_2$]-a-NI.[SA]$_2$* (*MAD* 5, 56, i 10), *E$_2$-a?-ba-lik* (*MAD* 4, 4:12), *'Ay(y)a-qarrād* 'Ay(y)a-Is-A-Warrior (*E$_2$-a-UR.SAG*, *MAD* 5, 56, iii 4), *'Ay(y)a-rabi* 'Ay(y)a-Is-Great (*E$_2$-a-ra-bi$_2$*, *MAD* 4, 7:4; *MAD* 5, 62:19; *MO* A 11:22; B 1:10; *RSO* 32, p. 88, v; *MAD* 1, 37:4; 300:3; 279:4; 326, ii 3; *ITT* I, 1300; *HSS* X, 153, v 12; *E$_2$-a-GAL*, *MDP* 14, 6 i),

'Ay(y)a-rēṣī 'Ay(y)a-Is-My-Helper (*E_2-a-ri_2-zi*, *MAD* 5, 70:11), *'Ay(y)a-šadu* 'Ay(y)a-Is-A-Mountain (*E_2-a-sa-tu*, *MAD* 3, p. 264), *'Ay(y)a-šar* 'Ay(y)a-Is-King (*E_2-a-sar*, *MAD* 5, 45, ii 12; 56, iii 5), *'Ay(y)a-ṭāb* 'Ay(y)a-Is-Good (*E_2-a-DUG_3*, *JCS* 1, p. 348b; *MAD* 5, 45, ii 9), *'Ay(y)a-watar* 'Ay(y)a-Is-Surpassing (*E_2-a-DIRIG*, *MAD* 1, 305:10-13), *Ayyar-'Ay(y)a* Man-Of-'Ay(y)a (*A-ar-E_2-a*, *MO* A 7:3, 15; 10:10), *Akū(n)-'Ay(y)a* I-Have-Proved-True-O-'Ay(y)a (*A-ku-E_2-a*, *MO* C 16:10),[109] *BALA-E_2-a* (*MO* A 15:12; *MAD* 5, 7:6), *Enna-'Ay(y)a* Mercy-O-'Ay(y)a[110] (*En-na-E_2-a*, *MO* D 13:2; 7:1; 9:15; 14:6), *Iddi(n)-'Ay(y)a* 'Ay(y)a-Gave (*I-ti-E_2-a*, *MAD* 5, 74:8; *MO* C 11:9; *Iraq* 7, p. 42), *Ikrub-'Ay(y)a* 'Ay(y)a-Blessed (*Ik-ru-ub-E_2-a*, *MO* C 18:19; D 12:2), *Ikūn-'Ay(y)a* 'Ay(y)a-Proved-True (*I-ku-E_2-a*, *MO* C 19:11), *I-mi-E_2-a* (*MAD* 5, 70:2), *Išīm-'Ay(y)a* 'Ay(y)a-Determined (*I-šim-E_2-a*, *MAD* 5, 19:6), *Kalab-'Ay(y)a* Dog-Of-'Ay(y)a (*Ga-la-ab-E_2-a*, *MAD* 5, 19:4; *MO* D 11:4), *Puzur-'Ay(y)a* Protection-Of-'Ay(y)a (*PU_3.ŠA-E_2-a*, *MO* C 5:8; 16:11; *MAD* 1, 326, i 10; *PU_3.ŠA-E_3-a*, Nik., *Dok*. II. 1), *Šumu-'Ay(y)a* Name-Of-'Ay(y)a (*Su-mu-E_2-a*, *MO* C 11:2; *Su_4-mu-E_2-a*, *RSO* 32, p. 93), *Šu-'Ay(y)a* He-Of-'Ay(y)a (*Šu-E_3-a*, *MCS* 9/1, 243 rev.; *CST* 5), *Ur-'Ay(y)a* Man-Of-'Ay(y)a (*Ur-E_2-a*, *MAD* 1, 255, iii 1), *Warad-'Ay(y)a* Slave-Of-'Ay(y)a (*$ARAD_2$-E_2-a*, *MAD* 5, 80:5).

This divine name is consistently written syllabically in the Sargonic period as *E_2-a*,[111] but as Gelb has pointed out, *e_2* has the value *'a_3* in the Sargonic period, while the *e_2* value is not attested until Ur III.[112] The value *'a_3*, moreover, appears to be derived from **ḥa*,[113] which, assuming the name is Semitic, would suggest a root **ḥ-x-x*. It is impossible to fill in the two missing radicals in a truly convincing manner, however. The pronunciation of *'a_3-a* with internal *-y(y)-* is suggested by the alphabetic writing of this name as *ey* in the Hurrian pantheon list from Ras Shamra[114] and by the deity's assimilation to the goddess Ay(y)a in a trilingual vocabulary from the same site,[115] but the character of this *-y(y)-* is problematic.[116] If it were part of the root, one could consider *ḥyy*, "to live," as a possible etymology,[117] but if the *-y-* represents a simple glide, that etymology is extremely dubious. Nevertheless, since the name is written without the determinative and occurs almost exclusively in Akkadian contexts, it is probably Semitic.[118]

'Ay(y)a's identification with Enki indicates that he is a water deity of some sort,[119] perhaps a Semitic god of fresh water springs and spring-fed pools. He takes on a social character as a wise, cunning, and creative deity who is basically favorable to man.[120]

20. Enlil

Sargonic: Ibbi-Enlil Enlil-Named (I$_3$-bi$_2$-^{d}En-lil$_2$, MAD 3, p. 194). Irīš-Enlil Enlil-Rejoiced (I-ri$_2$-iš$_x$(LAM+KUR)-^{d}En-lil$_2$, BIN 8, 123:12), Li-bur-ki-^{d}En-lil$_2$ (BIN 8, 203:6),[121] Puzur-Enlil Protection-Of-Enlil (PU$_3$.ŠA-^{d}En-[lil$_2$], ITT I, 1472, 1:5), Ra'im-Enlil Beloved-Of-Enlil (Ra-im-^{d}En-lil$_2$, ITT I, 1437, 2),[122] Šu-Enlil He-Of-Enlil (Šu-^{d}En-lil$_2$, MAD 5, 25, i 2; 36, i 15; 47:5), Tukkil-Enlil Strengthen-O-Enlil (Du-kil-^{d}En-lil$_2$, CT 1, 1c).

After An, Enlil is the chief god in the Sumerian pantheon, who, as the storm, was seen as the embodiment of executive power in the universe, both in its positive and negative aspects.[123]

21. Erra

Sargonic: Erra-ālšu Erra-Is-His-City (^{d}Ir$_3$-ra-al-su, MDP 14, 76:6),[124] Erra-andul Erra-Is-Protection (Ir$_3$-ra-AN.DUL$_3$, MDP 28, 444:3), ^{d}Ir$_3$-ra-KAR$_3$ (MAD 1, 163, viii 8),[125] Erra-qarrād Erra-Is-A-Warrior (Ir$_3$-ra-UR.SAG, RTC 127, rev. v; MAD 1, 179:11), Ikū(n)-Erra Erra-Proved-True (I-ku-^{d}Ir$_3$-ra, MAD 5, 57, ii 5), I-mi/me-Ir$_3$-ra (ZA 12, p. 33; RT 19, p. 48), Išku(n)-Erra Erra-Placed (Iš-ku-Ir$_3$-ra, ITT IV, 7449), Iddi(n)-Erra Erra-Gave (I-ti-Ir$_3$-ra, MCS 9/1, 251:8; MCS 4, 3:2), ME-Ir$_3$-ra (FM 49:3), Puzur-Erra Protection-Of-Erra (PU$_3$.ŠA-Ir$_3$-ra, MAD 1, 183:12; MCS 9/1, 245:18), Ur-Erra Man-Of-Erra (Ur-Ir$_3$-ra, MAD 1, 237, rev. ii; MDP 14, 19:16; Ur-^{d}Ir$_3$-ra, OIP 14, 91:3).[126]

In recent years scholars have produced a relatively extensive literature on the god Erra, due primarily to the interest created in the Erra epic by the publication of Gössmann's monograph.[127] Nevertheless, many questions are still unanswered. There remains a curious lack of uniformity in the reading of the divine name. While the older readings Lubara,[128] Dibbarra,[129] Gir(r)a,[130] and

Ur(r)a[131] have largely disappeared from modern scholarly works, the most recent studies still fluctuate between *Ira*,[132] *Irra*,[133] *Era*,[134] and *Erra*.[135] Though the god is generally assumed to be Akkadian,[136] to belong to the Akkadian layer of the population,[137] or at least to be non-Sumerian,[138] no one has presented a detailed discussion of the origin of the deity, much less proposed a serious etymology. And even the character of Erra, about which so much has been written, remains inadequately delineated.

The divine name is normally written with the signs *(^{d})ER_3.RA*,[139] but several variants and a gloss also occur:

1. *^{d}Er-ra*: This orthography occurs in the Old Babylonian hymn to the gods of the night, AO 6769 (*RA* 32, p. 182:16), where the duplicate has *$^{d}Er_3$-ra* (*ZA* 43, p. 306:16).

2. *Er-ra*: The pronunciation of *$^{d}ER_3RA$* is given as *Er-ra* by the second column of the unpublished god list UM 55-21-322 (3N-T 408), obv. 11. This orthography also occurs in the personal name *Išbi-Erra* (*Iš!-bi-er-r[a]*, *CT* 30, 10, K 3843, rev. 4) and in a syllabic writing of the related divine name *$^{d}Er_3$-ra-gal* (*Er-ra-ga-al*, *UM* X/2, 13:7). One should also note the compound divine name from Mari, *Ištar-er-ra-kal* (*ARMT* 7, p. 196f.), though there may be some question about this reading.

3. *E-ra*: This writing occurs in several Old Assyrian personal names along with the more traditional *Er_3-ra* (*E-ra-da-an*, *EL* I, 211:9, 15; *E-ra-di_2/di_3*, *CCT* 5, 48d:6; *TC* 2, 28:14; *TC* 3, 251A:7; 23:19; *ICK* I, 61:26; *Šu-E-ra*, *EL* II, 293:20; Hirsch, *AfO* Beih. 13, p. 32).

4. *$^{d}Er_3{}^{er}$-ra*: This gloss occurs in Meek's fragment of a god list (*RA* 17, p. 159, K 8220, line 7).

5. *$^{d}Er_3$-ra_2*: One finds this unusual orthography in the theological text *UM* X/4, 12, i 9, where the duplicate has *[^{d}]Er_3-ra* (*BBR* II, 27, i 11).

6. *$^{d}Er_x$-ra*: The reading *$^{d}Er_x$-ra* for *$^{d}GIR_3$.RA* seems quite certain from the gloss *$^{d}GIR_3{}^{er}$-r[a]* (*CT* 25, 39:27).[140]

On the basis of these variant orthographies one may not only dismiss the older readings of the divine name, one may raise serious questions about the widely adopted reading Era (or Ira) as well. Apparently this reading is based on the idea that ER_3 is an ideogram for Era followed by the phonetic complement ra--a conception which Gössmann argues for as follows:

> From the fact that the syllable ra may also be lacking behind the ideogram, it follows that it does not belong to its phonetic stock, but is to be considered as a phonetic complement.[141]

Gössmann's argument, however, is vitiated by the fact that all the references he gives for the absence of the phonetic complement, i.e., Išbi-Era, Era-kāmi-nišē, Era-ḫābit, Era-nisu, and Išgum-Era,[142] actually represent the orthography Er_3-ra. The evidence for the divine name written simply $^dER_3$ or ER_3 is exceedingly slim. The name Ipqu-Erra occurs once in the orthography $Ip-qu_2-er_3$,[143] but this is probably just a scribal error for $Ip-qu_2-er_3$-ra, which is the way the man's name is written elsewhere.[144] Assuming the names have been read correctly, Schneider's IR_3 might possibly be a theophoric element in a couple of names where it is preceded by the determinative ($^dIR_3$-dan, $Puzur_2$-$^dIR_3$), but it is doubtful that a theophoric element IR_3 occurs in any of the names Schneider cites as containing the element written without the determinative.[145] Most of them are clearly to be explained differently, e.g., IR_3-e-^{d}Babbar = Ir'e-Šāmaš Šamaš-Shepherded, and Ir_3-zu-ni = Warassuni Their-Slave. Moreover, the passage in the Sumerian hymn to Nergal treated by van Dijk is broken, so one cannot be sure that the -ra is missing.[146]

On the other hand, the syllable writings ^{d}Er-ra and Er-ra strongly suggest that the doubling of the r be taken seriously, and this suggestion is reinforced by the occurrence of Erra at the end of the line in the Old Babylonian poem mentioned above, since the next to the last syllable in a line of Old Babylonian poetry is characteristically long. No objection to this conclusion can be raised from the Old Assyrian E-ra, for Old Assyrian orthography normally uses defective writing to render double consonants.[147] Finally, the reading Erra is preferable to Irra, even if i were the original vowel, since i was normally spoken as e before an *r* which closes the syllable.[148]

Having established the correct reading of the divine name as *Erra*, one may now raise the question of its linguistic affinities. Is the name derived from Sumerian, Akkadian, or some other language? The evidence points toward the second alternative. Erra, written *^{d}Er$_{3}$-ra*, *Er$_{3}$-ra*, *^{d}Er-ra*, or *Er-ra*, occurs almost exclusively in Akkadian sources.[149] The name is first attested in the Sargonic period as a theophoric element in the Old Semitic personal names listed above, and it remains a very popular theophoric element in Akkadian names through the Old Babylonian period.[150] Like most of the other syllabically written Akkadian divine names, it is normally spelled in these early periods without the determinative for deity.

Moreover, a plausible Semitic etymology of the name lies to hand. Erra could be a *pirs*, *pars*, or *paris* formation from the root **ḥ-r-r*, "to scorch, char,"[151] followed by the *-a* ending typical of many early Akkadian proper names as well as early loan words into Sumerian.[152] Any of these forms--**ḥirra*, **ḥarra*, or **ḥarira*--could in the normal course of development become *Erra* in Old Akkadian.[153] Since the *pars* formation is used for abstracts formed from verbs,[154] *pirs* to denote the verbal action as such as well as its result,[155] and *paris* as the normal form of the verbal adjective,[156] Erra could accordingly mean either "scorching" or "scorched." The fact that *Išum*, "Fire," is Erra's *ālik maḫrīšu*, "the one who goes before him,"[157] however, favors the latter interpretation and suggests that Erra was originally seen as the personification of the natural phenomenon resulting from a grass or forest fire--"scorched earth."[158] This interpretation could also explain the troublesome conjugal relationship between Erra and Mamma, a mother goddess embodying fertility.[159] Since the burning off of fields is a well-known agricultural device for maintaining a high yield, the connection between Erra (scorched earth) and Mamma (fertility) is not as remote as some scholars have assumed. Moreover, the later humanizing characterization of Erra can be easily explained as a natural development from this proposed origin.

The most characteristic portrayal of Erra is as a warrior,[160] and, more specifically, as a warrior whose main weapon is famine. Actually the texts associate Erra far more closely with famine than with plague, though it has become a scholarly commonplace to refer to Erra as a god of pestilence. *Hušaḫḫu* (*SU.KU*$_2$), "famine," for instance, occurs as a gloss for *ukulti Erra* in the expression *ukulti Erra ina māti ibašši*, "there will be a devouring of Erra (famine) in the land."[161] Much of the imagery of the badly broken second and third tablets of the Erra epic also seems to reflect the circumstances of famine,[162] and Erra constantly occurs in contexts with famine in such a way that their proximity appears more than coincidental.[163] Note especially the following passage:

> *nišē Aribi ittīšu ušabalkitma iḫtanabbatū ḫubut Amurri ummānātīya ša ina miṣir mātīšu ašbū uma' 'era ṣīruššu abiktašunu iškunū nišē Aribi mala itbûni urassipū ina kakki kultāri mūšabīšunu išātu ušāhizū ipqidū ana išāti .... [Yauta' adi] Aribi ša lapān kakkīya innabtū ušamqit Erra qardu sun[qu ina bīrīšu]nu iššakinma ana būrī[šunu ēku]lū šērē mārīšun.* "He caused the people of Arabia to revolt with him, and they kept plundering Amurru. My troops who were stationed on the border of his country I sent against him. They defeated them and struck down in battle all the people of Arabia who had revolted. They set the tents, their dwellings, on fire (and) consigned them to the fire .... Yauta' together with the Arabs who had fled from my weapons warrior Erra cut down. Famine was set in their midst, and for their hunger they ate the flesh of their own children."[164]

What makes this juxtaposition of Erra and famine particularly significant for my argument, however, is the observation that famine can be the result of crop or grass fires--whatever their source--which turn fields or pasture into "scorched earth." The passage just cited, as well as a more mythological account of the same event--

Ištar ... eli Aribi izannun nabli Erra qardu anuntu kuṣṣurma urassipa gārîya. "Ištar ... was raining fire upon Arabia. The warrior Erra engaging (them) in battle, struck down my foes."[165]

-- points precisely in this direction. From the context of these two passages one could suppose that the Assyrians deliberately set grass fires to deprive the fugitive Arabs of sustenance, thus provoking the dire famine.[166] At any rate it is striking to find famine following the same sequence of fire and Erra as reflected in the epic's portrayal of Išum as Erra's ālik maḫri.[167]

Thus there appears to be no difficulty in deriving Erra's role as a god of famine from his original character as "scorched earth." The same is true, of course, for Erra's martial character, since it would have been an all too common experience that "scorched earth" often springs from the burning and devastation created by war. Erra, then, as the personification of "scorched earth," which often results from war and may lead to famine, develops quite naturally into a warrior figure closely associated with famine.

The Erra epic, however, adds yet another stroke to this portrait and gives added support to our argument when it pictures Erra as the instigating spirit behind riot and rebellion. This is clearly the god's main role in the fourth tablet of the epic. Having tricked Marduk into assigning to him the authority over heaven and earth, Erra takes on human form, enters Babylon, and as an effective demagogue soon gathers a large crowd of leaderless Babylonians.[168] He incites this rabble, and though they are not warriors, they arm themselves and destroy what order is left in the city.[169] They speak sedition against the governor and indulge in wanton destruction and arson, barricading the city gate and burning their own sanctuaries.[170] Erra takes the lead in the riot,[171] and soon the whole city is bathed in the blood of senseless murder.[172] Finally the governor, under the god's influence,[173] becomes furious at these outrages and orders his troops to put down the insurrection, but he orders it done with all the brutality and indiscriminate killing and plunder normally reserved for the enemy.[174] Even when Erra is persuaded to return Akkad to favor, his character as the instigator of internal dissension is clear:

> *tâmtim tâmtim [sic] Subartâ Subartû Aššurâ Aššurû Elamâ Elamû Kaššâ Kaššû Sutâ Sutû Gutâ Gutû Lullubâ Lullubû māta mātu bīta bītu amēla amēlu aḫa aḫu lā igammilūma linārū aḫāmeš.* "Sea shall not spare sea, Subartian shall not spare Subartian, Assyrian shall not spare Assyrian, Elamite shall not spare Elamite, Kassite shall not spare Kassite, Sutian shall not spare Sutian, Gutian shall not spare Gutian, Lullubian shall not spare Lullubian, land shall not spare land, house shall not spare house, man shall not spare man, (and) brother shall not spare brother. Let them kill one another.[175]

There is nothing in this portrayal of Erra which would suggest that he was a god of plague. He is pictured as a revolutionary pure and simple, and this development from the original conception of the god is easily understood when one considers the mindless burning, actually attested in the text, so characteristic of anarchy and rebellion. One thinks almost involuntarily of the modern radicals' cry, "Burn, baby, burn!"

What, then, is one to make of Erra's characterization as a god of plague, hallowed by a long and apparently unbroken scholarly concensus? Actually the evidence for this view is not as impressive as scholars have assumed. It is true that Erra is identified with Nergal who, among other things, is a god of pestilence,[176] but the syncretism reflected in the identification of two originally separate deities often obscures basic differences in the original character of the gods involved. In defense of the traditional view one could also point to Erra's epithet *bēl šibṭi u šag(g)ašti*,[177] since *šibṭu* sometimes occurs in lists with *di'u* and *mutānu* where a reference to some kind of disease would seem appropriate.[178] But the basic meaning of *šibṭu* as a *pirs* formation from *šabāṭu*, "to slay, smite,"[179] would seem to be "slaying, smiting, massacre." It cannot always refer to plague, since in one case Assurbanipal establishes the *šibṭu*: *ina libbi nišē lā kanšūti šibṭu aškun*, "in the midst of the rebellious people I instituted a massacre."[180] Thus where *šibṭu* is paired with its synonym *šag(g)aštu*, "slaughter," the more general meaning "affray" or "massacre" seems more appropriate than "plague." In fact, in one instance where the epithet *bēl šibṭu u šag(g)ašti* is used of Erra, the text goes on to describe his joint intervention with Aššur and Adad in the following terms: "Let them overthrow his kingdom, take away his throne, (and) make him sit bound before his enemy. Let them establish want (*sunqu*), hunger (*bubūtu*), and famine (*ḫušaḫḫu*) in his land, (and) let them destroy his name and seed from the land."[181] Note that pestilence is not specifically mentioned, while war is clearly alluded to, and three different terms for famine are used. This general meaning of "affray" or "massacre" would also seem to fit the occurrence in the epilogue of the Erra epic where the "sword of the affray" stands in contrast to "peace, safety, well-being," particularly since the epic has dealt with war, famine, and insurrection, not plague:

> *nâru ša iṣarraḫu ul imât ina šibṭi .... ina bīti ašar ṭuppu šâšu šaknu Erra līgugma lišgišū ilū Sibittu paṭar šibṭi ul iṭeḫḫîšu šalimtu šaknassu.* "The singer who sings (the epic) will not die in an affray .... in the house where this tablet is deposited, though Erra rage and the Divine Seven slaughter, the sword of the affray will not draw near it, but well-being will be appointed for it."[182]

One could even interpret the expression *lipit Erra*, which is normally taken as a reference to plague,[183] in the light of *ukulti Erra* and see it as referring primarily to famine.

It is not necessary, however, to deny any connection between Erra and plague. Epidemics spread very rapidly among the victims of famine and often stem, like famine itself, from the dislocations brought on by war.[184] Thus it would be very strange if a god intimately involved in war and famine developed no connections with pestilence.[185] Whatever connection Erra has to pestilence, however, seems secondary to his character as a god of war, anarchy, and famine, and this basic characterization grows easily out of the original phenomenon in which Erra was experienced and which has given the god his name--scorched earth.

Since Old Semitic names normally stress the favorable aspects of a deity, it is not surprising that Erra's rather forbidding nature is obscured in them. Only *Erra-qarrād* gives a general indication of the negative side of his character.[186] Just as other gods of similar nature, Erra could protect men from the evils he embodied, and it is no doubt for this reason that he was given a cult. Nevertheless, this element of polarity should not be allowed to obscure the basically hostile character of Erra.

If the divine name *^{d}GÌR-ra* can be explained as a Sumerian rendering of Erra as I have suggested,[187] the apparent identification of *^{d}GÌR-ra* and Nergal[188] suggests that the later equation of Erra and Nergal had already taken place during the Sargonic period.[189] Presumably texts from Kutha would show a high percentage of names with Erra as the theophoric element, but as yet such texts are not available. The present evidence limits the names with Erra to the Akkad and Diyala regions.[190]

22. *Gazur*

Sargonic: *Ummu-Gazur* Gazur-Is-A-Mother (*AMA- Ga-zur$_x$(SAG)*, *FM* 20:2).

Gazur is the Old Akkadian name for the city of Nuzi.

23. *Ḫanīš*

Sargonic: *Enpiq-Ḫanīš* Ḫanīš-Came-Forth (*En-bi$_2$-ik-^{d}Ḫa-ni-iš*, *UCP* 9, p. 205, 83:44),[191] *Rīm-Ḫanīš* Mercy-Of-Ḫanīš (*Ri-im-Ḫa-ni-iš*, *ITT* I, 1371; *RTC* 122:6), *Šu-Ḫanīš* He-Of-Ḫanīš (*Šu-Ḫa-ni-iš*, *ZA* 12, p. 335).

From the standpoint of orthography this divine name could be either an active or passive participle, but since *ḫanāšum*, "to submit," is a verb of passive-intransitive action, it cannot mean "the one who causes submission," and the simple passive participle, "the submissive one," does not give an adequate meaning.[192] It seems best, therefore, to read it as *Ḫanīš*, but to take it as a substantized substitute formation to the G infinitive on the analogy of such forms as *šalīmum*, *šagīmum*, *dalīum*, and *ḫasīsum*.[193] The meaning of the divine name, then, would be "Submission," which goes well with the name of the god who almost always accompanies him, *Šullat*, "Despoilment."[194]

In the later material Ḫanīš is usually written ideographically as *LUGAL*.[195] He is identified with the storm god Adad in *An-Anum*,[196] but in the Gilgamesh epic he and Šullat precede Adad.[197] There he is apparently portrayed as the low-hanging first line of clouds in a rapidly approaching storm front, while Adad is the dark, massive thunderhead which follows. This neat distinction may be a secondary harmonization between two originally independent storm gods, but it is at least clear that Ḫanīš was a storm god. In an Old Babylonian Narām-Sîn epic, Narām-Sîn is said to have "made the lightning of his god Ḫanīš his weapons."[198]

24. *Ḫarīm*

Sargonic: *Ḫarīm-bēlī* Ḫarīm-Is-My-Lord (*^{d}[Ḫa]-ri$_2$-im-be-li$_2$*, *MAD* 5, 20:6), *Puzur-Ḫarīm* Protection-Of-Ḫarīm (*PU$_3$.ŠA-^{d}Ḫa-ri$_2$-im*, *ITT* I, 1287:5; II/2, p. 22, 4388), *Mut-Ḫarīm* Man-Of-Ḫarīm(?) (*DAM-^{d}Ḫa-ri-im*, *ITT* V, p. 39, 9451-9453).[199]

^{d}Ḫa-ri/ri$_2$-im is probably to be derived from the root *ḫarāmum*, "to separate," which appears to be etymologically related to the common Semitic *ḥrm*.[200] If it were a genuine Akkadian root, however, it should have become *erēmum*, since the *ḥ* was lost in Akkadian. This suggests that the root, which has a very limited attestation in Akkadian, may have been borrowed from a non-Akkadian dialect in which the *ḥ* was still preserved, and to express this sound the Akkadians used their *ḫ*.[201] If this is the case, the divine name is probably non-Akkadian Semitic also, and one could interpret the name as *Ḫarīm*, the deified sacred enclosure.[202]

25. *Īda-il(um)*(?)

Sargonic: *Šu-Īda-il(um)* He-Of-Īda-il(um) (*Šu-I-da-DINGIR*, *HSS* X, 145, iii 13; 147:7; 155, v 11).

Since *šu* does not regularly occur in front of the other personal names in the same lists, the theoretically possible rendering of the context as "x *PI* belonging to *Īda-il(um)* " hardly seems possible. That leaves two possibilities for interpreting the passage. One could translate the phrase *šu Īda-il(um)* as "the man (slave) of Īda-il(um) (his human master)," and understand it as a substitute expression for the slave's real name, or one could interpret Īda-il(um) as a compound divine name analogous to the well-known Mari divine names Ya/ikrub-El and Ya/itūr-Mēr.[203]

26. Il

Presargonic: Enna-Il Mercy-O-Il (En-na-il, MAD 3, p. 52; CT 32, 7, iii 9; Orient. NS 36, p. 61; I-na-il, WF 107 iv),[204] Ibūr-Il Il-Stayed-In-Good-Health (I-bu$_3$-ur$_2$-il, TSS 479:2),[205] Ikū(n)-Il Il-Proved-True (I-ku-il, CT 5, 3, iv 2; Orient. NS 36, p. 61), Ikū(n)-ku(m)-Il Il-Proved-True-To-You[206] (I-ku-gu-il, Orient. NS 36, p. 61), Iblul-Il Il-Mixed[207] (Ib-lul-Il, TME V, 31, ii 5), Išlul-Il Il-Drew-Out[208] (Iš-lul-il$_x$,[209] BIN 8, 11:45; Iš-lul-il, WF 38, i 2; 72, vi 7; Orient. NS 36, pp. 61-62; TMH V, 31, ii 1), Ištup-Il Il-Preserved (Iš-dup-Il, CT 32, 8, bottom iii 2; MAD 3, p. 291; Orient. NS 36, pp. 61-62), Išu-Il Il-Exists[210] (I-šu-Il, SKL, p. 106), Īsi-Il Il-Went-Forth (I-zi-Il, BIN 8, 11:7),[211] Rabi-Il Il-Is-Great (RA-bi$_2$-Il, OIP 14, 51, vii 5), Uš-mi-il (Orient. NS 36, p. 62), Il-dūr Il-Is-A-Wall (Il-BAD$_3$, Orient. NS 36, p. 62), Il-ilī Il-Is-My-God (I$_3$-li$_2$-li$_2$, BIN 8, 16:8), Puzur-Il Protection-Of-Il (PU$_3$.ŠA-Il, Orient. NS 36, pp. 61-62).

Sargonic: Dūr-Il Il-Is-A-Wall (BAD$_3$-Il, MO D 5:9), Enna-Il Mercy-O-Il (En-na-Il, HSS X, 36, ii 9), Īda-Il Il-Knew[212] (I-da-Il, MO B 4:12), Sa-ri$_2$-il (MAD 1, 269:4),[213] Il-bēlī Il-Is-My-Lord (Il$_2$-be-li$_2$, MAD 1, 3, v 4),[214] Il-ilī Il-Is-My-God (I$_3$-li$_2$-li$_2$, MO A 16:13; FM 37:12; MAD 1, 212:6; CT 44, 48:21; HSS X, 188, ii 25; 216:5; BIN 8, 142:4; MAD 5, 9, i 16; 56, i 15; I-li$_2$-li$_2$, HSS X, 29:27; 34, ii 6; 36, vi 17; 38, ii 8; 72, iv 5; 115:8; 205:6; MAD 5, 5:8; 9, rev. i 15; 18:8; 28:2, 29:1), Il-ipqī Il-Is-My-Grace (Il$_2$-ip-gi, HSS X, 33, iii 2).[215]

A close examination of the names listed above confirms the view that Il sometimes occurs as the proper name of a specific deity in the Old Semitic names.[216] Morphologically il could be either the absolute or the predicate state of ilum, but there are strong syntactical arguments against taking il in either of these senses in the above names. (1) In the verbal-sentence names such as Išlul-Il or Ištup-il the element il functions as the subject and thus should be in the status rectus, not the absolute or predicate state. Therefore it cannot be merely the general word "god," or it would have the case ending and mimation of the normal nominative form, Išlul-ilum.[217] (2) The occurrence of il in a nominal sentence name with a stative as the other element of the name is also hard to explain on any other analysis than that il is a proper divine name serving as the subject of the nominal sentence.[218] (3) Finally, the occurrence of il as the nomen rectum in the genitive-construction name Puzur-Il offers conclusive proof that il must be taken as a proper divine name, since ilum in such a position would be declined in the genitive case with mimation, Puzur-ilim.[219]

Though the existence of Il as a proper divine name seems established, the lack of non-onomastic evidence makes it difficult to characterize him. Il is etymologically the same as 'el in the other Semitic languages, and while the meaning of the root is not certain,[220] the fact that it is common Semitic is significant.[221] Moreover, Ugaritic most clearly, but some of the other cognate languages as well, share a common usage of the root with Old Akkadian[222]--it occurs both as a generic term for god and as the proper name of a specific deity. This etymological relation to the other Semitic languages and especially the continuity in the usage of the root between Old Akkadian and some of the cognates suggests a continuity in the conception of the deity that justifies using these non-Akkadian sources to give more depth to what may be gleaned from the Old Akkadian material, though the resulting picture remains quite tentative.

The Old Semitic verbal-sentence names as a rule are closely tied up with the experience of childbirth and infancy, and those with Il as the subject are no exception. Iblul-Il, if it is correctly interpreted as a mythopoeic expression for conception and the subsequent development of the fetus in the mother's womb, points to Il's role in the formation of the new child. Išlul-Il, on the other hand, points to Il's part in the actual act of giving birth. He takes the role of the midwife. Ikū(n)-Il and Ikū(n)-ku(m)-Il refer back to the oracle from the deity in which the child was promised,[223] and at the same time they refer to the successful completion of the childbirth by which Il demonstrated the truthfulness of his promise.[224] Ištup-Il could refer to the survival of the baby from complications in the actual childbirth,[225] or it could refer to the newborn baby's subsequent recovery from an illness.[226] Finally, Īda-Il is a more general expression of the god's concern, but it could very well grow out of the specific successes experienced in negotiating childbirth and early childhood illnesses.[227]

In spite of the fact that these names follow the normal pattern of such names in relating to the birth experience, they, nevertheless, do contribute something to a characterization of the Old Akkadian Il. The specificity with which Išlul-Il and Iblul-Il refer to aspects of the birth experience is most striking, for one cannot find the same kind of specificity with any of the other gods except DINGIR, and one may suspect that Il is hiding behind the ideogram in these instances.[228] In other words, the connection between Il and human childbirth seems to be dictated by more than a mere convention of relating verbal-sentence names to the birth experience. The connection appears intrinsic to the nature of Il himself. This conclusion, moreover, is supported by the picture given of the Ugaritic 'El, who is called 'ab 'adm, "father of mankind,"[229] and who, at least in the Keret epic, plays the role of the god responsible for the birth of human children.[230]

Turning to the nominal-sentence and genitive-construction names, one may add a few more strokes to Il's portrait. Puzur-Il is of little help, since puzrum is used in this same construction with a dozen or more other deities.[231] Rabi-Il offers a bit more help, since, strangely enough, rabi is not used too widely in the Old Semitic names. It occurs as the predicate in theophoric names with Eštar, 'Ayya, Šamaš, and PI-li-ir.[232] One is justified in concluding from this that Il was a high god like Eštar, 'Ayya, and Šamaš. Il-dūr points to Il's willingness to protect his ward, while Il-ipqī stresses the gracious, friendly character of the deity, who, as Il-bēlī and Il-ilī indicate, could be a man's personal god.

The picture, then, that the Old Akkadian names give of Il is a portrait of a high, but gracious god, who is interested in man's welfare, and who is particularly active in the giving of children. This characterization corresponds in great part to what we know of 'El in the rest of the Semitic world.[233] The resemblance is so close in fact that several of the Old Akkadian Il names have their parallels among the 'El names from other Semitic areas: (1) Ikū(n)-Il = 'l'mn (Sab., Phoen.);(2) Ištup-Il = 'lḏhr (Qat., Min., or Sab.);(3) Īda-Il = 'lydʿ (Sab.), 'lmydʿ (Min.), 'elyādāʿ (Heb.);(4) Rabi-Il - 'lrb (Min., Sab.), 'Ilrb (Ug.);(5) Enna-Il = Ḥnn'l, Ḥnw'l (Phoen.), Ḥanni-'el (Heb.), Ḥn'il, Annēlos, Annēlou (Saf., Nab.);(6) Išlul-Il = Nšl'l (Saf.).[234]

27. Il-aba (DINGIR.A.MAL)

Sargonic: Il-aba-ālšu Il-aba-Is-His-City (Il$_3$-a-ba$_4$-al-su, ITT II/2, p. 27, 4491), Il-aba-andul Il-aba-Is-The-Protection (Il$_4$-a-ba -an-dul$_3$, UET 8/2, 14, v 4), Il-aba-iš-takal Trust-In-Il-aba (Il$_3$-a-ba$_4$-iš-da-gal, MO C 13:24; 19:28), Il(um)-Il-aba Il-aba-Is-(The)-God (DINGIR-Il$_3$-a-ba$_4$, MDP 14, 51, rev. ii; 71, rev. iv), Kašid-Il-aba Il-aba-Has-Arrived (Ga-si-id-Il$_3$-a-ba$_4$, RTC 95),[235] Rīssu-Il-aba Il-aba-Is-His-Helper (Ri-zu-Il$_3$-a-ba$_4$, MCS 9, 1:242, 256).

The correct reading of the divine name DINGIR.A.MAL was disputed for a long time,[236] and that made it impossible to be sure whether he was Semitic or not.[237] An unpublished god list gives the reading of the name as I-la-ba,[238] however, and that should settle the issue, particularly since he does not normally appear outside Akkadian contexts. The name Il-aba, "Il-Is-The-Father," suggests that the god is originally a form of the god Il. He plays a brief but important role before fading into obscurity at the end of the Sargonic period.[239]

28. Il-ab (DINGIR.AB)

Sargonic: Pu-Il-ab (Pu$_3$-DINGIR.AB, MAD 1, 182:4, 11), Ur-Il-ab Man-Of-Il-ab (Ur-DINGIR.AB, MO D 14:13).[240]

The problem in interpreting this divine name is the question of how to read the signs. If one could read the name as Il$_3$-ab, one could either regard it as a variant orthography for Il$_3$-a-ba$_4$ or identify it with the Ugaritic god 'El'eb.[241] If, on the other hand, DINGIR is to be read as a determinative, it is doubtful whether ^{d}AB should be considered Semitic. Either way DINGIR.AB is a very old deity. He is mentioned in the Fara god list,[242] and in the list published by de Genouillac,[243] where the identification with Enlil known from the later An-Anum[244] is already foreshadowed.[245] He also occurs in a few names from the later periods, but he never seems to have been overwhelmingly popular.

29. Illa

Sargonic: Ennī-Illa Mercy-For-Me-O-Illa (En-ni-Il$_2$-la, OIP 14, 143:23), Puzur-Illa Protection-Of-Illa (PU$_3$.ŠA-Il-la, MO B 5:10).

Illa occurs in the position normally occupied by the divine name, so it appears to be tho name of a deity.[246] The god is otherwise unknown, however.[247] Perhaps one should consider a Semitic derivation from the word illum, "partner."[248]

30. Illat

Presargonic: Ištup-Illat Illat-Preserved (Iš-dup-Il$_2$(?)-at?, TMH V, 5:2).

Sargonic: Ela-Illat Illat-Is-God (E-la-^{d}Il-at, ITT I, 1460:7).[249]

The element illat occurs in a large group of other names, but always in the last position.[250] Following the analogy of Eštar/Su'en/Addu/Šamaš-illat, illat in those names may best be interpreted as the predicate state of illatum, "clan." The god Illat, who is unquestionably attested later,[251] is probably a personification of the group solidarity felt in the clan.

31. Il-mār (?)

Presargonic: Il-mār-dūr Il-mār-Is-A-Wall (Il-DUMU-BAD$_3$, Orient. NS 36, p. 65).

Sargonic: Bēlī-Il-mār Il-mār-Is-My-Lord (Be-li$_2$-DINGIR-ma-ar, ITT I, 1472, ii 7).

The interpretation of these two names is very questionable. If they have been interpreted correctly, Il-mār, "Il-Is-A-Son," would appear to represent a manifestation of Il analogous to Il-aba.

32. (Ilu)mer

Presargonic: KA-Me-er (PSBA XX, ii 8).

Sargonic: DINGIR-MA-Me-er (FM 2:5; MO B 5:3; MDP 14, 6, ii 1; HSS X, 13, ii 9; MAD 5, 66, ii 3), E_3-lu-Me-er (RTC 127, rev. vi), KA-Me-er (MAD 1, 162:4; FM 9:4), Ni-wa-ar-Me-er (Syria 21, p. 153).

The etymology and origin of the god (Ilu)mer is a difficult problem. The ideogram IM has a Sumerian reading me-er, "wind,"[252] so one could argue that Mer was a Sumerian name for the storm god.[253] There are two difficulties with this, however. The divine name is sometimes written without the determinative, and his attestation is limited, apart from the god lists, to Akkadian sources.

33. Inin

Sargonic: I-nin-a-na-ak (HSS X, 107:10; 179:20), Inin-il(um) Inin-Is-(The)-God (I-nin-DINGIR, MAD 5, 67, ii 1), Inin-laba Inin-Is-A-Lion (I-nin-la-ba, BIN 8, 160:21; HSS X, 211:15; MAD 5, 57, rev. ii 2; MAD 4, 10:14), I-nin-me-šum (MO A 7:18), Inin-šadu Inin-Is-A-Mountain (I-nin-sa-tu, RSO 32, p. 93; MAD 1, 163, ii 33; MO C 16:28; D 14:5), Ininum (I-nin-um, MDP 14, 72 iii; MAD 5, 62:24; 102:8; I-nin-num_2, MAD 1, 163, viii 33; FM 2:7; JCS X, p. 26, iv 3; I-nin-[nu]?, MAD 5, 34:2).

Inin in Inin-laba and Inin-šadu holds the same position normally occupied by a proper divine name in these constructions,[254] which suggests that Inin is also a proper divine name.[255] If this analysis is correct, the name should probably be explained as a pirs form from *anānum, "to skirmish."[256] Inin, "Skirmishing," then, would be a goddess of war similar to Annunītum and Ši-laba.

34. Išar

Sargonic: Išar-iš-takal Trust-In-Išar (I-sar-iš-da-gal, HSS X, 210:12), Ūṣe-Išar Išar-Went-Forth (U-ṣi-I-sar, MDP 14, 6, ii 16).

The first name compared with Il-aba-iš-takal, Su'en-iš-ti/takal, Eštar-iš-takal, Il-iš-takal, and Mamma-iš-takal strongly suggests that Išar must be interpreted here as a divine name.[257] If one compares the second name to Ūsi-Malik, it also points in the same direction,[258] and this interpretation appears secured by an Ur III god list that includes the divine name ᵈIšar.[259] Etymologically the name Išar is an adjective with a wide range of meaning,[260] but the divine name probably has the meaning, "The Just One," which presumably relates to a judicial function he performs in the underworld. He appears to be an underworld deity, because the word occurs in the later period as one element in several divine names, most of whom are clearly underworld gods.[261]

35. Išḫara

Sargonic: ME?-Iš?-ḫa-ra (MAD 1, 232, ii 10), Pu-Išḫara Mouth-Of-Išḫara (Pu₃-ᵈIš-ḫa-ra, MAD 1, 33, obv. 3), Šu-Išḫara He-Of-Išḫara (Šu-ᵈIš-ḫa-ra, MAD 1, 328, rev. 2).

The etymology and origin of Išḫara is still unclear, and her character can still not be sharply focused.[262] She is a guarantor of oaths,[263] "mistress of judgement and oracles,"[264] "merciful mother of the people,"[265] "mistress of the inhabited places,"[266] and a late text makes her the queen of the city Kisurra.[267] She is similar to Ištar, with whom she is sometimes identified,[268] in that she seems to combine traits of a goddess of love and a goddess of war at the same time.[269] Išḫara also appears to have some connection with the underworld, since she is the mother of the Sebettum.[270]

36. (Ištar)/Eštar

Presargonic: Enbi-Eštar Fruit-Of-Eštar (En-bi₂-Eš₄-dar, BE 1/2, 104:6; i-GURUNⁿⁱ⁻ⁱᵇ-Eš₄-dar, SKL, p. 96, n. 159),[271] Šu-Eštar He-Of-Eštar (Šu-Eš₄-dar, CT 5, 3:3), Eš₄-dar-ra[272] (PSBA XX, ii 18), Eštar-ummī Eštar-Is-My-Mother (Eš₄-dar-um-me, BIN 8, 23:10), Eštar-mutī Eštar-Is-My-Man(?) (Eš₄-dar-mu-ti, SKL, p. 108).[273]

Sargonic: Eštar-ālšu Eštar-Is-His-City (Eš₄-dar-al-su, MO B 2:1; FM 16:5), Eštar-asû Eštar-Is-A-Doctor (Eš₄-dar-AZU.A, MDP 14, 33 ii; Eš₄-dar-a-zu, BIN 8, 259:3; MAD 1, 163, vii 6), Eštar-balag Eštar-Is-A-Harp (Eš₄-dar-BALAG, FM 49:7), Eš₄-dar-BALA (CST 4; MCS 9/2, 243), Eš₄-dar-ba-lik (MAD 1, 7, i 10), Eš₄-dar-BI₂

(MAD 1, index), Eštar-damqat Eštar-Is-Gracious (Eš$_4$-dar-dam-ga-at, FM 28:5; 30:2; MAD 1, 7, rev. i 6; 11, i 4), Eštar-dān Eštar-Is-Strong (Eš$_4$-dar-dan, MAD 5, 9, rev. ii 12), Eštar-dannat Eštar-Is-Strong (Eš$_4$-dar-da-na-at, MDP 14, 75; MAD 1, 163, iii 4, 27), Eštar-dāri Eštar-Is-Eternal[274] (Eš$_4$-dar-da-ri$_2$, FM 33:29), Eštar-dūrī Eštar-Is-My-Wall (Eš$_4$-dar-BAD$_3$-ri$_2$, MAD 5, 56, ii 11), Eštar-tukultī Eštar-Is-My-Trust (Eš$_4$-dar-du-gul-ti, MAD 1, 163, ii 36; 115:10; FM 19:18; 30:9; MAD 1, 298:12), Eštar-bīt(um) Eštar-Is-(The)-Household (Eš$_4$-dar-E$_2$, MDP 14, 74:9; MAD 1, 326:14; MAD 5, 10, i 11), Eštar-rabiat Eštar-Is-Great (Eš$_4$-dar-ra-bi$_2$-at, FM 30:3; Eš$_4$-dar-GAL, FM 10:17), Eštar-illat Eštar-Is-The-Clan (Eš$_4$-dar-il$_3$-la-at, MAD 1, 116, i 6), Eštar-imittī Eštar-Is-My-Support (Eš$_4$-dar-i-mi-ti, FM 23:3), Eštar-iš-takal Trust-In-Eštar (Eš$_4$-dar-iš-da-gal, RTC 127, rev. v), Eš$_4$-dar-iš (MAD 1, 163, i 19),[275] Eš$_4$-dar-KAR$_3$ (MAD 1, several times), Eštar-laba Eštar-Is-A-Lion (Eš$_4$-dar-la-ba, MAD 1, 260), Eštar-malkat Eštar-Is-A-Princess (Eš$_4$-dar-ma-al-ga-at, MAD 1, 163, iii 25), Eštar-m(a)-ilī Only-Eštar-Is-My-God (Eš$_4$-dar-me-li$_2$,[276] MAD 1, 3, iii 6). Eštar-ṣil Eštar-Is-Protection (Eš$_4$-dar-MI, FM 23:6; 50:3), Eštar-mūda Eštar-Is-Wise (Eš$_4$-dar-mu-da, MAD 1, 326, iii 6), Eš$_4$-dar-NI.SA (MAD 1, 163, iii 17; MAD 5, 9, ii 6), Eš$_4$-dar-NI.SU (BIN 8, 143:10), Eštar-nu''id Praise-Eštar (Eš$_4$-dar-nu-id, MAD 1, several times; MAD 5, 4:2), Eštar-nuḫšī Eštar-Is-My-Wealth (Eš$_4$-dar-nu-uḫ-si, MAD 1, 163, i 21), Eštar-nūrī Eštar-Is-My-Light (Eš$_4$-dar-nu-ri$_2$, MAD, 163, iii 12), Eštar-paluḫ Eštar-Is-Awe-Inspiring (Eš$_4$-dar-ba-luḫ, MAD 5, 20:2), Eštar-rēṣī Eštar-Is-My-Helper (Eš$_4$-dar-ri$_2$-zi, MAD 1, 290:4), Eštar-šadu Eštar-Is-A-Mountain (Eš$_4$-dar-sa-tu, FM 3:3), Eštar-ummī Eštar-Is-My-Mother (Eš$_4$-dar-um-mi, HSS X, 66:14), Eštar-qarrād Eštar-Is-A-Warrior (Eš$_4$-dar-UR.SAG, FM 14:16; 33:51; MAD 1, 317, iii 7), A-ma-an-Eš$_4$-dar[277] (Ward, SCWA, no. 217), Āmur-Eštar I-Saw-Eštar[278] (A-mur-Eš$_4$-dar, RTC 127, rev. iv), Taddi(n)-Eštar Eštar-Gave (Da-ti-Eš$_4$-dar, MAD 1, 255, vi 2),[279] E-ma-an-Eš$_4$-dar (MAD 1, 66:3), Ilī-Eštar My-God-Is-Eštar (I$_3$-li$_2$-Eš$_4$-dar, Iraq I, pl. III a; = Ward, SCWA, no. 387), Iddi(n)-Eštar Eštar-Gave (I-ti-Es$_4$-dar, MO D 7:5; MDP 14, 71, rev. 4), Išma-Eštar Eštar-Heard (Iš-ma$_2$-Eš$_4$-dar, MAD 5,

70:13), Maṣiam-Eštar Enough-For-Me-O-Eštar! (Ma?-zi-am-Eš$_4$-dar, Coll. de Clerq I, 121), Nūr-Eštar Light-Of-Eštar (Nu-ur$_2$-Eš$_4$-dar, MDP 14, 50), Puzur-Eštar Protection-Of-Eštar (PU$_3$.ŠA-Eš$_4$-dar, MO C 11:5; OIP 14, 176, several times; MAD 1, 332:2; HSS X, 98.6; JCS X, p. 26, v 12; MAD 5, 11:6; 34:3; 45, i 9), Šu-Eštar He-Of-Eštar (Šu-Eš$_4$-dar, MO B 5:5; FM 33:45; CST 4; MDP 18, 68; MDP 14, 47; RSO 32, p. 90; AnOr 7, 372; MAD 1, several times; HSS X, 20, rev. 5; BIN 8, 144:12), Ūbil-Eštar Eštar-Pardoned[280] (U-bil$_2$-Eš$_4$-dar, CT 21, 1d), [Um]mī-Eštar Eštar-Is-My-Mother ([Um]-mi-Eš$_4$-dar, MAD 5, 9, i 6), Ur-Eštar Man-Of-Eštar (Ur-Eš$_4$-dar, MAD 1, index).[281]

Old Akkadian Eštar,[282] later Ištar, derives from a form ʿAṯtar which occurs as the name of a male deity in Ugaritic, South Arabic, and, in the double name ʿAštar-Kamoš, among the Moabites.[283] A corresponding feminine formation, ʿAṯtart/ʿAštart, is also attested as the name of a goddess in Ugaritic, Hebrew, Phoenician, and in Presargonic material from Mari.[284] Apparently the two names originally designated the planet Venus under its two aspects as morning star (male = ʿAṯtar) and evening star (female = ʿAṯtart).[285] This distinction was preserved only in the west, however. In the east the masculine form usurped both functions, and the feminine form dropped out of normal use.[286] Nevertheless, the East Semites appear to have retained a memory of the androgynous character of Venus which allowed the Akkadian *ʿAṯtar to develop as a goddess contrary to its grammatical gender.[287] This development is anomalous in spite of its latent possibility, however, so one must suspect Sumerian influence.

The names Eštar-laba, Eštar-qarrād, possibly Eštar-pāliq(BA.LIK) Eštar-Is-A-Slayer(?), and evidence from the royal inscriptions[288] show that Eštar had already been typed as a war goddess in the Old Akkadian period, and while this aspect of her character is not as easy to detect in the personal names, she probably was also considered a sex goddess.[289] How the Akkadians originally combined these two seemingly incongruous elements is unclear. It may be that the Semites originally assigned the war aspect to the male ʿAṯtar and the love aspect to the female ʿAṯtart,[290] but the union of these two aspects in one goddess also occurs with Ugaritic ʿAnat,[291] and probably with Ugaritic ʿAṯtart,[292] so it may merely reflect the typing of the goddess as a young, marriageable girl.[293] As such she would be the object of sexual desire, but since in early nomadic society the young women egged on the young warriors in battle with praise and taunts,[294] she could also be seen as the personification of the rage of battle. In the later tradition, at any rate, both aspects are combined in the one portrait of Eštar as the independent, willful, and spoiled young noblewoman whose seductive and voluptuous charm hides a fickle heart and a vicious temper.[295]

37. Ištarān

Presargonic: Ištup-Ištarān Ištarān-Preserved (Iš-dup-ᵈKA.DI, Orient. NS 36, p. 65).

Sargonic: Ur-Ištarān Man-Of-Ištarān (Ur-ᵈKA.DI, MAD 5, 59:14'; 112:3; MCS 9/2, 255; BRM 3, 101; CST 4).

The god Ištarān[296] has a good Semitic name[297] and must be considered Semitic.[298] He was the city god of Der,[299] and Narām-Sîn made offerings to him.[300]

38. Išum

Presargonic: Ur-Išum Man-Of-Išum (Ur-I_3-šum, OIP 14, 48, ii 7).

Sargonic: Šumšu-Išum His-Name-Is-Išum (Šum-su-I_3-šum, BIN 8, 265:2).[301]

Išum has a Semitic etymology,[302] is written without the determinative, and is limited to Akkadian sources, so he is clearly Semitic.[303] The name is a masculine form of išātum, "fire," which elsewhere in Akkadian always appears in the feminine.[304] This original connection to the natural phenomenon has been obscured by the subsequent humanizing of the deity, but it still shows through in places. In the Erra epic he is called a torch[305] and is the forerunner of Erra, "scorched earth."[306] His most common epithets, nāgir mūši, "herald of the night,"[307] nāgir sūqi šaqummi, "herald of the quiet street,"[308] and muttallik mūši, "night watchman,"[309] might derive from the night watchman's use of a torch in making his rounds,[310] but since these epithets are shared by and possibly borrowed from the Sumerian Ḫendursağa, it is not clear how intrinsic they are to the Akkadian deity.

As the herald of Erra[311] and the counselor of Nergal,[312] Išum belongs to the underworld deities.[313] But fire can be a blessing as well as a bane,[314] so Išum, unlike Erra or Nergal, with whom he is occasionally identified,[315] is favorably inclined toward man.[316] In the Erra epic he is the general who stirs up Erra, because he enjoys a good fight, but he is appalled by Erra's excesses and finally succeeds in appeasing him.[317] Išum's family ties are unclear, perhaps because of his identification with the Sumerian Ḫendursağa, the son of Enlil.[318] An Old Babylonian text makes him the brother of Ištar and the son of Ninlil.[319] His wife is variously given as Šubula[320] or Ninmug,[321] who is identified with Meme.[322]

The Old Akkadian references are limited to Adab and the Lagash region[323] and throw no light on the god's character.

39. Kar(r)um

Sargonic: Iš-ma$_2$-KAR$_2$ (MDP 14, 66:4; 71 iv; MAD 5, 5:4; 9, i 2; 18:3; 36:4), Iš-ma$_2$-GAR$_2$ (MO A 14:19; MAD 1, several times; ITT I, 1456:2).[324]

Kar(r)um appears to be an Akkadian element, but its meaning is unknown.[325] It normally occurs in the predicate position as an epithet for different divine names,[326] so one should probably not regard it as a divine name, but as a substitute for one.

40. Keš

Sargonic: Puzur-Keš Protection-Of-Keš (PU$_3$.ŠA-Keš$_3$^{ki}, MAD 1, 237, rev. 8), Ur-Keš Man-Of-Keš (Ur-Keš$_3$^{ki}, MAD 1, 135, rev. 8; MO C 11:11).[327]

Keš, which serves as the theophoric element in these names, is a city in middle Babylonia.[328]

41. Ki-ki

Sargonic: Šu-Ki-ki (HSS X, 51, i 5; 52, i 6).

Ki-ki appears to be a Hurrian element used in an Akkadian name formation.[329] Whether Ki-ki is the name of a Hurrian deity, however, is not clear.

42. *Kiti*

Sargonic: *ME-Ki-de$_3$* (*FM* 33:35).

Kiti is a deified city name. In line 50 of the same text one finds *in Ki-te$_4$^{ki}*, "in the city Kiti."[330] The city is also mentioned in an inscription of Belakum of Ešnunna[331] and in a geographical list from Harmal.[332] Although the city has not been definitely located, the references to it all come from the Diyala region, so it was probably in that general area.[333]

43. *Laba*

Sargonic: *Āmur-Laba* I-Saw-The-Lion (*A-mur-La-ba*, *RTC* 197:2; 198:4), *Itbe-Laba* The-Lion-Arose (*It-be-La-ba*, *MAD* 5, 9, i 11; 21:10).

Laba is normally used as an epithet for other divine names,[334] so it is probably just an epithet used here as a substitute for a proper divine name. The final -*a* is difficult, but the epithet may have acquired this fixed form because of its normal occurrence as a predicate in -*a*.

44. *Lā'im*?

Presargonic: *I-ku-la-im* (*CT* 32, 8, iv a3).

One could interpret this name as *Ikū(n)-Lā'im* and take Lā'im as a theophoric element, perhaps as the G participle from the root *la'āmum*, "to devour," which would make Lā'im, "The Devourer." A god Lā'im, however, is not elsewhere attested,[335] so the interpretation of the personal name above remains doubtful.

45. *Lamassum*?

Sargonic: *^{d}KAL-a-bi* (*CST* 2:7), *Ur-^{d}KAL* (*CST* 21, iii 5), *A-mur-KAL.LA* (*MDP* 14, 43:5).

The correct reading of *^{d}KAL* and *KAL.LA* in these names is not sure, but Lamassum is a possible reading, at least of *^{d}KAL*,[336] and it occurs in syllabic orthography in the Ur III period.[337]

46. *Malik*

Sargonic:[338] *Malik-ṣīnšu* Malik-Is-His-Helper (*^{d}MA-lik-zi-in-su*, *MO* A 11:9), *Ir'am-Malik* Malik-Loved (*Ir$_3$-am-^{d}MA-lik*, *MO* B 3:8; 5:15), *Ir'e-Malik*

Malik-Shepherded (Ir_3-e-^{d}Ma-lik, MO A 14:5), Puzur-Malik Protection-Of-Malik (PU_3.ŠA-^{d}Ma-lik, MAD 3, p. 176), Šum-Malik Name-Of-Malik (Šum-Ma-lik, RSO 32, p. 92; Šum-^{d}Ma-lik, RTC 163; ITT I, 1134), Ūṣi-Malik Malik-Went-Forth (U-ṣi-^{d}Ma-lik, De Sarzec, DC II, p. LVII).

The divine name Malik is probably the absolute form of a noun malkum or malikum, "prince, king."[339] The name is normally written with the determinative, but this is probably just a device to distinguish the divine name from the same word used as an epithet. Most likely the divine name itself was originally an epithet that split off and became an independent divine name.[340] It is impossible to prove conclusively, but there are indications that the epithet was originally attached to the god Dagan. The two deities appear in several Old Semitic names of the same formation,[341] both have clear and closely related underworld connections,[342] and both have very close ties to the city of Mari.[343]

47. Mamma[344]

Presargonic: Pu-Mamma Mouth-Of-Mamma (KA-Ma-ma, OIP 14, 71, ii 1), Puzra-Mamma Protection-Of-Mamma (PU_3.ŠA-ra-Ma-ma, TMH V, 149, ii 2), Ur-Mamma Man-Of-Mamma (Ur-Ma-ma, CT 5, 3, 5).

Sargonic: Mamma-asû Mamma-Is-A-Doctor (Ma-ma-a-zu, MAD 1, 77:2; 163, ii 35), Mamma-huršān Mamma-Is-A-Mountain (Ma-ma-hur-sag, CST 2:16; 17:2; MCS 9/1, 242:12), Mamma-iš-takal Trust-In-Mamma (Ma-ma-iš-da-gal, MAD 1, 163, viii 9), Mamma-šarrat Mamma-Is-Queen (Ma-ma-sa-ra-at, MAD 1, several times), Mamma-šadu Mamma-Is-A-Mountain (Ma-ma-sa-tu, MAD 1, 116, i 7; BIN 8, 148:24), Mamma-šu'at Mamma-Is-A-Lady (Ma-ma-šu-at, MAD 1, 163, v 11), Mamma-ummī Mamma-Is-My-Mother (Ma-ma-um-mi, MAD 1, 163, i 31, 38; MDP 14, 75:6), Būr-Mamma Calf-Of-Mamma (Bur-Ma-ma, RTC 254, rev. ii), Pu-Mamma Mouth-Of-Mamma (KA-Ma-ma, MO C 10:15; 18:23; FM 25:1; HSS X, 188, ii 19), Puzur-Mamma Protection-Of-Mamma (PU_3.ŠA-Ma-ma, MAD 1, several times; MAD 5, 62:8, 10; MO A 8:22; D 12:9; MCS 9/1, 242:20), Šu-Mamma He-Of-Mamma (Šu-Ma-ma, MAD 1, several times; MAD 4, 160:3; MAD 5, 92:5; FM 12:9; 14:2; RSO 32, p. 91; MDP 14, 19:32; HSS X, 205:5; 153, v 16; RTC 127, rev. ii 4; CST 3:9; MCS 9/1, 245:24; Su-Ma-ma, BIN 8, 121:40),

Ummī-Mamma Mamma-Is-My-Mother (Um-mi-Ma-ma, MAD 1, 7, i 5; 132:5), Ur-Mamma Man-Of-Mamma (Ur-Ma-ma, MAD 1, 215:20).

Mamma/Mammi appears to be a baby word for mother.[345] Baby words do not have etymologies, so it is impossible to attribute the divine name to any linguistic group on that basis. It should not be Sumerian, however, since it is written without the determinative normal with Sumerian divine names,[346] and it occurs only in Akkadian sources. Both these facts suggest that the name is Akkadian.

The name itself indicates that the goddess was experienced from the very beginning as the power manifesting itself in motherhood, and giving birth remains the deity's basic role even in the later texts. In the Atraḫasīs epic, where she is identified with Nintu,[347] Bēlet-ilī,[348] and perhaps Dingirmaḫ,[349] the gods summon Mammi and give her the task of creating mankind,[350] which she accomplishes by mixing the blood of a slain god with clay.[351]

According to the Erra epic Mamma is the spouse of Erra,[352] and a god list makes her the wife of Nergal,[353] while yet a third text designates Ninazu, another underworld deity, as her offspring.[354] This connection to the underworld has been questioned, but on insufficient grounds.[355] Actually one should not be surprised to find a mother goddess related to the underworld, since often they are only particular embodiments of "Mother Earth," who is not only the mysterious source of new life, but also the womb to which the dying return.[356]

The names Mamma-ummī and Ummī-Mamma relate directly to Mamma's character, though one could address his personal goddess as mother even if she were not by nature a mother goddess. Šarratum and šu'atum, which occur in two of the other names, are also known as epithets of Mamma.[357] They represent a certain socializing of the divine figure away from the natural phenomenon in which she was originally experienced. Finally, the epithet asû may reflect the medical role Mamma filled as the divine midwife during human childbirth.[358]

48. Ma-na

Sargonic: Šu-Ma-na (HSS X, 155, ii 11).

Ma-na does not occur elsewhere as a divine name, but it does occur as a month name in the Old Babylonian period at Mari.[359] Perhaps this name should be interpreted as He-(Who-Was-Born-In)-The-Month-Mana.[360]

49. Meme

Presargonic: Šu-Meme He-Of-Meme (Šu-me-me, BIN 8, 154:37), Meme-turāḫ Meme-Is-A-Mountain-Goat (Me-me-tu-ra-aḫ, UET II, pl. L 49, rev. 6).[361]

Meme may also be a baby word for mother. The name may be Akkadian since it occurs without the determinative in Old Semitic personal names. If so, her identification with Ninmug[362] suggests that Meme was the original name of the wife of Išum in the Akkadian tradition. The goddess is also identified with Ninkarrak[363] and Gula,[364] which indicates that she was more strongly impressed with the character of a healing deity than Mamma, but she also retains certain traits of the fertility goddess as well.[365]

50. Meslam[366]

Presargonic: Meslam-il Meslam-Is-God (Meslam-il, Orient. NS 36, p. 66).

Meslam was the name of Nergal's temple in Kutha.[367]

51. Mummu

Sargonic: Mummu-šadu Mummu-Is-A-Mountain (Mu-mu-sa-tu, MAD 3, p. 264), Ši-Mummu She-Is-Mummu (Si-Mu-mu, HSS X, 196:6).

The origin and etymology of Mummu is questionable.[368] There are at least two and possibly four distinct homonyms: (1) the mummu derived from Sumerian mud-mud, "creator, fashioner," (2) mummu, "thunder," (3) mummu referring to a household object, and (4) the mummu which is used as a synonym of kuṣṣum, "cold."[369] The first one seems more appropriate since it is attested elsewhere as a divine name, but if the Sumerian etymology is correct, one would have expected the name to have been written with a determinative.

52. Nanna[370]

Sargonic: Pu-Nanna Mouth-Of-Nanna (Pu_3-Na-na, HSS X, 33, v 5), Šu-Nanna

He-Of-Nanna (Šu-Na-na, FM 9:1; BIN 8, 235:3; MAD 1, several times).

The lack of the determinative suggests that this deity is Semitic, but whether it may be identified with the love goddess Nana is questionable. Nanna also appears at Mari in the name Warad-^{d}Na-na,[371] and should probably be equated with the goddess ^{d}Na-an-ni,[372] who occurs in the Mari pantheon[373] and in Ur III proper names.[374] Sometimes the name is inflected,[375] but this does not fully explain the variation in the final vowel, for Na-an-ni in ^{fd}Na-an-ni-šar-ra is obviously nominative. The character of this goddess is unfortunately unknown.[376]

53. Nāru

Presargonic: Iddi(n)-Nāru The-River-Gave (I-ti-^{d}ID$_2$, BA 31, p. 176, ^{d}ID$_2$-bi$_2$-bi$_2$ (PBS 13, 27, rev. 1).

Sargonic: Nāru-laba The-River-Is-A-Lion (^{d}ID$_2$-la-ba, MAD 3, p. 191), Iddi(n)-Nāru The-River-Gave (I-ti-^{d}ID$_2$, MAD 1, 215:24; 265:6; I-ti-ID$_2$, RSO 32, p. 89), Pu$_3$-su-^{d}ID$_2$ (MAD 1, 233, i 6), Puzur-Nāri Protection-Of-The-River (PU$_3$.ŠA-^{d}ID$_2$, MAD 1, 237:10), Šu-Nāri He-Of-The-River (Šu-ID$_2$, Iraq 7, p. 66).

The correct reading of this divine name is not sure. In the later period the logogram ^{d}ID$_2$ is construed as a masculine while nārum is feminine, so the CAD argues that the logogram should be read Id.[377] Whether one can assume the same for the Old Akkadian period, however, is questionable. Id is a Sumerian loan word which apparently replaced a genuine Semitic name for the river god,[378] and it is possible that the replacement is later than the Old Akkadian period.

The river god received a social character primarily from the role the river played in the river ordeal, so it is primarily thought of as a judge, just as in Ugarit.[379] It is also thought of as a creative god, however, probably because of Mesopotamia's dependence on the rivers for life.[380]

54. Nazi (Nanse)[381]

Sargonic: Ibbi-Nazi Nazi-Named (I-bi$_2$-^{d}AB+KU$_6$, MAD 5, 36, i 8).[382]

Nazi is a Sumerian fish goddess who interprets dreams and is concerned with justice.[383]

55. Ninlil

Sargonic: Ninlil-iš-kīn With-Ninlil-It-Is-Sure (Nin-lil$_2$-iš-gi-in, FM 33:48).

Ninlil is a borrowed Sumerian goddess, the spouse of Enlil.[384]

56. ^{d}Nin-š[um]?

Sargonic: Um-me-^{d}Nin-š[um]? (MDP 14, 74:1).

This divine name is questionable because of the break in the text. The beginning of the sign looks like a good šum, but it is hard to be sure. The line appears to have extended around to the side so it might be possible to include another sign in the divine name. Possibly ^{d}Nin-TAG.TAG[385] should be read, but that would be crowding the space a bit.

57. Nisaba

Sargonic: Nisaba-ālšu Nisaba-Is-His-City (^{d}Nisaba-al-su, MDP 14, 78:2), Nisaba-ipqī Nisaba-Is-My-Grace (^{d}Nisaba-ip-ki, MAD 1, 258, rev. 6).[386]

Nisaba is a Sumerian grain goddess.[387]

58. Nūnu

Sargonic: Dān-Nūnu Nūnu-Is-Strong (Dan-Nu-nu, MAD 1, 98:4; Da-Nu-nu, MAD 1, 2, iii 7), Šu-Nūnu He-Of-Nūnu (Šu-Nu-nu, MO A 15:15, 17; Su$_4$-Nu-nu, MDP 14, 6, ii 3), Puzur-Nūni Protection-Of-Nūnu (PU$_3$.ŠA-Nu-ni, MO B 3:12; MAD 5, 9, i 9).[388]

The divine name Nu-nu is written without the determinative and may occur in Hebrew onomastica[389] as well as in Old Assyrian[390] and Old Babylonian names,[391] so a Sumerian derivation is unlikely. While little is known of the deity, he is identified with the Sumerian deity Lugal-du$_6$-ku$_3$-ga,[392] who has connections with the apsû.[393] He is closely tied to Enmešara and is clearly an underworld deity.[394] Perhaps, therefore, one should interpret the divine name as nūnu(m), "fish," and see the god as the power originally experienced as the fish of the sweet-water lagoons.

59. Padān

Sargonic: Enna-Padāh Mercy-O-Padan (E-na-Pa$_2$-dan, MAD 1, 81:4).

Padān is clearly attested as a divine name in the Ur III period, where the name is written with the determinative and is designated as the recipient of certain offerings.[395] The name, however, is merely the absolute state of padānum, "road."[396] The god Padān, then, is the deified road.

60. PI-li-ir

Sargonic: Ra-bi$_2$-PI-li-ir (MDP 14, 82:3).

PI-li-ir perhaps represents an Elamite deity used in an Akkadian name. It is hardly Akkadian.

61. Rašap

Sargonic: Īṣi-Rašap Rašap-Went-Forth (I-zi-Ra-sa-ap, MDP 14, 72 ii).

Rašap is a pars or paras formation from a root unattested in Akkadian, but well known in West Semitic, which together with the West Semitic element īṣi suggests one is dealing with a West Semitic deity. The name is to be connected etymologically with Middle Hebrew rešep and Jewish Aramaic rišpā, "flame." The plural of the word is used in the Old Testament for flames,[397] but the singular occurs in contexts where it must mean something like pestilence.[398] "Flame," however, appears to be the original meaning of the root. The meaning pestilence only occurs in passages where at least a trace of mythological flavor is left, which suggests that this meaning is secondarily derived from the character of the West Semitic god Rašap, "Flame," who was regarded as a god of pestilence.[399] In a list of gods from Ugarit he is identified with the similar Mesopotamian deity Nergal,[400] and the later Greeks identified him with Apollo.[401] The link between Rašap's name "Flame" and his character as a god of pestilence may very possibly be the high fever which accompanies many epidemic diseases.

62. Su'en

Presargonic: Su'en-šar Su'en-Is-King (ZU.EN-LUGAL, YOS IX, 1), Puzur-Su'en Protection-Of-Su'en (PU$_3$.ŠA-^{d}EN.ZU, SKL, p. 106), Šu-Su'en He-Of-Su'en (Šu-^{d}EN.ZU, SKL, p. 106).

Sargonic: Su'en-ayyar Su'en-Is-A-Young-Man (^{d}EN.ZU-a-ar, MO A 7:14), Su'en-ālšu Su'en-Is-His-City (^{d}EN.ZU-al-su, MO A 4:17; MAD 5, 65:12), Su'en-dūr

Su'en-Is-A-Wall (^{d}EN.ZU-BAD$_3$, MAD 1, 252:13), Su'en-bānī Su'en-Is-My-Creator (^{d}EN.ZU-ba-ni, MAD 1, 228:7; 237:8), Su'en-dān Su'en-Is-Strong (^{d}EN.ZU-dan, MAD 1, 250, iii 4), Su'en-bīt(um) Su'en-Is-(The)-Household (^{d}EN.ZU-E$_2$, MAD 1, several times), ^{d}EN.ZU-GIŠ.RIN$_2$ (MAD 1, 232, iii 11; MO A 10:6), Su'en-gāmil Su'en-Is-Merciful (^{d}EN.ZU-ga-mi-el, MDP 28, 525), Su'en-irībam Su'en-Compensated-For-Me (^{d}EN.ZU!-i-ri-ba-am, UET 1, 275, vi), Su'en-iš-takal Trust-In-Su'en (^{d}EN.ZU-iš-da-⟨gal⟩, MAD 5, 45, rev. i 5), ^{d}EN.ZU-KAR$_2$ (RA 9, 34, v), ^{d}EN.ZU-KAR$_3$ (MAD 1, 255, iv 4), Su'enum (^{d}EN.ZU-num$_2$, MAD 1, 232, ii 14), Su'en-mūda Su'en-Is-Wise (^{d}EN.ZU-mu-da, MAD 1, several times), ^{d}EN.ZU-NI.SA$_2$ (MAD 5, 56, i 6), Su'en-šar Su'en-Is-King (^{d}EN.ZU-sar, MAD 1, several times), Su'en-damiq Su'en-Is-Gracious (^{d}EN.ZU-SIG$_5$, MAD 1, 208:3), Su'en-rē'i Su'en-Is-A-Shepherd (^{d}EN.ZU-SIPA, MAD 1, 232, iii 3), Su'en-qarrād Su'en-Is-A-Warrior (^{d}EN.ZU-UR.SAG, MAD 1, 215:35; 249:4), Amma-Su'en Su'en-Is-The-Paternal-Uncle (A-ma-^{d}EN.ZU, MO A 5:3), Āmur-Su'en I-Saw-Su'en (A-mur-^{d}EN.[ZU], MAD 1, 254, iii 1), Bēlī-Su'en Su'en-Is-My-Lord (Be-li$_2$-^{d}EN.ZU, MAD 5, 14:5), Tukkil-Su'en Strengthen-O-Su'en (Du-kil-^{d}EN.ZU, MAD 1, 233, i 3), Enna-Su'en Mercy-O-Su'en (E-na-^{d}EN.ZU, MAD 1, 207:9; 215:36; 255, ii 8), Kalî-Su'en Su'en-Is-My-All (Ga-li$_2$-^{d}EN.[ZU], MAD 1, 233, iii 14), Amat-Su'en Handmaid-Of-Su'en (GEME$_2$-^{d}EN.ZU, OIP 14, 189:5), Ibbi-Su'en Su'en-Named (I-bi$_2$-^{d}EN.ZU, MAD 1, 241:9; RSO 32, p. 87; MO A 4:1), Īda-Su'en Su'en-Knew (I-da-^{d}EN.ZU, FM 12:1; MAD 5, 53, rev. 6), Il'e-Su'en Su'en-Prevailed (Il$_2$-e-^{d}EN.ZU, MAD 1, 219:10), Ilī-Su'en Su'en-Is-My-God (I$_3$-li$_2$-^{d}EN.ZU, MAD 3, 29), Imgur-Su'en Su'en-Agreed (Im-gu[r-^{d}]EN.ZU, MAD 5, 66, i 2), Īmi-Su'en (I-mi-^{d}EN.ZU, MO A 6:14; 7:10; MAD 5, 5:5; CST 3:8; E$_3$-mi-^{d}EN.ZU, MAD 5, 64, ii' 2'), Išar-Su'en Su'en-Is-Just (I-sar-^{d}EN.ZU, BIN 8, 152:43), ME-^{d}EN.ZU (MAD 1, 265:7), Ištup-Su'en Su'en-Preserved (Iš-dup-^{d}EN.ZU, MO A 3:8; 18; 5:1; D 10:8), Itūr-Su'en Su'en-Returned (I-dur-^{d}EN.ZU, MAD 1, 216:4; 232, i 9; 255, ii 15; HSS X, 24:4; 45:2; 153, iii 5), Išma-Su'en Su'en-Heard (Iš-ma$_2$-^{d}EN.ZU, MAD 1, 215:14; MAD 5, 7:9; 19:5), Kurub-Su'en Pray-To-Su'en (Ku-ru-ub-^{d}EN.ZU, MAD 1, 55, iv 2), Nabi-Su'en Named-Of-Su'en (Na-bi$_2$-^{d}EN.ZU, MAD 5, 42.9), Narām-Su'en Beloved-Of-Su'en

(*$^{(d)}$Na-ra-am-^{d}EN.ZU*, royal name; *UCP* 9, no. 83), *Puzur-Su'en* Protection-Of-Su'en (*PU$_3$.ŠA-^{d}EN.ZU*, *SKL*, p. 120; *MAD* 5, 51:5; 9, rev. ii 10; *HSS* X, 12:8), *Qibi-Su'en* Speak-O-Su'en (*Qi$_2$-bi$_2$-^{d}EN.ZU*, *RA* 24, p. 96, = *MAD* 5, 1:2), *Šīrat-Su'en* Crescent-Of-Su'en (*Si-ra-at-^{d}EN.ZU*, *MAD* 1, 205:2), *Šumu-Su'en* Name-Of-Su'en (*Su-mu-^{d}EN.ZU*, *MO* C 15:29), *Šu-Su'en* He-Of-Su'en (*Šu-^{d}EN.ZU*, *ITT* II/2, p. 33, 4596), *Ur-Su'en* Man-Of-Su'en (*Ur-^{d}EN.ZU*, *MO* C 16:12).

This divine name is normally written *^{d}EN.ZU* in the Old Akkadian period, but there are two exceptions in the Presargonic material where it occurs once as *^{d}ZU.EN*[402] and another time as simple *ZU.EN*.[403] Since the pronunciation implied by this variant orthography is also supported by the Old Assyrian writings *su$_2$-en* and *su$_2$-in*[404] as well as by the later development of the name to *Sîn*,[405] one should probably assume that the writing *^{d}EN.ZU* was viewed as an anagram in Akkadian contexts to be read as *^{d}Su$_2$-en*.[406]

There is no clear Semitic etymology for the name even though it also occurs in South Arabic,[407] but the commonly assumed Sumerian derivation has its difficulties as well.[408] Whatever the ultimate origin of the name, the Akkadians seem to have been responsible for introducing it into the Sumerian south, where as a moon god Su'en was identified with the similar Sumerian Nanna, the city god of Ur.[409] Even in the later period Su'en does not achieve a sharply delineated social character much beyond his obvious astral aspect,[410] and in the Old Akkadian period a clear social character is totally absent.

63. *Šadu*

Sargonic: *Īnu(n)-Šadu* The-Mountain-Granted-A-Favor (*I-nu-sa-tu*, *BIN* 8, 298:9).[411]

Šadu normally functions as an epithet for other divine names,[412] so it is probably just an epithet used as a substitute for a proper divine name here.

64. *Šakan*

Presargonic: *Iddi(n)-Šakan* Šakan-Gave (*I-ti-^{d}Ša-^{ga}gan*, *Orient*. NS 36, p. 65).

Sargonic: *Šakan-qarrād* Šakan-Is-A-Warrior (*Ša$_2$-gan$_2$-UR.SAG*, *HSS* X, 18:7).

Šakan is the Sumerian god of the wild animals who live in the steppe, and he also has chthonic aspects.[413]

65. Šalim

Sargonic: *Ikū(n)-Šalim* Šalim-Proved-True (*I-gu-Sa_2-lim*, *HSS* X, 211:14; *JCS* X, p. 26, vi 9), *Kūn-Šalim* Be-True-O-Šalim (*Ku-un-Sa_2-lim*, Iraq 7, p. 66, F 1159), *ME-Sa_2-lim* (*RSO* 32, p. 80).[414]

Šalim is the absolute state of the verbal adjective from *šalāmum*, "to be well, whole, complete." The verb occurs in the expression *šalām šamši*, "sunset," used as an idiom for "west,"[415] and since the verbal adjective expresses the result of the verbal action, Šalim should probably be translated as "Twilight" or "Dusk." This would correspond to the West Semitic evidence where the god Šalim is attested in close relationship with Šaḥr, "Dawn."[416] On the basis of the West Semitic material one may probably assume that Šalim was favorable to man,[417] but that is all one can say about the deity's character. He seems to have disappeared from the Akkadian pantheon fairly early, though a feminine counterpart, Šalimtum, is attested quite late.[418]

66. Šamaš

Presargonic: *Ibbi-Šamaš* Šamaš-Named (*I-bi_2-^{d}UTU*, *DP*, pl. 2, i 9), *Ikū(n)-Šamaš* Šamaš-Proved-True (*I-gu-^{d}UTU*, *CT* 5, 2, no. 2146), *Išme-Šamaš* Šamaš-Heard (*Iš-me-^{d}UTU*, *SKL*, p. 109).

Sargonic: *Šamaš-illat* Šamaš-Is-The-Clan (*^{d}UTU-il-la-at*, *RTC* 108; *^{d}UTU-il-at*, *RTC* 180, rev. 8), *Šamaš-lidīn* Let-Šamaš Judge[419] (*^{d}UTU-li-din*, *MAD* 5, 53, rev. 2), *Šamaš-mūda* Šamaš-Is-Wise (*^{d}UTU-mu-da*, *MAD* 3, p. 18), *Šamaš-rabi* Šamaš-Is-Great (*^{d}UTU-ra-bi_2*, *ITT* I, 1372; *RTC* 133, rev. 7; *BIN* 8, 194:13), *Šamaš-šadu* Šamaš-Is-A-Mountain (*^{d}UTU-sa-[tu]*, *HSS* X, 188, i 23), *Āmur-Šamaš* I-Saw-Šamaš (*A-mur-^{d}UTU*, *MAD* 5, 9, ii 15), *I-ri-^{d}UTU* (*RTC* 246:15), *Ir'e-Šamaš* Šamaš-Shepherded (*Ir_3-a-^{d}UTU*, *MAD* 1, 7, rev. ii 6; *HSS* X, 42:10; 63:4; 144:2; 154, iv 2; 188, ii 2; *CT* 1, 1b:12), *Kurub-Šamaš* Pray-To-Šamaš (*Ku-ru-ub-^{d}UTU*, *MDP* 14, 71, rev. iv, 5), *Pu-Šamaš* Mouth-Of-Šamaš (*Pu_3-^{d}UTU*, *MAD* 1, 2, vi 5; 34:4; 57, rev. 8; *Pu_3-Ša-mu-sa?*, *MAD* 5, 51:2), *Puzur-Šamaš* Protection-Of-

Šamaš (PU₃.ŠA-dUTU, CT 44, 48:11; PU₃.ŠA-dŠa-mu-uš, MAD 1, 215:10; 241:14), Šarru-kī-Šamaš The-King-Is-Like-Šamaš (Šar-ru-ki-dUTU, CST 14:4), Šu-Šamaš He-Of-Šamaš (Šu-dUTU, MDP 14, 72, rev. iv 11), Tamḫur-Šamaš Šamaš-Received(?) (Dam-ḫur-dUTU, MAD 3, p. 173), Tūlid-Šamaš Šamaš-Gave-Birth (Tu-li-‹id›-dUTU, MDP 14, 78, x 4), Ummī-Šamaš Šamaš-Is-My-Mother (Um-mi-dUTU, MAD 1, 7, ii 12; 53, i 2; 163, i 7).[420]

Although the ideogrum dUTU occurs as the theophoric element in all but two of these names, it probably stands for Semitic Šamaš, since the names are clearly Semitic.[421] Šamaš is the common Semitic word for "sun," so the deity is clearly the power experienced in that phenomenon, but the gender of the deity is not so obvious. At Ugarit,[422] in the Amarna letters from Canaan,[423] and among the Arabs the deity was considered a goddess.[424] The Old Akkadian personal names Tamḫur/Tūlid-Šamaš probably point in the same direction,[425] and Ummī-Šamaš certainly does.[426] On the other hand, the name Šarru-kī-Šamaš points to Šamaš being masculine in line with the later Akkadian tradition. This is probably a secondary development due to the influence of the Sumerian Utu, but it was already at work in the Old Akkadian period, and probably quite advanced, since the Old Akkadian seals usually picture the sun deity as a man.[427]

If the name Šamaš-lidīn has been correctly interpreted, it points to the characterization of Šamaš in the later tradition as the great all-seeing judge who preserves the right.[428] This is probably a fundamental element in the original characterization of the Semitic sun goddess, since the Ugaritic Šapš is also seen as a judge.[429]

67. (Ilū)-šibi

Presargonic: E₂-DINGIR-Si-bi₂ (TSA 12, viii 7), SA-DINGIR-Si-bi₂ (TSA 11, vii 13; Nikolski, Dok. I, vii 13; 6, viii 12),[430] Ur-DINGIR-Si-bi₂ (TSA 10, vi 4).

One cannot be sure from these names, but Šibi may represent the seven gods who normally occur in the later material under the orthography DINGIR.IMIN.BI or DINGIR.Si-bit-te.[431] They are basically gods of war and destruction belonging to the Erra circle,[432] but there is a polarity in their nature in that they are sometimes hostile to man,[433] sometimes favorable.[434] Perhaps they may best be seen as professional soldiers who do not care which side they fight for as long as they can take part in a good fight.[435]

68. Tibar

Sargonic: Dān-Tibar Tibar-Is-Strong (Dan-Ti-bar, HSS X, 185, ii 14), Šu-Tibar He-Of-Tibar (Šu-Ti-bar, MAD 1, 163, ix 21; HSS X, 108:11, 23; 129:4; 153, vii 10).

Tibar seems to be a deified mountain name like A/Ebiḫ, since it appears as the name of a mountain in a copy of a Narām-Sîn inscription.[436] The personal names in which it serves as the theophoric element all come from the Diyala region. This distribution suggests that Mount Tibar is to be located somewhere in the general Gazur area.[437]

69. Tirum

Sargonic: Šu-Tirum He-Of-Tirum (Šu-Ti-ru-um, MAD 1, 81:1), Ti-ru-ša-ki (HSS X, 129:13; 197:9).

Tiru(m) is probably an Elamite deity, though very little is known about him.[438]

70. Tišpāk

Sargonic: Abī-Tišpāk Tišpāk-Is-My-Father (A-bi$_2$-^{d}SUḪ, MAD 1, 163, ii 42; MAD 4, 3:2), Warad-Tišpāk Slave-Of-Tišpāk (ARAD$_2$-^{d}SUḪ, FM 13:2), E-ma-^{d}SUḪ (MAD 3, p. 46), ME-^{d}SUḪ (MAD 1, 132:4), Izammar-Tišpāk Tišpāk-Protects (I-za-mar-^{d}SUḪ, MAD 1, 336:5),[439] Pu-Tišpāk Mouth-Of-Tišpāk (Pu$_3$-^{d}SUḪ, FM 4:4, 10; MAD 1, 45, i 10), Šat-Tišpāk She-Of-Tišpāk (Ša-at-^{d}SUḪ, MAD 1, 18:4), Tišpākum (^{d}SUḪ-kum, MAD 1, several times).

Tišpāk is normally considered neither Akkadian nor Sumerian.[440] Yet the god is attested almost exclusively in Akkadian sources, and Jacobsen has suggested a possible Semitic etymology for the name.[441] He appears to regard Tišpāk as a pitrās form from šapākum with metathesis of consonants, šitpāk to tišpāk, and the nominalization of an original adjectival meaning, "downpouring (rain)," to "the downpouring one, downpour."[442] There are grammatical difficulties with this etymology which make the derivation less than sure,[443] but it does fit the character of Tišpāk well, since according to the Labbu myth he fights the sea dragon[444] in typical storm god fashion.[445] It is true that the text is broken, so one could question if this victory was actually attributed to Tišpāk,[446] but the description of Tišpāk's statue which has him treading on the serpent with both feet leaves little doubt that such a tradition about him was current.[447] If this analysis of Tišpāk as "Downpour" is correct, it would explain both his warlike epithet ^d^Marduk ša ummānu, "Marduk of the army,"[448] and the more peaceful epithet ^d^Ninurta ša ramkūt, "Ninurta of the libation?-priests."[449] It might also explain the curious Old Akkadian reference to Tišpāk as abarak ti'amtim, "steward of the sea."[450]

All these names are from the Eshnunna region where by the Sargonic period Tišpāk was replacing Ninazu as the city god, though Ninazu is still mentioned in the temple hymns of Enḫeduanna.[451] It is in this capacity as city god that one should probably understand Tišpāk's role as guarantor of oaths in the Old Akkadian material from the Eshnunna region.[452]

71. Tutu

Sargonic: Bīt(um)-Tutu Tutu-Is-(The)-Household (Bi-Tu-tu, JCS X, p. 26, v 8; E_2-Tu-tu, HSS X, 105, i 6; 106:2; 180:3), Šat-Tutu She-Of-Tutu (Ša-at-Tu-tu, UET 1, 17),[453] Warad-Tutu Slave-Of-Tutu ($ARAD_2$Tu-tu, FM 4:12).

Tutu may be the same deity who is etymologized as Sumerian[454] and figures in the recitation of the fifty names of Marduk,[455] with whom he is identified.[456] The occurrence of the name without the determinative is strange, however. It is possible that Tutu is not really Sumerian despite the popular etymology, but if not, the linguistic affiliation of the name is unclear.[457]

72. U_3

Sargonic: Laba-U_3 U_3-Is-A-Lion (La-ba-U_3, RSO 32, pp. 87-88), U_3-ilī U_3-Is-My-God (U_3-i_3-li_2, BIN 8, 143:14; 144:22, 29, 38; MO D 12:8; MAD 5,

15:5-6; 69, i 4', 11'; 101, ii' 6, 15).

U_3 in these names seems to function as a theophoric element, but the correct reading and interpretation of U_3 is problematic.

73. Ulmaš

Sargonic: Nabi-Ulmaš Named-Of-Ulmaš (Na-bi-Ul_3-maš, MAD 1, 220:11), Ukīn-Ulmaš Ulmaš-Established (U-gi-in-Ul-maš, AO 17/18, no. 229).

Ulmaš occurs in the temple name E-Ulmaš, which was the designation for the temple of Eštar in Akkad, the temple of Annunītum in Sippar, and possibly the temple of Antu in Uruk.[458] Ulmaš^{ki} occurs in the temple hymns of Enḫeduanna as the name of the city in which Inanna's temple E-Ulmaš is located.[459] It is doubtful, however, whether Ulmaš was a separate city. It was probably just a name derived from the temple for the part of Akkad in which the temple E-Ulmaš stood.

74. Ūmum

Sargonic: Iddin-Ūmum Ūmum-Gave (I-din-U_4-mu-um, UET VIII/2, 14 iii), Ūmu-ilī Ūmu-Is-My-God (U_3-mu-i_3-li, OIP 14, 51, iv 6).

As the subject of this verbal-sentence name U_4-mu-um obviously functions here as a theophoric element. The final m is due to mimation, so one should probably equate the deity with the $^{d}U_2$-mu known from later god lists.[460] This deity is closely connected to the Šamaš circle,[461] and this suggests that the god Ūmu(m), "Day," is nothing else than the deified day.[462] A similar deity is found in the Ugaritic pantheon,[463] he is invoked along with the deified night in the Aramaic Sefire treaty,[464] and a copy of a Narām-Sîn inscription bears witness to a related deification of at least certain special days.[465] The same divine name may also occur in other Sargonic inscriptions in the absolute state.[466]

75. Zababa

Sargonic: Ibbi-Zababa Zababa-Named (I-bi_2-^{d}Za-ba_4-ba_4, MAD 5, 45, i 1), Puzur-Zababa Protection-Of-Zababa (PU_3.ŠA-^{d}Za-ba_4-ba_4, MC B 3:6; MAD 5, 9, i 10, 22; 17:19; 45, iii 15; 62:9), Šu-Zababa He-Of-Zababa (Šu-^{d}Za-ba_4-ba_4, MAD

5, 33, ii 7).

The origin and even the reading of ^{d}*Za-ba*$_4$*-ba*$_4$ is debated. On the basis of the equation *il-ba-ba* = ^{d}*za-ba*$_4$*-ba*$_4$[467] some scholars have opted for a reading ^{d}*Il*$_x$*-ba*$_4$*-ba*$_4$.[468] A value *il*$_x$ for *za* is not otherwise attested, however, and an unpublished god list gives the pronunciation of ^{d}*Za-ba*$_4$*-ba*$_4$ as *Za-ba-ba*,[469] so Weidner is probably correct in assuming an error in the Assyrian tradition with its peculiar *il-ba-ba*.[470] The question still remains, though, whether the god is Semitic. Zababa is attested in some of the most ancient Sumerian material,[471] but his occurrence in the later Sumerian literature is rather rare.[472] In other words the Sumerian evidence is ambiguous. On the other hand, the name is usually written with the determinative, which suggests that the god is non-Akkadian, though it would not rule out an ultimately Semitic derivation for the divine name.[473]

By nature Zababa is a war god. *An-Anum* identifies him with Marduk of the battle,[474] Hammurabi calls on him to smash the weapons of his enemy on the field of battle,[475] and he accompanies the army of Akkad on campaign in a Narām-Sîn legend.[476] As a war god he is sometimes identified with the similar Ningirsu and Ninurta,[477] and his spouse is variously given as Ištar or Baba.[478] He was the city god of Kish,[479] and this is the city from which all the Old Akkadian personal names listed above come.

76. *Zu*

Sargonic: *Zu-a-lum* (*MAD* 1, 254, i 3),[480] *Ibbi-Zu* Zu-Named (*I-bi*$_2$*-Zu*, *RSO* 32, p. 92; *MAD* 1, 252:11), *I-mi-Zu* (*MAD* 1, 216:5; 241:8; 254, ii 12), *Iddi(n)-Zu* Zu-Gave (*I-ti-Zu*, *OIP* 14, 6), *Puzur-Zu* Protection-Of-Zu (*PU*$_3$*.ŠA-Zu*, *MAD* 1, 250, iii 14; 215:38).

The element *zu* in these names occurs in the position normally occupied by a divine name, and the other elements in these names usually occur with a divine name,[481] so *zu* is probably a divine name. It is questionable, however, whether one can connect this deity with the adversary of Ninurta/Ningirsu in the Zû myth, since Landsberger has presented a convincing case for reading the name of the storm bird as Anzû rather than ^{d}Zû.[482]

Summary

Of the divine names listed above, Alim, Annum, Apsûm, Baba, Enlil, Nazi, Ninlil, Nisaba, and Šakan are Sumerian, though Annum and Apsûm have been Akkadianized by the addition of case ending and mimation. Thus one may dismiss them from consideration in discussing the Old Semitic pantheon. Ki-ki, Nin-š[um]?, PI-li-ir, and Tirum also appear to be non-Semitic, and (Ilu)mer, Išḫara, Lā'im, Ma-na, Mummu, Tutu, U_3, Zababa, and Zu are either of dubious Semitic origin or just too obscure to merit further comment. One could also raise serious questions about the origin of the deified place names, but here the more important consideration is the fact that the Old Semites deified them, not that they named them. On the other hand, Karrum, Laba, and Šadu are clearly Semitic, but they appear to be epithets rather than proper divine names, so they will be omitted from the discussion too.

Among the remaining Semitic deities the most important, if we may judge from the frequency of their employment in the personal names, is undoubtedly the group of astral deities: Ay(y)a, Eštar, Su'en, Šalim, Šamaš, Ūmum, and perhaps Ištarān, though an astral significance for him is somewhat problematic. Three of these, Šamaš, Su'en, and Eštar, which compose the triad, sun, moon, and Venus, are three of the four deities which occur most often in the Old Semitic personal names. Since each of these three deities occurs in other Semitic languages as well,[483] the importance of this triad among the Semitic inhabitants of Mesopotamia prior to Ur III probably reflects a dominant role for the astral deities during the Proto-Semitic period. This would agree nicely with the commonly assumed semi-nomadic background of the early Semites, for the veneration of the heavenly bodies appears to be a religious response typical of semi-nomadic herdsmen or shepherds, but highly untypical of settled farming communities.[484]

'Ayya (Ea), the god of fresh-water springs, is the other most popular deity in the Old Semitic personal names, a fact that may also point to a semi-nomadic past, since his popularity could reflect the concern of semi-nomadic herdsmen to find water for their animals. 'Ayya, however, is only one, though the most important, of a large group of deities which reflect the deification of topographical phenomenon. In his case, and even more drastically in the case of Erra, the original connection with the topographical phenomenon has faded, but in other cases it remains quite obvious. Mountains (Abiḫ and Tibar), rivers (Nāru, Balīḫ, Daban, and Durul), the road (Padān), cities (Ālum, Abra?, Admu?, Gazur, Keš, and Kiti), and temples (Bītum, Ḫarīm, Meslam, and Ulmaš) were on occasion deified and used as the theophoric element in personal names. This tendency to deify geographical or topographical phenomena is one of the most striking things about the Old Semitic piety disclosed by the theophoric personal names and deserves further consideration.

The deification of rivers and mountains is the least problematic expression of this piety, since it is not totally different from the deification of heavenly bodies. Both may go back to a primary experience of awe before the natural phenomenon.[485] One may even suspect that the same is true of the deification of the road, for who has not sensed the aura of mystery, foreboding, and promise that envelops a road leading to the unknown. Certainly there are strong hints that this experience was also shared by the ancient Mesopotamians.[486]

On the other hand, the deification of the temple, while it springs from an experience of the numinous, is somewhat more secondary. Those places where the numinous was encountered were separated from the ordinary and considered holy places because of the awe they acquired as places where the deity had revealed himself. They often became the centers of a cult on the assumption that the appearance of the deity at that spot indicated a willingness on the part of the deity to be worshipped there. Normally they would begin as simple open-air sanctuaries around a sacred tree, stone, or the like, until finally in the course of time an elaborate temple was built. The later temple continued to share in the original holiness of the place, but the awesomeness of the site was no doubt heightened by a well-constructed and appropriately lighted temple. Ultimately, however, the quasi-divine character that the temple possessed was derived from the numinous experience of the deity encountered there.

In what sense one should speak of the deification of the city is an even more problematic matter. It is possible that the semi-nomadic Semites were awed by their first encounters with the great cities of Mesopotamia, but one should note that none of the deified cities ever attained the status of major gods--Aššur is a more complex figure than a mere deified city. Thus if one may legitimately speak of the deification of cities, it should probably be understood on the same functional level as the use of royal names for the theophoric element. Just as the king could be considered the god of his land or city because of the functions he fulfilled in Mesopotamian society,[487] so the city, which seen as a legal personality[488] provided protection, community, and legal redress, could be regarded as performing on one level the function of a deity, and thus in some sense divine.

One should also note the deification of social phenomena as it is reflected in the gods Amurru, Illat, and perhaps Illa. In some respects it seems very similar to the deification of geographical phenomena, and, in fact, one could debate whether a theophoric element like <u>bītum</u> fit in one group or the other.

Rain is a critical factor for human existence in much of Mesopotamia, and the storms that bring it are often awesome displays of irresistible power, so it is not surprising to find the early Semites worshipping a large number of storm gods: Addu, Dagan, Ḫanīš, (Ilu)mer, and Tišpāk. Originally most of these were probably extremely limited, local manifestations of the power in the storm--Tišpāk is perhaps the best example, since he does not occur outside the Eshnunna region in the Old Akkadian period--but certain ones like Addu and Dagan gradually gained a much wider significance, while others like Ḫanīš remained about the same or even declined in importance. These different local manifestations grasped the essence of the storm differently, however, as the meanings of their names indicate.

Erra, Išar, Išum, Malik, Nūnu, Rašap, and Šibi as well as Dagan, Mamma, and Meme, who also have underworld connections, show that the chthonic deities played a significant, if comparably modest, role in the early Semitic piety. The Erra epic appears to reflect this early tradition, since several of the companions of Erra in that epic correspond to these ancient underworld deities. One should also note the interesting and recurring connection between fire and the underworld.

Mamma, Meme, and Il all play major roles as deities concerned with fertility, though Meme also functions as a healing deity, and Il's role was probably broader still. Eštar, besides being an astral deity, shares traits of a sex goddess with Ay(y)a and characteristics of a war deity with Inin, Il-aba, and some of the storm gods and underworld deities. Lamassum is a protective deity, though this is probably not a proper name. Finally there is the unfortunately large group of deities of indeterminate character which includes Ab(b)a, Ašar?, Īda-Il(um)?, Il-mār, and Nanna.

Several of these deities, Ab(b)a, Anda, Dagan, Ḫarīm, Rašap, are apparently Old Amorite, or at least West Semitic, in origin. Rašap, though well attested in West Semitic, does not occur in later Akkadian, and the one name cited above in which this theophoric element occurs contains the Amorite verbal element Īṣi.[489] Dagan was adopted into the Akkadian pantheon, but at this period he still shows traces of being a foreign deity. Neither Ab(b)a, Ḫarīm, nor Nanna are well known, but there are indications that all three are Amorite. Addu appears to be good Akkadian, but the form Anda is attested primarily in the West in later periods, and so may reflect Old Amorite.

Sixteen of the Semitic deities (Abiḫ, Abra?, Addu, Ay(y)a, Ālum, 'Ay(y)a, Il, Illat, Il-mār, Eštar, Ištarān, Išum, Mamma, Nāru, Su'en, and Šamaš) occur in both the Presargonic and Sargonic personal names, three (Meme, Meslam, and Šibi) occur only in the Presargonic period, and the rest are limited to the Sargonic names. It is questionable whether one should make much of this distribution, however, since the available evidence for the Presargonic period is not sufficient to draw many conclusions about the number of Semitic deities worshipped in Mesopotamia during that time.

[1]The interpretation of this name and the Ikūn-DN names is suggested by the Old Assyrian Ikūppāša<Ikūn-pāša Her-Mouth-Proved-True, and the Old Akkadian Pūšu-kīn His-Mouth-Is-Reliable. Presumably the deity had promised a child through an oracle, and when the promised child was born, the parent(s) celebrated the deity's faithfulness by the name they gave the little one.

[2]This assumes that GI$_4$ is just an orthographic variant of GI.

[3]A-ba in the first name could be interpreted as the predicate state of abum with inverted word order, but A-ba-GI is not open to this possibility. The Ur III names A-ba-GAL and A-ba-na-da (MAD 3, p. 11) support the interpretation of A-ba as a divine name, and the deity is attested in a god list under precisely the same orthography (SLT 122, vii 13).

[4]Cf. D. O. Edzard, ZZB, p. 66, n. 306. I. J. Gelb, on the contrary, sees two separate deities behind these orthographies: Abba, a male deity, and Aba, a female deity (MAD 2, p. 148). The evidence for Abba's masculinity, however, is limited to the name's occurrence as subject of a third masculine singular verb in the Old Babylonian period, and D. O. Edzard has since proved that the agreement in gender in the Old Babylonian verbal-sentence names is between the verb and the person named, not between the verb and the divine subject ("^{m}Ningal-gāmil, ^{f}Ištar-damqat. Die Genuskongruenz im akkadischen theophoren Personennamen," ZA nF 21 [1963], p. 127), hence Gelb's examples do not prove that Abba was male, and without this distinction in gender it is hazardous to postulate two separate deities on the basis of orthography. The orthographic differences can be explained just as easily by the contrast between full versus defective spelling.

[5]Gelb cites the Old Babylonian names ^{d}A-ba-ri-mi-it, ^{d}A-ba-ri-ša-at, and Ta-din-A-ba (MAD 2, p. 148), and since there is no evidence for the theoretically possible name formation *Taddin-Masculine Deity in female names (Edzard, "Die Genuskongruenz," ZA nF 21 [1963], p. 127), the deity is probably feminine.

[6]^{d}MAR.TU ^{d}A-ba (PBS XX 14, no. 323). If this inscription is interpreted by analogy with seals bearing the inscription ^{d}Adad ^{d}Šala or ^{d}Šamaš ^{d}Ay(y)a, it suggests that Ab(b)a may have been regarded as a spouse of Amurru (cf. Jean Bottéro, ARMT 7, pp. 195-196). J. R. Kupper rejected this view on the grounds that (1) nothing indicated Ab(b)a was feminine, and (2) it is often written without the determinative, and hence was probably a foreign name (IDAG, p. 61, n. 3). The first objection has proved false, and the omission of the determinative is not at all unusual with genuine Semitic names. It is true that there is more evidence for Ašratum as the spouse of Amurru (IDAG, pp. 61-63), but there is no reason to doubt there were other traditions.

[7]F. Thureau-Dangin, "Notes assyriologiques," RA 31 (1934), p. 85. When this name is spelled out phonetically in the Ur III and Old Assyrian sources, it begins with a-, in the later texts with e- (I. J. Gelb, "Studies in the Topography of Western Asia," AJSL 55 [1938], p. 68).

[8]RLA 2, p. 264.

[9]Cf. the similar theophoric use of such topographical names as Balīḫ, Durul, Gazur, Keš, Kiti, and especially Tibar, another mountain.

[10]Gelb, "Studies in Topography," AJSL 55 (1938), p. 68.

[11]For a very brief sketch of the contents of this myth see S. N. Kramer, Sumerian Mythology: A Study of Spiritual and Literary Achievement in the Third Millennium B.C. (Philadelphia: American Philosophical Society, 1944), pp. 82-83.

[12]Julius Lewy, "The Old West Semitic Sun-God Ḫammu," HUCA 18 (1944), p. 460, n. 162. The first radical cannot be '3-5, since the normal phonetic change '3-5 + a to e does not take place in this name in Ur III. '1-2 is also difficult, since that leaves unexplained why the change from a to e does develop in the later period.

[13]ʿApra-Rašpu, ʿApr(a)-'el, ʿApr-(a)baʿal, ʿApr(a)-d(a)gal, ʿApru-ʿanu, ʿApru-hq, and ʿApru-'as'apa' (W. F. Albright, "Northwest-Semitic Names in a List of Egyptian Slaves from the Eighteenth Century B.C.," JAOS 74 [1954],

p. 225). Albright first interpreted these names as composed of a construct noun *ʿapru, "fosterling," before the name of a god or land, but while he keeps the genitive construction, he now takes *ʿaparu, "dust," as the first element and interprets the formation as Dust-(On-Which)-DN-(Treads) (Yahweh and the Gods of Canaan: A Historical Analysis of Two Contrasting Faiths [Garden City: Doubleday & Co., 1968], p. 66, n. 49).

[14]It occurs in Old Assyrian texts as a place name (Margarete Falkner, AfO 18 [1957-58], p. 2).

[15]Ad-da-lum, which could be analyzed as Adda-(i)lum (J. Bottéro, ADS, p. 31), also occurs in a Presargonic text (WF, VAT 12654, 1). The element Ad-da could be analyzed differently, however, e.g., AD.DA = abu (ŠL 145:39; MAD 3, p. 11. To this meaning of AD.DA one should compare the Ugaritic words 'ad and 'adanu, both of which mean "father" [UT, p. 351, Nr. 71; p. 352, Nr. 86; Ugaritica V, pp. 232-233, II 9'], and the expression a-ad-da-a with which Yasmaḫ-Addu addresses his father Šamšī-Adad in the Mari letters, and which some scholars translate as "Daddy" [UT, p. 351, Nr. 71; but cf. ARMT XV, pp. 140-141]), and since it occurs in other Fara names which do not appear to be Semitic--Ad-da-da, Ad-da-tur (WF, p. 21)--it is best not to include it as a Semitic name. For the same reason the name Ad-da (Presargonic: WF, pp. 20-21; Sargonic: MDP 18, 74; CST 15; MAD 1; OIP 14, 191; HSS X, several times) is not included, though it could be analyzed as a hypocoristic formation analogous to Eš₄-dar-ra (PSBA XX, ii 18).

[16]The element ba-na is difficult (cf. MAD 3, p. 99). A contracted form of bania, "is gracious," is the first thing that comes to mind, but this contraction is not normal in Old Akkadian.

[17]The verbal element in this name could be from wapûm (GAG % 106o; CAD a, II, pp. 201-202) or from nabā'um, since Old Akkadian did not distinguish between voiced and voiceless stops, and doubling was not normally indicated in the writing. Nabā'um, however, is probably to be preferred due to its widespread occurrence in the Old Babylonian names of this formation.

But what does the name mean? Stamm rejected the earlier view that equated (šumam) nabā'um with "to call into existence, to create," and suggested that these names really mean that the god, not the father, names the child (ANG, p. 141). This interpretation will not stand up, though, for as Stamm himself noted, it is not at all clear how the name given by the god relates to the name Ibbi-DN (ANG, p. 141). Addu would hardly name the child Addu-Named-(The-Child)! Another possibility is to translate nabā'um as "to call," since šumam nabā'um does occur in historical inscriptions with the meaning "to appoint to an office," but in the words of Stamm, "the names lack the necessary information as to what the god called the bearer" (ANG, pp. 141-142). The idiom is also used in prayers where it seems to imply a return of the deity's favor and hence healing and salvation: ibi šumī šūrika ūmīya, "Name my name, prolong my days" (BMS 5:3); ulli rēšīya ibi šumu qibītukka liššemû zikrū'a, "Raise my head, name (my) name, by your command let my words be heard" (KAR 59, rev. 6-7); and see W. G. Lambert, "Literary Style in First Millennium Mesopotamia," AOS 53, pp. 127, 129, line 31. This usage might have some bearing on the name type Ibbi-DN, but the related formation Šumu-DN, Name-Of-DN, suggests that one should look for a more intimate connection to the birth experience. Hence, the earlier view which interpreted (šumam) nabā'um as describing the name bearer's (pro)creation remains the most probable interpretation of the name type Ibbi-DN.

At the same time Šumu-DN suggests that Ibbi-DN means more than DN-Created. S. Dean McBride, Jr., has argued persuasively in an unpublished Harvard dissertation that šumum in the personal names is an abstraction which "defines the being of one person given form in another" so that "the terms 'hypostasis' and 'manifestation' seem not at all inappropriate to what is meant" ("The Deuteronomic Name Theology," 1969, p. 99). Thus the name type Šumu-DN would describe the name bearer as "the progeny-manifestation" of the deity named, who is probably to be identified with the personal god because of the personal god's well-known role as the progenitor of human offspring (ibid., pp. 132-133,

155, n. 111). In this light the meaning of the name formation *Ibbi-DN* could perhaps be paraphrased as DN-Manifested-Himself-In-The-Child.

[18]This name contains the theophoric element *Anda*, but *i-zi* is a crux. It is commonly derived from **wḍʿ* and considered a G verbal form (H. B. Huffmon, *APNMT*, pp. 184-185). There is some evidence for *īṣi* as an allomorph of *ūṣi* in Old Babylonian (*CAD* A 2, p. 383), and though Gelb says there is no clear evidence for it in Old Akkadian (*MAD* 2, p. 184), it seems the most probable interpretation. The allomorph's limited attestation in good Akkadian, moreover, probably indicates that the origin of the allomorph is non-Akkadian, especially in view of its popularity in Amorite names. This fact taken in conjunction with the "Western" form the theophoric element assumes in this name suggests that this name is Old Amorite rather than Old Akkadian (see p. 60).

For the interpretation of the name one should compare *Šu-mu-um-li-ṣi*/ *Šumum-līṣi*/ Let-The Name-Go-Out (*CT* 4, 17a:19), and the use of *waṣāʾum* in birth contexts: *līṣa kīma ṣēri*, "Let him come forth (from the womb) like a snake" (*KAR* 196, rev. 44). Following the interpretation suggested in the preceding note, one could paraphrase *Īṣi-Anda* as The-New-Child-Went-Forth-From-The-Womb-As-A-Manifestation-Of-Anda.

[19]This interpretation assumes that the child is given in fulfillment of an oracle. There is a grammatical difficulty, however, since one expects *miḫir* in the construct, not *meḫri*. The reading *Meḫrī-Addu*, Addu-Is-My-Weir, is grammatically better, but *meḫrum*, "weir," does not seem to be used in a transferred sense to imply protection. A third possibility, *Meḫrī-Addu* My-Counterpart-(The-Child)-Is-(A-Manifestation-Of)-Addu, is perhaps too speculative.

[20]This is the only two-element name in which the theophoric element is written *ad-da*. It is possible, therefore, that it should be read as an ideogram for *abum* as suggested in note 15 above.

[21]Cf. Ur III *Ša-ᵈIM* (*ITT* II/1, p. 9, 638). *Ša* is probably just a

secondary form of šu according to Gelb (MAD 3, p. 254).

[22]MAD 3, p. 70.

[23]Cf. Huffmon, APNMT, p. 158; and PRU IV, 248a. The final -a vowel is troublesome but well attested with the divine name (see in addition to the variant spellings of Nqmd in PRU IV, p. 248a, the long list of names with the theophoric element written A-ad-da in PBS XI/2, 25, ii 3-25).

[24]MAD 3, p. 18.

[25]Cyrus Gordon, UT, p. 389; H. Donner and W. Röllig, KAI III, p. 58.

[26]Marvin Pope, WM, p. 254.

[27]MAD 3, p. 12.

[28]Cf. the names Ad-mu-e-ra-aḫ, ^{f}Ta-aḫ-zi-^{d}Ad-mu, ^{f}Ad-mu-ni-ri, ^{f}Ta-aḫ-ṣi$_{2}$-in-Ad-mu, ^{fd}Ad-mu-ba-la-ṭi$_{3}$, I-din-^{d}Ad-mu, and Qi$_{2}$-iš-ti-Ad-mu (APNMT, pp. 158-159).

[29]Maurice Birot, "Textes économiques de Mari (IV)," RA 50 (1956), p. 66, n. 9.

[30]Anne Draffkorn Kilmer, "The First Tablet of Malku = Šarru Together with Its Explicit Version," JAOS 83 (1963), p. 437, line 198. For the root as primae w see Arthur Ungrad, "Zum Sanherib-Prisma I R 37-42," ZA 38 (1929), p. 200.

[31]Giorgio Buccellati, AUP, p. 130.

[32]Georges Dossin, "Un 'panthéon' d'Ur III a Mari," RA 61 (1967), pp. 99-100:14.

[33]This interpretation was also suggested by Birot, RA 50 (1956), p. 66, n. 9. It would not necessarily rule out Buccellati's derivation. Note the Palestinian place name, 'ādām (Joshua 3:16). One should observe, however, that the Amorite name Ad-mu-a, if it is correctly analyzed as containing our element + 3fs suffix, 'admu-ha Her-(God)-Admu (so Buccellati, AUP, p. 130), supports the interpretation of the name as a deified kinship term analogous to ḫammum.

[34]Albrecht Goetze, "An Old Babylonian Itinerary," JCS 7 (1953), p. 53,

iii, 11; p. 6; Birot, RA 50 (1956), p. 66, n. 9.

[35] For the interpretation of this name see n. 15 above.

[36] One should also note the name E_2-a-a (MO C, 5:5), but it is not clear how it should be read. Does it contain the name of the goddess Ay(y)a, the god 'Ay(y)a (Ea), or perhaps neither?

[37] Vincent Scheil, Une saison de fouilles à Sippar, Mémoires publiés par les membres de l'Institute français d'archéologie orientale du Caire, I/1 (Cairo, 1902), p. 136, No. 576. The reading with a double -yy- is suggested, since simple -y- is not normally preserved in Akkadian between vowels (GAG §22e).

[38] The attestation for the deity Ay(y)a does not become extensive until the Old Babylonian period. Deimel's reference to ^{d}A-a in SF, VAT 12761, 10, is incorrect, and as Bottéro noted (ADS, p. 32), its occurrence in personal names in WF, VAT 9117:6; 12497:9; and 12729:12 is by no means sure. It may occur in a few personal names of the Ur III period (Engelbert Huber, Die Personennamen in den Keilschrifturkunden aus der Zeit der Könige von Ur und "Nisin," AB XXI [Leipzig: J. C. Hinrichs, 1907], p. 167; Tom B. Jones and John W. Synder, Sumerian Economic Texts from the Third Ur Dynasty [Minneapolis: University of Minnesota, 1961], p. 358), but most, if not all, of these names could be explained differently.

[39] Her Sumerian name ^{d}Sud-aga$_2$/^{d}Su$_3$-ud-aga$_2$/^{d}Su$_3$-ud-da-aga$_2$ apparently means "meteor" (Adam Falkenstein, "Sù-ud-ága," ZA nF 18 [1957], p. 306); ^{d}Nin-mul-si$_4$-a, "Lady-Of-The-Red-Star"; and ^{d}Sir-ri-ga$_2$-ga$_2$, ^{d}Sur-ga$_2$-ga$_2$, Zab-utu, and Utu-bil-bil also appear to relate to light phenomena, but their interpretation is less clear (RLA 1, p. 1).

[40] One could consider a derivation from the root hw/yy, "to fall," or from hy', "to be shapely, well-formed."

[41] For this translation see Rivkah Harris, "The Nadītu Woman," in SPAO, p. 117.

[42] ^{d}Nin-ag$_2$-ag$_2$ (= Bēlet-râmi ?) Mistress-Of-Loving, Nin-ul-šu-tag

(=*Bēlet-ulṣa-zu''unat*) Mistress-Adorned-With-Voluptuousness, and the Akkadian *Ay(y)a ša maštaki* Ay(y)a-Of-The-Harem, all point in this direction.

[43] Cf. *RLA* 1, p. 1.

[44] Harris, *SPAO*, p. 106.

[45] If this name is correctly analyzed, it must be understood on the analogy of such names as *DN-dūrī* DN-Is-My-Wall, i.e., the deity protects his ward just as a man's native city fulfilled that function in ancient Mesopotamian society.

[46] *CAD* a, p. 349, under *alimbû*.

[47] *CAD* a, p. 349, under *alimu*.

[48] *BA* occurs quite often as the predicate element in the Old Semitic names, but its reading and meaning are unsure.

[49] It is possible that one should assume inverted order in this name and take *Da-ad* as the theophoric element. The evidence for *Da-ad* as a divine name in Old Akkadian, however, is not convincing (but cf. *MAD* 3, p. 104).

[50] *MAD* 3, pp. 4-6.

[51] One could read *aḫum* instead of *ālum* in several of these names since *LUM* also has the value *ḪUM*. In favor of the reading *ālum* is the fact that *aḫum* in the Presargonic and Sargonic names, when it is written with unambiguous signs, normally does not have mimation. There are not enough references to *ālum* written with unambiguous signs to make this argument decisive, however.

[52] This name can be interpreted either as a hypocoristic formed from the theophoric element or as the use of a geographical designation in place of a man's real name, "the Amorite."

[53] One could also read *DINGIR* as *ilim*, but it would make little sense to say the god Amurru was like a god. For semantic reasons it seems preferable to read *DINGIR* as the name of a particular god, *Il*.

[54] One could also read this name as *Ibrī-Amurru* Amurru-Is-My-Friend.

[55] Due to the character of the source for these last two names--a list of transliterated names gathered from scattered sources that are not indi-

cated--one cannot be positive about the precise reading of either of these names. They could very easily be the same name, as the difference between ur and ib is very slight.

[56]Cf. especially the Mardu myth where the god is pictured as a barbaric nomad (S. N. Kramer, The Sumerians: Their History, Culture, and Character [Chicago: University of Chicago Press, 1963], p. 253). For the Amorite problem see G. Buccellati, AUP, and the literature cited there.

[57]J.-R. Kupper, IDAG, pp. 87-88. That means that L. R. Bailey's identification of the god as a lunar deity is not convincing ("Israelite 'Ēl Šadday and Amorite Bêl Šadê," JBL 87 [1968], p. 437). As Kupper had already pointed out (IDAG, p. 79), the connection with Sîn does not come until the Old Babylonian period; in Ur III Amurru is put in the Enki circle.

[58]D. O. Edzard, WM, pp. 97-98.

[59]RLA 1, p. 102; IDAG, pp. 62-63, 67. Note especially his epithets bēl šadê and bēl ṣērim.

[60]CAD ṣ, pp. 145-146.

[61]Kupper denies this (IDAG, p. 64, n. 2), but it is clear that Amurru is listed with underworld deities in An-Anum (RLA 1, pp. 102-103; H. Zimmern, "Zur Herstellung der grossen babylonischen Götterliste An = (ilu) Anum," BSGW LXIII/4 [1911], p. 123).

[62]One could also read this name as a statement of more general theological import: Annu-bān(i)-ilī Annu-Is-The-Creator-Of-The-Gods.

[63]The unambiguous syllable spelling of the last example suggests that Annum was treated as indeclinable in these names, since Annum is clearly not inflected as a genitive. Cf. Išum in the name Ur-Išum.

[64]Jacques de Morgan, Mission scientifique en Perse, IV/1 (Paris: E. Leroux, 1896), p. 161:13-15; F. Thureau-Dangin, SAKI, p. 172.

[65]Wolfram von Soden, AHw, p. 55.

[66]Cf. W. G. Lambert and A. R. Millard, Atra-ḫasīs, The Babylonian Story of the Flood (Oxford: Clarendon Press, 1969), p. 50, I 136; and p. 52, I 169.

[67]The name A-bi$_2$-ap-sum$_6$(TAG) (CT 1, 1a) is not included, since the reading sum$_6$ for TAG is highly questionable. It is probably to be explained differently. Ur-ZU.AB could be Sumerian, and one could read I-bi$_2$-ZU.AB in Sumerian too (ŠL 142:66), but I-bi$_2$ occurs quite often in the Old Semitic names where a Sumerian rendering is out of the question (MAD 3, pp. 194-195), so it seems doubtful that it reflects anything but the normal Akkadian element when it appears in the predominantly Akkadian MO.

[68]AHw, p. 61. Bottéro, following Hommel and Zimmern, connects apsûm to the Semitic root 'ps, and particularly with the Hebrew expression apsē ereṣ, "the ends of the earth," which he sees as rooted in the cosmological conception of the sweet water ocean which surrounds the earth (ADS, p. 35). Bottéro's treatment, however, suffers from a lack of philological method. The Akkadian word is apsûm, with a long final vowel that shows it was borrowed from Sumerian ab.zu/su$_2$. The Semitic root 'ps would have a long final vowel only in the plural, but the Akkadian apsû(m) is singular as the occasional mimation shows. Moreover, 'ps does not denote the sweet waters under the earth, but "nothingness," and then "the ceasing, the not being" of the earth, i.e., where the earth stops.

[69]AHw, p. 61; Thorkild Jacobsen, "Formative Tendencies in Sumerian Religion," BANE, p. 270; = Tammuz, p. 5.

[70]One could also consider Ālī-Ašar My-City-Is-Ašar or with inverted order Ašar-Is-My-City.

[71]MAD 3, p. 76.

[72]Huffmon, APNMT, p. 172.

[73]APNMT, p. 172.

[74]UET I, 12:1. A god Ašar is also known from Dura-Europa and Palmyrene (M. Höfner, "Die Stammesgruppen Nord- und Zentralarabiens in vorislamischer Zeit," WM I/3-4, p. 426). He is portrayed mounted on a horse, and scholars have usually identified him as an Arabic deity (Jacob Hoftijzer, Religio Aramaica, Godsdienstige Verschijnselen in Aramese Teksten [Leiden: Ex Oriente

Lux, 1968], p. 42, n. 102; Daniel Schlumberger, La Palmyrène du nord-ouest [Paris: Paul Geuthner, 1951], pp. 121, 125-128, especially p. 125, n. 6; Comte du Mesnil du Buisson, "Les origines du panthéon palmyrenion," Mélanges de l'Université Saint Joseph XXXIX/3 [Beirut, 1964], 169-195). For an attempt at an etymology of the name see H. Ingholt and J. Starcky, "Recueil épigraphique," in the volume by Schlumberger cited above, inscription 2, note 1, at the end. Whether this later Ašar has anything to do with the much earlier Mesopotamian deity may be questioned, but the possibility should not be ruled out a priori.

[75]MAD 3, p. 5. This also holds true of Ālī-DN.

[76]Ba-ba-lum could be interpreted differently, but the parallel with Ba-ba-DINGIR makes the above interpretation more probable.

[77]This interpretation is offered only as a possibility, since it has little comparative support. Another possibility, Mut(um)-Baba Baba-Is-(The)-Man, finds some support in the names Mu-tum-DINGIR and Eš$_4$-dar-mu-ti. If the divine name is taken as the subject in this name, it probably means that the deity provides the protection expected of the man or husband. If mutum is the subject, however, it might mean that the new child was a manifestation of the deity (cf. above, n. 17). It is also possible that this particular name is pure Sumerian and should be omitted from the list.

[78]Edzard, WM, p. 45. The writing ba-ba is known, however, along with some other variant orthographies (RLA 1, p. 432; cf. T. Jacobsen, The Sumerian King List, AS 11, pp.104-105, n. 196). A Goetze pointed to the name Ba-u$_2$-ga-al, which he interpreted as Bau-(u)kal Bau-Is-Holding-(The-Child), as evidence for the earlier reading of the divine name as Bau ("Diverse Names in an Old Babylonian Pay-List," BASOR 95 [1944], p. 21), but his interpretation of the personal name is open to doubt.

[79]SF, VAT 12760, rev. i.

[80]Edzard, WM, p. 45.

[81]Ibid.

[82]This name is to be interpreted in the light of the suggestions made above (n. 17). Assuming that the suffix refers to the father, the meaning of the name may be paraphrased His-Progeny-Is-(A-Manifestation-Of-)-*Balīḫ*.

[83]*Bēlī-Balīḫ/Su'en*, *Kurub-Balīḫ/Su'en*, *Šumšu-Balīḫ/Išum*.

[84]T. Jacobsen, *SKL*, p. 81, n. 76; A. Goetze, "An Old Babylonian Itinerary," *JCS* 7 (1953), p. 53, iii 8, *[UD-x-KAM A]p-qum ša* ^{d}*Balīḫu(KASKAL.KUR)*, "the x day *Apqum* (source) of the divine *Balīḫu*.

[85]This reading of *Ba-lu-uḫ*$_2$*-E*$_2$ is confirmed by the Old Babylonian name ^{m}*Pa-luḫ-bi-tum* (*PBS* 8/1, 101, ii 5, 14).

[86]One could also read this name as *Idī-Bītum* The-Temple-Is-My-Strength, but the derivation from *nadānum* with the assimilation of the final *-n* to the beginning aleph of the second element is supported by Gelb's example from Ur III where the same man's name is written once *I-din-E*$_2$*-a* and another time *I-ti-E*$_2$*-a* (*MAD* 2, pp. 120-121). A derivation from **yadā'*$_4$*um* is excluded, since one would expect either the form *Īda* showing the retention of *'*$_4$ or **Īde* with a reflex following the loss of *'*$_4$. The same pattern is found with *šamā'*$_4$*um*, which usually occurs in the names as *iš-ma/ma*$_2$, but occasionally as *iš-me*. If the interpretation as *Iddin-Bītum* is correct, Stamm's view that *bītum* does not occur in thanksgiving or entreaty names as a theophoric element (*ANG*, p. 91) will not hold for the Old Akkadian material.

[87]See, for example, the names given in *CAD* b, p. 287: *E*$_2$*-še-mi*, *E*$_2$*-kīma-ilim-šēmi*, *Bītum-dayyān*, and *Bītum-muballiṭ*. Note also the Neo-Babylonian, *bītu ana Marduk bēlīya damiqtī tizkaram*, "O temple, recommend me to my lord, Marduk" (*CAD* b, p. 287b).

[88]Literally *Mouth-Of-D/Ṭaban*, but that could be ambiguous used with the name of a river. The personal name probably means that the child had been promised by an oracle from the deity (by the mouth of the deity).

[89]*RLA* 2, p. 96.

[90]*Ibid.*

[91]Both *Durul* and *D/Ṭaban* occur as river names in the date formula for

for Samsuiluna's thirty-second year (RLA 2, p. 185).

[92]See n. 18 above.

[93]The interpretation of this name is open to question. Perhaps one should understand it as Dagan-Sent-(The-Child).

[94]Stamm took ubarum as the equivalent of Hebrew gēr and translated it as "Schutzbefohlener" (ANG, p. 264), but the term seems to imply more than just a rootless sojourner in need of protection. At least in a later period the ubarum appears to have been a foreigner representing in some fashion his native land and as such given special treatment by the palace of the country in which he was living (Elena Cassin, "Quelques remarques à propos des archives administratives de Nuzi," BA 52 [1958], pp. 27-28). On the whole question of ubarum see Henri Cazelles, "Hébreu, Ubru et Hapiru," Syria 35 (1958), pp. 198-217; Martin David, "Beiträge zu den altassyrischen Briefen aus Kappadokien," OLZ 36 (1933), pp. 214-215, n. 8; Hildegard Lewy, "The Nuzian Feudal System," Orient. NS 11 (1942), pp. 321-322, n. 1; E. A. Speiser, AASOR XVI, p. 124; A. Goetze, AASOR XXXI, pp. 109-110; Jean Nougayrol, PRU III, p. 237; Bruno Meissner, MAOG III/3, p. 45.

[95]Cf. W. F. Albright, "Gilgames and Engidu, Mesopotamian Genii of Fecundity," JAOS 40 (1920), p. 319, n. 27, but correct dgg to dgn (Hans Wehr, Arabisches Wörterbuch für die Schriftsprache der Gegenwart [Leipzig: Otto Harrasowitz, 1952], p. 245). The divine name is attested in Akkadian and Ugaritic, and the Philistines adopted the deity when they entered Palestine (Judges 16:23; 1 Samuel 5:2), which suggests that Dagan was also worshipped by the Canaanites far to the south of Ugarit.

Since the name occurs regularly in Akkadian contexts, not Sumerian, the deity is hardly Sumerian. One can always assign the name to an unknown pre-Sumerian, non-Semitic group, but that solves nothing and does not seem necessary. It is true that Dagan is normally written with the determinative, but this may be because he was originally from a non-Akkadian Semitic group. He is not attested in any of the Presargonic Old Semitic names (unless E_2-nim-dDa-gan [D. O. Edzard, "Pantheon und Kult in Mari," CRRA XV (1967), p. 51, n. 7] is from that period, though he does occur in a Presargonic inscription from Mari written without the determinative (ibid., p. 53, n. 1), and even in the Sargonic and later periods Dagan's main cultic centers lie west of the Euphrates at Mari, Tuttul, and Terqa, not in Akkad proper. Cf. W. von Soden, "Zur Einteilung der semitischen Sprachen," WZKM 56 (1960), pp. 185-186.

96 RLA 2, p. 100. For further evidence on this identification see W. G. Lambert, "Enmeduranki and Related Matters," JCS 21 (1967), p. 131; A. Goetze, "An Inscription of Simbar-Šīḫu," JCS 19 (1965), pp. 127-128; CT 46, 39:111; and STT I, 19:58.

97 RLA 2, p. 100.

98 Baʿl is cited as Dagan's son in the Ugaritic material (MRS X, No. 6, i 51-52; No. 14 [Krt]:77-78), a fragment from northern Mesopotamia makes Dagan the father of Addu (CRRA III [1954], p. 129), and the Hurrians identified Dagan with Kumarbi, the father of the storm god, Tešub (E. Laroche, "Notes sur le panthéon hourrite de Ras Shamra," JAOS 88 [1968], p. 150). Elsewhere Kumarbi = Enlil (Edzard, WM, p. 185), but Laroche has convincingly explained that equation as due to prior identification of Dagan and Enlil (Ugaritica V, pp. 524-525). Note also UET VI/2, 398, obv. 17-18: dUraš rabu zāri reštû abūšu ušarbi šīmassu ina pān(IGI) dDagan dNingirsu, Great Uraš, primordial primordial progenitor, his father, exalted his (Marduk's) destiny before Dagan (and)? Ningirsu." Or should these two divine names be read as a compound name, Dagan-Ningirsu?

99 Cf. especially the myth of Enlil and Ninlil, which explains why some of Enlil's children belong to the underworld (Thorkild Jacobsen, "Sumerian Mythology: A Review Article," JNES [1946], pp. 132-136; = Tammuz, pp. 110-111).

100 For the Ugaritic material see René Dussaud, "Deux stèles de Ras Shamra portant une dédicace au dieu Dagon," Syria 16 (1935), pp. 177-180; and David Neiman, "PGR: A Canaanite Cult-Object in the Old Testament," JBL 67 (1948), pp. 55-60. For Mari see ARM III 40 and II 90.

[101] ARM X 63:15.

[102] F. Thureau-Dangin, "Un acte de donation de Marduk-zâkir-šumi," RA 16 (1919), pp. 145, 148.

[103] S. N. Kramer, The Sumerians: Their History, Culture, and Character (Chicago: University of Chicago Press, 1963), pp. 119-121.

[104] Dgn, "grain," which occurs in Aramaic, Hebrew, and Phoenician, is probably derived from the name of the god precisely because he was the power that caused the grain to grow. Kumarbi is also closely linked with grain, so closely in fact that his name is sometimes replaced by the word for grain, ḫalki = NISABA (Ugaritica V, p. 524).

[105] Dagan also had a political role in the Sargonic period, but see the chapter on the royal pantheon for that aspect of his character.

[106] The meaning of this name is unclear. The problem is what to do with the element imi. As Stamm has pointed out, the element is always predicative (ANG, p. 57), and even Martin Noth, who once connected it with the nominal element emu, "father-in-law" ("Gemeinsemitische Erscheinungen in der israelitischen Namengebung," ZDMG nF 6 [1927], p. 34, n. 3), later decided that was very doubtful (IPN, p. 79). B. Gemser derives it from amûm and translates it by "DN has spoken" (De Beteekenis der Persoonsnamen voor onze Kennis van het Leven en Denken der oude Babyloniers en Assyriers [Wageningen, 1924], p. 81). He then interprets it as probably another expression for "to call into existence" (ibid.). The difficulty with this derivation is that the root for the word "to speak" is actually awûm, not amûm. It occurs in Old Akkadian, but with the spelling i-wi, not i-mi (MAD 3, p. 2). Gelb allows the possibility of this derivation, however (ibid.), since he thinks the w to m change can be observed in certain cases for Old Akkadian (MAD 2, p. 123). Of the examples he cites, however, only the last is absolutely sure. Na-mu-ru-um may be the verbal adjective of the N stem of amārum, nammurum<nanmurum, and Na-me-er could be interpreted as an N stem imperative of the same root. Even the example of I-lu-Me-er compared with A-ḫu-We-er does not really solve the

problem in the name under discussion. The etymology of W/Mer is not sure, and the actual order of attestation would point to a m to w change rather than a w to m. Goetze considers it an Amorite element ("Šakkanakkus of the Ur III Empire," JCS 17 [1963], p. 4, n. 34), for which see the Mari name Yami-ila/Pl-mi-i-la (ARM VIII, 9:2), but note APNMT, p. 211. William Moran has recently come out in support of Goetze's view against Huffmon (JAOS 90 [1970], pp. 530-531).

[107]L. Legrain, "Quelques tablettes d'Ur," RA 30 (1933), p. 121, U. 7012; RLA 2, p. 255. Note the date formula for Samsuiluna's thirty-second year: mu id$_2$ dur-ul$_3$ u$_3$ ta$_3$-ba-an mu-un-ba-al, "year that he dredged the river Durul and the river Ṭaban" (RLA 2, p. 185, no. 177).

[108]Cf. Hans Hirsch, "Die Inschriften der Könige von Agade," AfO 20 (1963), p. 32, n. 349; Falkenstein, "Kleine Beiträge," ZA nf 11 (1939), pp. 69-70; MAD 2, p. 81, no. 142; Landsberger, MSL 2, pp. 79-80.

[109]The interpretation of this name is not sure, but the translation suggested above has the merit of relating it to the birth experience. The parent had promised a certain offering if the god would give a child, the child came, and now the parent records the fulfillment of his vow by the very name he gives the child. While the writer knows of no specific passage in Akkadian where a person promises the god a votive offering if the god will grant a child, there can be little doubt that this was common enough practice. The gods often demanded votive gifts in turn for favors: marṣum ina marṣīšu ilum usannaqšūma ikribīšu ušaddanšūma iballuṭ, "the god will press the sick man in his sickness and make him hand over the promised votive gift, and then he will get well" (CAD b, p. 54c). These offerings might be made prior to receiving the divine gift as in the case of this sick man, but they could also be made after the god had granted the child. That way one could put more pressure on the god, since if he did not grant the request, he would lose the promised offering. There are some medical texts that indicate this was done and that the promised votive offerings were not always promptly paid.

Several texts that deal with illnesses of young babies diagnose the cause of the illness as an unpaid votive offering: šumma la'û ina tulî ummīšu ittanadlah ik-ri-bu ṣab-tu-šu$_2$, "If the baby constantly frets at its mother's breast, an (unpaid) votive offering has seized him" (TDP 220:20, 228:103ff., 109; 230:113). One could also consider interpreting the name as I-Have-Become-Lasting-(In-My-Heir)-O-'Ay(y)a.

[110]The meaning of the element en-na has been the subject of an extensive debate. Ungnad interpreted it as the imperative of enēnum with ventive ending (MAS, p. 29), but this interpretation is difficult, since the same element appears to occur in the writings en-nam, en-ni, en-nu, and en-um (MAD 3, p. 52-53). The last three cannot be interpreted as masculine singular imperatives. Julius Lewy, working from the Old Assyrian material, wanted to take the element as ēnum, an old word for "lord," which would be ēnā in Amorite according to Lewy ("Die altassyrischen Rechtsurkunden vom Kültepe," MVAeG 35/3, [1935], pp. 170f., n. 2; "Zur Amoriterfrage," ZA nF 4, [1929], p. 245, n. 3), but Stamm pointed out this would be strange, since Old Assyrian, which has another word for lord, bēlum, lacks the name type *Bēlum-Aššur (ANG, p. 133, n. 1). Thureau-Dangin in a series of articles tried to equate the element with a word he found in mathematical texts in parallel with mi-nam ("Notes sur la terminologie des textes mathématiques," RA 28 [1931], pp. 195-196; "Notes assyriologiques," RA 30 [1933], p. 185, n. 6; "Notes assyriologiques," RA 31 [1934], p. 51, no. 3). He took the word as an interrogative and interpreted a name like Ennam-Sîn as How-Much-(Longer)-O-Sîn, understanding the name as the exclamation of a woman in travail (RA 31 [1934], p. 51, no. 3). Von Soden accepted Thureau-Dangin's interrogative pronoun as proven, though he did not think it occurred in the proper names ("Der hymnisch-epische Dialekt des Akkadischen," ZA 41 [1933], p. 99, n. 1), but by 1938, Thureau-Dangin had decided the EN.NA(M) of the mathematical texts was a Sumerian writing for minu (Textes mathématiques babyloniens [Leiden, 1938], p. 234; cf. Neugebauer and Sachs, Mathematical Cuneiform Texts, AOS 29 [New Haven

1945], p. 162), so the interrogative dropped out of the discussion about the name. Von Soden originally wanted to see the element in the names as a deictic particle related to the en in enma (ZA 41, p. 99), but this runs into trouble with the form en-ni which implies a first person pronominal suffix, and hence a noun, so von Soden changed his mind and along with CAD interpreted the element in the names as a noun ennum, "favor, friendliness, mercy," or the like, used as an exclamation (AHw, p. 219; CAD e, p. 170). As an exclamation there would be no problem explaining the occurrence either of pronominal endings or of the different case endings, though Gelb while accepting this explanation for ennum and ennī, for some unexplained reason, does not believe the form ennam could be derived from a noun (MAD 3, pp. 51-52).

111 The E_3-a writings are all from the Gutian period.

112 MAD 2, pp. 88-89.

113 MAD 2, p. 89. This makes it highly unlikely that the element e_2-a in such names as E_2-a-ba-ni could be the interrogative ay, "where," since the original consonant in that element was a simple aleph (Ugaritic), and Old Akkadian usually writes ay as a-a (MAD 3, p. 2).

114 E. Laroche, "Notes sur le Panthéon Hourrite de Ras Shamra," JAOS 88 (1968), p. 148; Ugaritica V, pp. 518-525.

115 Ugaritica V, p. 248, n. 6. The assimilation was precipitated by the need to find a masculine counterpart to Ay(y)a, the wife of the Akkadian sun god Šamaš, since the West Semitic Šapšu was a goddess, and therefore needed a husband, not a wife, but the choice of E_2-a was clearly more dependent on the similarity between his name and Ay(y)a than on any resemblance in essential nature.

116 One could question the very presence of this -y(y)- on the basis that it is found only at Ugarit, while in Mesopotamia proper one never finds a variant E_2-ya or E_2-ya_8 in spite of the hundreds and hundreds of occurrences of E_2-a. The author does not find this argument from silence convincing, however. The writing of the divine name was obviously fixed in the tradition

quite early, E_3-a being the only clearly attested variant known to this writer, and when traditional orthography dominates to this extent, it is precisely in the peripheral areas where one must look for clues to actual pronunciation. After all, how many times is ^{d}A-a written ^{d}A-ya in Mesopotamia?

[117]One could then relate the divine name to the adjective ḥayy(um), "alive, living," which is used in Hebrew, Syriac, and Arabic to describe spring-fed or running water. This would agree with the later identification ^{d}na-aq-bu$_{IDIM}$, "source, spring," = $^{d}E_2$-a (CT 24, 14:48); the final -a would present some difficulty, since it does not show the nominative case ending -u which one might expect, but the ending -a is characteristic of many of the Old Semitic divine names, e.g., Anda, Ab(b)a, Ay(y)a, Erra, Mamma, and Nanna.

[118]RLA 2, p. 375.

[119]T. Jacobsen in The Intellectual Adventure of Ancient Man, ed. by Henri Frankfort (Chicago: University of Chicago Press [1946]), pp. 146-148; note also the Old Akkadian seal which pictures him with water flowing out of his shoulders (Edzard, WM, p. 57). This is also supported by the identifications a-a = ^{d}En-ki = [^{d}En]-ki (Edmond Sollberger, "A Three-Column Silbenvokabular A," AS 16, p. 22:3), and A_2 = E_2-a = En-ki (PBS V, 106 rev. iv 31), where a-a probably = mu, "water," and A_2 = id_2 = nāru, "river."

[120]Edzard, WM, pp. 56-57.

[121]This name is obscure because the verb bârum, "to be in good health," is normally intransitive, so the ki cannot be read as an accusative pronominal suffix.

[122]This name is the counterpart of the name formation Ir'am-DN DN-Loved. Ra'im designates the name bearer as the recipient of the verbal action expressed in ir'am.

[123]T. Jacobsen in The Intellectual Adventure of Ancient Man, ed. by Henri Frankfort (Chicago: University of Chicago Press [1946]), pp. 140-144.

[124]One could also consider an interpretation Erra-alšu Erra-Has-A-Claim-

Against-Him. This would assume that the name reflects the idiom, so much x PN al PN$_2$ išu, "PN has a claim of so much x against PN$_2$" (MAD 3, p. 72). The expressions ilum ikribī eli awīlim išu and ilum eli awīlim tākultam išu (CAD i, pp. 291-292) illustrate what background one should then suppose for the giving of the name. The parent had vowed to perform a certain offering if the god would grant a child, and with the birth of the child the parent confesses his obligation. There is no evidence for that name formation, however, while the pattern DN-bīt/dūr/illat/āl(um) is well attested.

[125]KAR$_3$ is a fairly common predicative element, but its meaning is unknown.

[126]Much of the following discussion of Erra is based on the author's recent article, "Erra--Scorched Earth," which appeared in the JCS 24 (1971), pp. 11-16. The characterization of Erra has been revised to meet specific objections to this earlier treatment, but my basic point of view remains unchanged.

[127]P. F. Gössmann, Das Era-Epos (Würzburg, 1955). See the literature cited in Rykle Borger, Handbuch der Keilschriftliteratur I (Berlin, 1967), pp. 157-158, and the discussion of Erra in D. O. Edzard, WM, pp. 63-64. (This manuscript was completed before I saw a copy of Luigi Cagni's L'Epopea di Erra, Studi Semitici 34 [Rome, 1969], but a rather hasty examination of the work suggested no revisions in the major theses of this study.)

[128]G. Smith, The Chaldean Account of Genesis (New York, 1876), p. 124.

[129]F. Delitzsch's notes in H. Delitzsch's translation of Smith's book, Chaldaische Genesis (Leipzig, 1876), p. 309.

[130]P. Jensen, Die Kosmologie der Babylonier (Strassburg, 1890), p. 145, n. 1; 445.

[131]Ibid. O. Schroeder argued for this reading of the name on the basis of the phrase u$_2$-ra ša ^{d}Nergal (CT 29, 1:10; VB 6, No. 97), which he mistakenly assumed to contain a syllabic writing of ^{d}ER$_3$.RA (SPAW (1916), p. 1193), and Schroeder was widely followed. R. Labat, for instance, gives Ura as the reading of ^{d}ER$_3$.(RA) in his Manuel d'épigraphie akkadienne (Paris, 1963^4), p.

59, sign 50, and R. Frankena still preserved this reading in his Tākultu, de sacrale maaltijd in het assyrische ritueel (Leiden, 1954), p. 117, no. 237, though he has since adopted the reading Irra.

[132] Cited as a possible reading by Gössmann, Das Era-Epos (Würzburg, 1955), p. 68.

[133] R. Frankena, "Untersuchungen zum Irra-Epos," BiOr 14 (1957), pp. 2-10.

[134] Gössmann, Das Era-Epos (Würzburg, 1955), p. 68; W. G. Lambert, "The Fifth Tablet of the Era Epic," Iraq 24 (1962), pp. 119-125.

[135] Edzard, WM, pp. 63-64.

[136] Ibid.

[137] A. Falkenstein, DLZ 79 (1958), p. 15.

[138] Gössmann, Das Era-Epos (Würzburg, 1955), p. 68.

[139] The determinative is usually omitted until the late Old Babylonian period.

[140] Tallqvist, Götter-epitheta, p. 329; Landsberger, MSL III, p. 209:563. In view of this phonetic equation it is hardly possible to regard ^{d}GIR$_{3}$.RA and ^{d}ER$_{3}$.RA, both of whom are gods of Kutha (TCS III, p. 44:463; CH II, 60), as two separate deities. Nevertheless, the distribution of the orthography ^{d}GIR$_{3}$.RA, limited largely as it is to Sumerian sources, suggests that this orthography is Sumerian, not Akkadian. It probably represents an old Sumerian spelling for the name of the god dating from a period when the original ḫ (see below) was still heard in traces. By Old Babylonian times, however, ^{d}GIR$_{3}$.RA had probably come to be read simply ^{d}Er$_{x}$-ra, the traces of ḫ having by then disappeared from pronunciation. The phonetic development posited here is quite possible. Gelb has cited evidence for E$_{2}$ = *ḫa (MAD 2, p. 25), and in view of the Sumerian correspondence E$_{2}$:GA$_{2}$ (MAD 2, p. 26), there is no difficulty in regarding GIR$_{3}$ as a Sumerian rendering of Semitic *ḫa/ir.

[141] Das Era-Epos (Würzburg, 1955), p. 68.

[142] Ibid.

[143] Charles F. Jean, Tell Sifr, Textes cunéiformes conservés au British

Museum (Paris: Geuthner, 1931), No. 35a.

144 The same man, *Ipqu-Erra*, the son of *Nabi-ilīšu*, is also mentioned in Jean's Nos. 39:33, 56:28; 38:21; and 57:20 under this normal orthography.

145 *Die Götternamen von Ur III*, AnOr 19, p. 38, no. 221.

146 *SGL* II, pp. 36 and 50, line 36. The copy has *^{d}Er$_3$[ ] mi$_2$ na-mu-un-e* (*TCL* 15, 26, rev. 9').

147 K. Hecker, *Grammatik der Kültepe-Texte*, *AnOr* 44, p. 14, % 7.

148 *GAG*, % 9h.

149 A. Poebel noted this as long ago as 1910, though he thought the name was ultimately of Sumerian origin (*Die sumerischen Personennamen zur Zeit der Dynastie von Larsam und der ersten Dynastie von Babylon* [Breslau, 1910], p. 20). The references to Erra in the hymn to Ninurta (Falkenstein, *SAHG*, p. 2) are really misleading since the text has *^{d}GIR$_3$.RA* (*BE* 29, 4, rev. 2). Falkenstein himself reads the name in this passage as *^{d}Gir$_3$-ra* in *ZA* nF 19 (1959), p. 201, without making any explicit connection to Erra.

150 A selection of the Ur III names may be found in Schneider, *Die Götternamen von Ur III*, *AnOr* 19, p. 38, no. 222. Hirsch gives the Old Assyrian names (*Untersuchungen zur altassyrischen Religion*, *AfO* Beih. 13, p. 32), and a partial listing of the Old Babylonian names may be found in Ranke, *EBPN*, p. 209.

151 The root occurs in Akkadian as *erēru* with precisely this meaning (Landsberger, *MSL* 9, p. 219). This meaning is also supported by biblical Hebrew: *ʿwry šḥr mʿly wʿṣmy ḥrh mny ḥrb*, "My skin blackens and peels, my bones are scorched with heat" (Job 30:30, Pope's translation in *The Anchor Bible*); *ky klw bʿšn ymy wʿṣmwty kmwqd nḥrw*, "For my days vanish in smoke and my bones are charred like a hearth" (Psalm 102:4); *hnh l'š ntn l'klh 't šny qṣwtyw 'klh h'š wtwkw nḥr hyṣlḥ lml'kh hnh bhywtw tmym l' yʿśh lml'kh 'p ky 'š 'klthw wyḥr wnʿśh ʿwd lml'kh*, "Lo, it is given to the fire for fuel. The fire has consumed both its ends and its middle is charred--can it be used for anything? Even when it was whole it was not used for anything; how much less,

when the fire has consumed it, and it is charred, can it ever be used for anything" (Ezekiel 15:4-5). The root is also attested in Jewish Aramaic, Ugaritic, and Arabic with similar meanings.

[152]*MAD* 2, pp. 141-142.

[153]For the *i* to *e* change see *MAD* 2, p. 125, though this development could have occurred later due to the following *r*, *GAG* % 9h. For **ḥa* to *e* see *MAD* 2, p. 124, and for the loss of *i* in the penult see *GAG* % 12b.

[154]*GAG* % 55b.

[155]*GAG* % 55c.

[156]*GAG* % 55f.

[157]Erra Epic I, 105 *passim*. (The references to this epic follow the line count in L. Cagni, *Das Erra-Epos Keilschrifttext, Studia Pohl* 5 [Rome, 1970]). Because the name *Išum* is a masculine form while the Akkadian word for fire is always feminine, *išātum*, this interpretation of the name has been questioned (Edzard, *WM*, p. 90), but the masculine form exists in Hebrew *ēš* and may well have existed in Proto-Akkadian--the name *Išum* is attested from the Presargonic period (*OIP* 14, 48, ii 7). The name is clearly Akkadian since it is written without the determinative in the early periods, is limited to Akkadian sources, and, though the case ending and mimation normally seem frozen, it is declined in at least one instance (*CT* 15, Pl. VI, vii 11). Moreover, Išum's connection with fire still shows through in places, as when Erra addresses him *attā dipārumma inaṭṭalū nūrka*, "you are the torch, and they shall behold your light" (Erra Epic I, 10).

[158]Note Arabic *ḥarra*, "stony area; volcanic country, lava field," and Hebrew *hᵉrērîm*, "rocky waste, lava-covered stretches."

[159]The very name Mamma, since it appears to be a baby word for mother (Edzard, *WM*, p. 105), indicates that the goddess was experienced from the very beginning as the power manifesting itself in motherhood, and giving birth remains the deity's basic role (Atra-ḫasīs Epic I, 192-197). The Erra Epic makes her the wife of Erra (I 20), and Weidner's god list gave her as the wife of

Nergal ("Altbabylonische Götterlisten," *AfO* 2 [1924], p. 17:19). Nevertheless, scholars have been bothered by this marriage of fertility and the underworld. Weidner thought Mamma in his list was just a mistake for Māmētu, who is attested as the wife of Nergal in several places (*ibid.*, p. 17, n. 7), and Edzard, who wrote after the Erra texts made a mistake unlikely, simply stated, "Mami and Mame as the spouses of Nergal or Erra are probably identical with Māmītu (abbreviations of the name) and have nothing to do with the mother goddess Mama, Mami" (*WM*, p. 95). It seems rather unlikely, however, that the Akkadian scribe would abbreviate the name of one goddess with the name of another, totally distinct goddess! It is easier to assume that we are dealing with different traditions and that Mamma is the wife of Nergal under his Akkadian name and form as Erra.

[160]His most common epithet is *qardu*, *qarrādu*, or *qurādu*, and he is given a number of other epithets which are also drawn from the realm of war (Tallqvist, *Götterepitheta*, p. 329).

[161]*CT* 39, 26:8.

[162]The outbreak of drought is quite clearly portrayed in II c 16-20:

> *ana Addi aqabbi kila puri[ ] erpeta duppirma purus šal[ga u zunna]....[ša] ina ūm? tuḫdi? irbû ina ūm ṣummê iqab[birūšu] ša uruḫ mê illiku ḫarrān turba'i [itâr]*, "To Adad I will speak, 'Withhold [?], drive away the clouds, and stop the sno[w and rain.'] ...[He who] grew up in a day of plenty they will bury in a day of want. He who went on a well-watered path will return on a dusty road."

The continuation of this passage in IIc and IIIa portrays Erra's proposed all-out assault on civilized society which would drag nature--mountains, seas, reed thickets, and wild animals--into the general devastation along with human society. Thus more than famine produced by drought is involved, but famine, or at least the shortages that result from Erra's depredations, is clearly one factor in the resulting collapse of the Babylonian social fabric so graphically described by the poet. Two of the motifs--conflict within the family between mother and daughter (IIc 34; IIIa 10) and the cessation of childbirth (IIIa 16-17)--also appear in the description of famine found in the Atra-ḫasīs epic (W. G. Lambert, Atra-ḫasīs, pp. 112-115), and several other motifs, such as the man going naked in the street (IIIa 20B), the lack of sacrificial animals (IIIa 22), and the sick man's vain request for meat (IIIa 24), are most easily explained as reflecting a similar situation of extreme shortage.

[163] R. D. Biggs, "More Babylonian 'Prophecies,'" Iraq 29 (1967), pp. 122-123:23-24; VS I, 71:70-71; VAB 7, pp. 32:125-126; 38:79-80; 76:57-59; 132:17-19; 378:7-9.

[164] VAB 7, pp. 132-134, vii 97-viii 19.

[165] VAB 7, p. 78:79-82.

[166] That would fit in perfectly with the similar strategic measure of blocking the Arabs from access to the watering places (VAB 7, p. 74:31-37), and it would explain the severity of the famine among the animals--"the young camels, donkey foals, calves, (and) lambs sucked seven times and more at the mothers who nursed them, yet could not satiate their stomachs with milk" (VAB 7, pp. 76-78; 65-67; 378, ii 13-15; CAD b, p. 35).

[167] The same sequence of fire and famine also occur in VAB 7, p. 32, iii 125, and the Assyrian curse formula, Adad ina biriq lemutti mâssu libriq ana mātīšu ḫušaḫḫa liddi, "May Adad strike his land with terrible lightening; may he cast famine upon his land" (AOT 1, pp. 66:61-62; 92:22-23; 142:28-31; 146:13; 148:12), could reflect a similar thought.

[168] IV 3-6.

[169] IV 7-11.

[170] IV 12-14.

[171] IV 15.

[172] IV 16-19.

[173] IV 20-22.

[174]IV 23-24.

[175]IV 131-135.

[176]CH II 69, compared with CH R XXVIII 24; AfO 2, p. 17:5; KAR 142, rev. iii 27. For Nergal see the study of E. von Weiher, Der babylonische Gott Nergal, AOAT 11 (Neukirchen, 1971).

[177]Tallqvist, Götter-epitheta, p. 329.

[178]CAD d, p. 165.

[179]Landsberger, MSL 2, p. 143. This derivation seems more probable than a derivation from šapāṭum, "to judge," though R. Frankena argues that the use of šiptu, "judgment," to designate an illness could be derived from the view that the sickness resulted from a judicial decision of the gods (Kanttekeningen van een Assyrioloog bij Ezechiel [Leiden: E. J. Brill, 1965], pp. 13-14).

[180]VAB 7, p. 80:120. Streck's interpretation of the word as šiptu, "Strafgericht," does not fit this passage where the context points to a blood bath rather than judicial proceedings.

[181]E. A. W. Budge and L. W. King, Annals of the Kings of Assyria I (London: British Museum, 1902), p. 167:19-23.

[182]V 53-58. Against this interpretation one could cite the use of the epic as an amulet (see JNES 19 [1960], p. 151), but one should remember that amulets are employed against other evils as well as against disease. Moreover, one cannot be sure that each of the evils listed in Reiner's amulets are in fact the names of illnesses.

[183]AHw, p. 554.

[184]Note the sequence of famine and pestilence in the Atra-ḫasīs Epic (Lambert, Atra-ḫasīs, pp. 108-110:42-61).

[185]The Old Babylonian Mari name, Ḫimiṭ-Erra Scorching/Fever-Of-Erra (ARM 13, 19:13), if "fever" is the correct translation of ḫimṭu here, would seem to reflect such a connection.

[186]UR.SAG occurs as an ideogram for qarrādu in the Tell Halaf duplicate to the Erra amulet published by Reiner:

dErra qarrād/UR.SAG DINGIR/DINGIR.ME/DINGIR.MEŠ, "Erra, warrior of the gods" (JNES 19 [1960], p. 151, n. 5).

187 Cf. note 140, above.

188 Cf. note 140, above.

189 KAR 142, iii 46.

190 The names from Lagash and Susa come from the Akkadian garrison stationed there, so they only attest the worship of Erra among the inhabitants of the Akkad area (Thorkild Jacobsen, "Early Political Development in Mesopotamia," ZA nF 18 [1957], p. 137, n. 103; = Tammuz, p. 394, n. 103). The other names are from Tell Asmar, Khafaje, and Adab. The absence of the divine name in the texts from Assyria is strange, since it occurs in Old Assyrian as well as Old Babylonian texts (H. Hirsch, Untersuchungen zur altassyrischen Religion, AfO Beih. 13 [Graz: 1961], p. 32).

191 Buccellati, AUP, p. 154.

192 I. J. Gelb, "Šullat and Ḫaniš," ArOr 18 1/2 (1950), p. 196.

193 GAG % 55 i.

194 I. J. Gelb, "Šullat and Ḫaniš," ArOr 18 1/2 (1950), p. 196.

195 Ibid., pp. 189-198.

196 CT 25, 16:4.

197 XI 96-99.

198 J. J. A. van Dijk, "Textes divers du Musée de Baghdad, II," Sumer 13 (1957), p. 99, pl. 16:12-13, biriq ilīšu Ḫaniš iškun kakkīšu.

199 See above, note 76. With a masculine deity one could also consider the rendering Wife-Of-Ḫarīm. Gelb suggests this name might be the same as DAM-?ḪA-ri_2-im-?A.ZU (RTC 96, rev. ii; MAD 3, p. 132), but the RTC passage is open to several other possibilities: 1 DAM Ḫa-ri_2-im A.ZU lu_2 Na-ḫi-iš-tum bar.sag. giš.ra.a.ka ki.UR.TUR.ta im.$laḫ_4$.$eš_2$, "One wife of Ḫarīm, the doctor, the men of Naḫištum led from UR.TUR because of a murder," or "One wife of Ḫarīm-asûm, the man of Naḫištum, they led from UR.TUR because of a murder."

200 AHw, p. 323.

[201]This process is attested in the way the Akkadian scribes handled the laryngals in the West Semitic names from Mari (A. Finet, *L'Accadien*, p. 17 % 10), and the quadrilingual vocabulary from Ugarit treats this very West Semitic root in precisely this fashion: *ḫa-ri-mu* (*Ugaritica* V. No. 137 II 39', 40', 42').

[202]Note the West Semitic personal names *Ḥarīm* (Heb.), *Mlkḥrm* (Pu.), and *Ḥrm* (Ug., F. Gröndahl, *Die Personennamen der Texte aus Ugarit*, *Studia Pohl* 1 [Rome, 1967], p. 136); and compare Arabic *ḥarīm*, "a sacred inviolable place, sanctuary, sacred precinct."

[203]*ARMT* XV, p. 160; *APNMT*, p. 271.

[204]One could take *il* in this name as the absolute state of the generic word *ilum*, "god," since it functions syntactically as a vocative (*GAG* % 62j).

[205]This interpretation of the name assumes that the child is seen as a manifestation of Il (cf.nn. 17-18). One could take *il* as a vocative and translate the name as He-Stayed-In-Good-Health-O-God, but the overwhelming majority of names formed on the pattern Preterite + DN have the divine name as the subject.

[206]This interpretation assumes that the loss of mimation on the dative suffix is due to assimilation to the following aleph.

[207]One could also consider *palālum* as the verbal root in this name, which would have the advantage of relating the verbal root to the element *pālil*, which also occurs in Old Akkadian names. The difficulty with this is that *palālum* is an i-class verb in its two clear occurrences (*AHw*, p. 813). *Balālum*, on the contrary, has the right thematic vowel, though its meaning, "to mix," seems a little strange. Perhaps one should understand it as a mythopoeic expression for the god molding the child in the womb analogous to Job 10:8-11. The D stem is used in the Atraḫasīs Epic to describe the creation of man by the mixing of clay with the blood and flesh of a slain god, *ilam ištēn liṭbuḫūma...ina šērīšu u damīšu Nintu liballil ṭiṭṭa ilumma u awīlum libtallilū puḫur ina ṭiṭṭi* (*CT* 46, 4, iii 22-27; *Atra-ḫasīs*, I 208-213).

[208]Stamm took the verbal element in this name in the normal Akkadian sense of "to plunder," and therefore assumed that it must indicate that sickness or death had raged in the family of the newborn child (_ANG_, p. 291). The root occurs in Hebrew, however, with the meaning, "draw out," and the old passive participle form of this root is related to childbirth in both Hebrew and Arabic: Talmudic Hebrew _šālīl_, "embryo, abortion"; Arabic _salīlun_, "newborn child."

[209]_Il$_x$(IL + KAR$_2$)_ appears to be a mere orthographic variant of _il_, cf. _MAD_ 2, pp. 78, no. 134-134a; 226, no. 134.

[210]This interpretation is based on a comparison with the Ugaritic name _yṯil_, taking _yṯ_ as the equivalent of Ugaritic _iṯ_, later Hebrew _yēš_ (cf. Uyechi as cited by Gröndahl, _Die Personennamen der Texte aus Ugarit_, _Studia Pohl_ 1 [Rome, 1967], p. 147). Albright's earlier attempt to interpret Hebrew _'iš/'eš-ba'al_ in the same fashion (_Archaeology and the Religion of Israel_ [Baltimore: The Johns Hopkins Press, 1942], p. 207, n. 62) is attractive, but the Ugaritic name _išb'l/i-ši-ba'al_ (Gröndahl, _Die Personennamen der Texte aus Ugarit_, p. 102) raises difficulties. How is one to explain the final _-i_ vowel in the syllabic writing, _i-ši_ (cf. I Chron. 11:11, where the Greek has _Iesebaal_), and can one assume that the forms _iṯ_ and _iš_ were used contemporaneously? See Moran's comments in _CBQ_ 16 (1954), pp. 237-238, but compare Mitchell Dahood, _Ugaritic-Hebrew Philology_ (Rome: Pontificial Biblical Institute, 1965), p. 52, no. 392, for another interpretation of the name. _Išu-Il_ cannot be rendered I-Have-The-"God" (the spirit of a deceased child) as the _CAD_ would render the related name _I-su-DINGIR_ (i, p. 102), since this would demand inflection with the accusative case, _Išu-ilam_.

[211]Cf. n. 18 above.

[212]Gelb suggests that the verbal element in this name could be the imperative plural of _N'D_ (_MAD_ 3, p. 17). If one takes _il_ as a divine name, that is morphologically possible here. Landsberger argued that the transitive verb _nâdum_ formed its imperative as _nād-nādā_ (_OLZ_ 1925 , p. 231) and his view was

accepted by von Soden (GAG % 107q), Stamm (ANG, pp. 22, 103-104, 134, 202), Goetze (Language XX [1944], p. 165), and others, but the evidence for this conclusion is not imposing. As far as I can see the evidence is primarily drawn from the personal names of the type DN-na-da, where the case of the DN is not evident. If the name Ilam-na-da actually existed, this would make Landsberger's case, but I know of no example where such a name is spelled out syllabically so that the first element is unambiguously shown to be in the accusative case. On the other hand, there are names where the element na-da must clearly be taken as a stative: A-bu-um-na-da (Muazzez Çiğ and Ratice Kizilyay, "Additions to Series B and C of Personal Names from Old Babylonian Nippur," AS 16, p. 54), A-ḫu-na-da (ibid., p. 51). Moreover, in the name list that these examples come from, the element nada consistently occurs in predicate position following an element that occurs in the preceding and following names as the subject of a nominal sentence, e.g.:

dŠamaš-ba-ni

dŠamaš-na-da

dŠamaš-NA.GAD

dŠamaš-na-ṣir

The Old Assyrian name, Be-LIM-na-da, would point in the same direction, since LIM is the normal writing for lum_2 (MAD 2, p. 150), and the parallel name formation Be-LIM-ba-ni, Be-lu-ba-ni, Bi-LIM-ba-ni (Stephens, PNC, p. 26), lends weight to this interpretation.

Nevertheless, the same element i-da also occurs before i_3-lum where a plural imperative would make no sense. Since there is no unambiguous example of the element before an accusative in Old Akkadian--the name type idā-ilam/bēlam/šarram Praise-The-God/Lord/King, is not attested--it is better to derive i-da from *$yad\bar{a}'_4um$.

The exact meaning of the name is not clear, and the fact that the same form is used for both present and preterite adds to the problem. It could be the beginning of a long sentence name, Il-Knows/Knew-That ..., but these are very rare in the Old Akkadian period. One could conceivably connect it to the Old Assyrian expression ilum lu i-di$_2$, "May the god be my witness!" (CAD i, p. 22), and translate, Il-Is-My-Witness. A third possibility, and the one the writer favors, is to connect the name with the later Ilī-i-da-an-ni My-God-Knows-Me (CAD i, p. 27), and take the verb in the sense of "to care for" (CAD i, p. 27).

213The interpretation of this name is unsure. One could read Šarrī-Il Il-Is-My-King, but šarrum is normally written sar-ru/ri$_2$ (MAD 3, pp. 286-287). Perhaps this should be taken as the stative of the verbal element iš-ri$_2$, which occurs in the name Iš-ri$_2$-DINGIR, but the meaning of that name is also dubious. There is some resemblance to Hebrew Yiśrā-'ēl, but this cannot be taken at face value, because W. F. Albright has argued on the basis of Egyptian material that the original pronunciation of the Hebrew name was *Yaśir'el (The Vocalization of the Egyptian Syllabic Orthography, AOS 5 [New Haven, 1934], p. 34, and literature cited there).

214Il in both this name and Il-bēlī is written with the sign il$_2$, which appears to be a simple orthographic variant of il, though it does not occur often enough to establish that point.

215There are other personal names which may contain the divine name Il, but they are either of doubtful interpretation or capable of other explanation: Presargonic: As$_2$-dan-il (WF, VAT 9074, 2; 9111, 6), Il-LAGAD+$^{zu}_{zu}$-Sar (WF, VAT 12520, 7), Il-tu(d)-tu(d) (WF, VAT 126548). However, if the Sargonic name A-mur-ru-k[i?-m]a?-DINGIR has been correctly restored, it should probably be listed here (see above, p. 15).

216The suggestion of Sollberger ("Selected Texts from American Collections," JCS X [1956], p. 16) and Bottéro (ADS, p. 39) that ilum should also be interpreted as a proper divine name is far more questionable. It will be treated in detail in chapter III.

217The only way il in these names can be explained as a syntactically conditioned form of ilum is by taking il as the vocative rather than as the subject, but such an analysis of the syntactical structure of these names has little to commend it. Ištup-il is a parallel name formation to Ištup-DINGIR, and the syntactical function of DINGIR in this name is clearly indicated by the corresponding genitive-construction name, Sa-at-be-DINGIR/Šaṭp(u)-ilim/. Since the verbal adjective šaṭpum designates the child as the object upon which the god performed the action implied in the verb šaṭāpum, DINGIR must be the subject of the verbal-sentence name:

a) Ištup-ilum The-God-Preserved

b) Šaṭp(u)-ilim Preserved-Of-The-God

But, if DINGIR is the subject in Ištup-DINGIR, il can hardly be refused that role in Ištup-Il, and that means that il cannot be explained as a syntactical form of ilum. The form can be explained as a proper divine name, however, since these normally stand without case endings and mimation in the Old Akkadian period (MAD 2, pp. 139f).

[218]To avoid this conclusion one must either assume a double predicate or interpret il as a vocative and take the stative as referring to the child, Rabi-il He-Is-Great-O-God. The first interpretation is very dubious since this is a rare name formation--it is attested in Ḫaš(i)ḫ-amir He-Was-Desired-He-Was-Seen (CAD h, p. 135), and possible in some names with i-sar as one component (CAD b, p. 126)--and the second interpretation is also improbable. There is no clear example where rabi in the nominal-sentence names refers to the child, but it does occur in unambiguous names as the predicate adjective with the divine name as subject: Ra-bi_2-i_3-lum, Eštar-rabiat.

[219]It is hardly possible to interpret this name as a nominal-sentence name with il as the predicate, since the numerous undisputed proper divine names which occur with puzur invariably occur in final position just as il does in Puzur-Il. For a nominal-sentence name that would be very peculiar, since as the grammatical analysis in the first chapter indicated, the proper divine names usually occur in first position in the nominal-sentence names, and they are almost invariably to be taken as the subject. One could assume

rare inverted word order and interpret *puzur* as the predicate (cf. Sollberger, *Texts From Cuneiform Sources I* [Locust Valley, N.Y.: J. J. Augustin, 1966], p. 162), but that would leave *il* without any satisfactory syntactical explanation. The interpretation of the name as a genitive-construction name remains the most probable. Only this interpretation is able to explain why *puzur*, which occurs in scores of names, is found outside of first position in only one instance (*MAD* 3, pp. 220-222). As the *nomen regens* in a construct chain it would have to be in first position.

[220]See the discussion in M. Pope, *El in the Ugaritic Texts* (Leiden, 1955), pp. 16-19.

[221]It is missing only in Ethiopic where it has apparently been replaced by another word (*ibid*., p. 1, n. 1).

[222]*Īṣi-il* is the only Il name which appears to be Old Amorite, though the possibility that others are should be left open.

[223]The Akkadian prayed for children, e.g., Etana's prayer (Samuel Langdon, "The Legend of Etana and the Eagle, or the Epical Poem 'The city they hated,'" *Babyloniaca* XII [1931], Pl. III 39-40), and one must suppose that their prayers were often given an oracular answer. Šamaš's answer to Etana could be interpreted this way, though it may not have been and probably was not the typical oracular answer to a prayer for children (*ibid*., 41-43). The number of omen texts that contain apodoses relating to childbirth indicate that the oracular answer to the prayer for children was given through the normal divinitory channels of extispicy (*YOS* X, 11 v 12-13; 17:40; 41:7), oil omens (*YOS* X, 57:6), dreams (*Dream Book*, p. 319, Sm 2073, z + 7, 13, 15), *etc*. Cf. *CAD* a, pp. 289f. For West Semitic parallels see the story of Hannah (1 Sam. 1) and the Keret Epic.

[224]The expression *annu kīnu*, "reliable yes" (*AHw*, p. 53), is a similar use of the root *KWN* in the context of an oracular promise.

[225]It can hardly refer to the survival of the mother, though this is mentioned in some texts which deal with difficulties in childbirth (*l ulladma*

ina''eš, "she will bear once and recover," AMT 45, 5:6; līlidma libluṭ ša libbīšu līšir, "Let her give birth, and let her recover. Let her offspring be normal," BA 10/1, p. 69; CAD e, p. 354), since the name Šaṭp(u)-ilim clearly indicates that the object of the verbal action implied in Išṭup-Il is the child.

[226]Cf. tablet 40 of TDP and CAD b, p. 54d. The word šaṭāpum does not occur in any of these passages, but it is a synonym of balāṭum and nêšum, which do occur, so in light of the rare attestation for šaṭāpum this is no serious objection.

[227]The names Īṣi-Il, Ibūr-Il, and Išu-Il also relate to childbirth, if they have been interpreted correctly. Išu-Il is the least clear, but one could understand it either in the sense that the new child is a manifestation of the god, or as a confession which sees the birth of the child as a demonstration of the effective presence of the deity.

[228]DINGIR occurs with petûm as well as with balālum and šalālum. It also occurs with banûm, but that tends to be a less specific reference to the god's character, since it occurs with several deities and probably implies only that the deity was the personal god of the individual named.

[229]Keret A, 37.

[230]It is to 'El that Keret prays for an heir (A 57-58); 'El gives Keret the directions on how to acquire the right bride (A 60ff.); and 'El is the god who blesses Keret with the promise of seven sons and several daughters (B ii-iii).

[231]MAD 3, pp. 220-221.

[232]Ibid., pp. 233-234.

[233]The Old Akkadian Il is conspicuously lacking in any of the warlike traits that have recently been suggested for the Canaanite 'El (P. D. Miller, Jr., "El the Warrior," Harvard Theological Review 60 [1967], pp. 411-431), but as Miller notes, there is no hint of this warlike character of 'El in the Ugaritic texts published up to now (ibid., p. 411). It appears to be a trait

preserved for the most part among the less urbanized population of southern Canaan (ibid., p. 431). Even its prominence there, however, may be the result of a partial coalescence of 'El, the creator and clan leader, who as such would be characterized by love for the clan and a zeal to defend it, with Baal, the cosmogonic creator and cosmic warrior. One should note, however, that Il-aba, who is most probably an Il figure, is a war god.

[234]For these 'El names see A. Murtonen, A Philological and Literary Treatise on the Old Testament Divine Names אל, אלוה, אלהים, and יהוה, Studia Orientalia Edidit Societas Orientalis Fennica XVIII/1 (Helsinki, 1952), p. 31. Murtonen interprets nšl as "bereave," but I would take it in the meaning "to extricate" and interpret it as referring specifically to childbirth just as with šalālum in Akkadian.

[235]This interpretation assumes that the new child was regarded as a manifestation of the deity (see notes 17 and 18 above). One could read the divine name as a vocative, however, He-Has-Arrived-O-Il-aba.

[236]Poebel tried to equate Zababa and DINGIR.A.MAL by reading the latter as Za^{m}-a-ma_3 (PBS IV, p. 230, n. 1; OLZ 1912, p. 484), but this will not work because they occur in the same text as separate deities ("Keilschrifttexte nach Kopien von T. G. Pinches," AfO 13 [1939-41], p. 46, obv. ii 5; p. 47, rev. ii 6) and are the city gods of different cities (TH 35, 41). Gelb reads the name as ^{d}A-ba_4 (MAD 2, p. 83), while Oppenheim reads it as ^{d}$Amba_3$ (according to Edith Porada, "Notes on the Sargonic Cylinder Seal," Iraq 22 [1960], p. 120, n. 34b). No unambiguous evidence for either reading was presented, however.

[237]Landsberger regards him as one of the early pre-Sumerian gods (according to Porada, ibid.), but that cannot be proved as long as the pre-Sumerian linguistic situation remains relatively unknown.

[238]UM 55-21-322, obv. 1. This reference was pointed out to the author by Prof. Sjöberg.

[239]He is mentioned only sporadically after the Old Akkadian period (RLA

1, p. 91). For further discussion see pp. 148-149.

240 Both these names could be interpreted as Sumerian (Sudi [KA + SU]-DINGIR.AB and Ur-DINGIR.AB), but that does not seem likely since they come from areas where the Akkadian names dominate. One should also consider the name DINGIR.AB (E. Sollberger, "Selected Texts from American Collections," JCS X [1956], A 26 iv 6 and v 9). Sollberger rendered this name Ilum-abī (ibid., p. 16), but that name is otherwise unattested in the Sargonic sources. It could be read as ^{d}Ab and interpreted as a hypocoristic name like Adda, or one could read it as Sumerian DINGIR.AB.(ak) Belonging-To-DINGIR.AB.

241 See W. F. Albright, Yahweh and the Gods of Canaan (London: Athlone Press, 1968), pp. 122-124; Ugaritica V, pp. 44-46.

242 SF, VAT 12761, 1.

243 H. de Genouillac, "Grande liste de noms divins sumériens," RA 20 (1923), p. 98, i 41.

244 CT 24, 22:98.

245 H. de Genouillac, "Grande liste de noms divins sumériens," RA 20 (1923), p. 98, i 38-48.

246 Compare Ennī-illa to En-ni-li$_2$, En-ni-ma-da-ad, and En-ni-Ma-mi (MAD 3, p. 52); Puzur-Illa to Puzur-Enlil/Su'en/Eštar/etc. (MAD 3, pp. 220-221).

247 It could hardly be a mistake for the more common illat(um), however, since it occurs in two separate names.

248 CAD i, p. 86. One could also consider a root *Ilā, "god," but the double l makes that doubtful.

249 The interpretation of this name is not sure, but the one offered above seems the most likely.

250 MAD 3, pp. 39-40.

251 CAD i, p. 84; PB 1561.

252 ŠL 399, 15.

253 Schlobies, Der akkadische Wettergott in Mesopotamien, MAOG 1/3 (Leipzig: E. Pfeiffer, 1925), p. 7.

[254] Cf. DINGIR/DINGIR-su/Eštar/^{d}ID$_2$-laba (MAD 3, pp. 159-160) and 'Ayya/Eštar/ilī/Addu/Mamma/Šamaš/^{d}Šulgi-šadu (MAD 3, p. 264).

[255] Gelb, "The Name of the Goddess Innin," JNES 19 (1960), p. 74.

[256] Jacobsen, "Ancient Mesopotamian Religion: The Central Concerns," PAPS 107/6 (1963), p. 476, n. 6; = Tammuz, pp. 322-324, n. 6.

[257] MAD 3, p. 295.

[258] Ibid., p. 70. There are several other names where Išar may represent a divine name, but they are less sure: Išar-aḫī (HSS X, 176:9; MAD 1, 219:6), Išar-bēlī (ITT I, 1472, iv 5; MCS 9/1, 235:14), Išar-bānī (RTC 249, i 6), Išar-ilī (MCS 4, p. 13, 3:10), Išar-šarrī (RTC 127, rev. iv 3), Abī-Išar (RTC 169), Abu-Išar (ITT IV, 7449:3), Aḫu-Išar (BIN 8, 144:14).

[259] Georges Dossin, "Un 'panthéon' d'Ur III a Mari," RA 61 (1967), pp. 99-100:28.

[260] It can mean, "normal, regular, straight, ordinary, prosperous, favorable, fair, just or correct" (CAD i, p. 224).

[261] PB 1473-1477; ^{d}I-šar-ma-ti-su, ^{d}I-šar-ki-di-su, ^{d}I-šar-be$_2$-ri-su, ^{d}I-šar-li-su, and ^{d}I-šar-pad-da are all identified with Nergal (E. F. Weidner, "Altbabylonische Götterlisten," AfO 2 [1924], pp. 16-17).

[262] Edzard, WM, p. 90.

[263] Ibid. This aspect is especially prominent among the Hittites where Išḫara was the queen or goddess of oaths and could inflict sickness on those who broke the oath; E. Douglas Van Buren, "The Scorpion in Mesopotamian Art and Religion," AfO 12 (1937), p. 3; Johannes Friedrich, "Der hethitische Soldateneid," ZA 35 (1924), pp. 166:22 and 186; Emil Forrer, "Die Inschriften und Sprachen des Hatti-Reiches," ZDMG nF 1 (1922), p. 245.

[264] Bezold, Cat. IV 1438.

[265] ABRT I, 3:17; BMS 7, rev. 59; 57:2.

[266] Šurpu II 172; CT 33, 3:29; III R 43, iv 28. She is also called "the mistress of the lands" (BMS 67:14), and among the Hittites "the lady of the mountains and rivers of Hittite land" (E. Douglas van Buren, "The Scorpion

in Mesopotamian Art and Religion," *AfO* 12 [1937], p. 3).

[267] II *R* 60:14. This is troublesome because Išḫara does not seem to have been part of the Kisurra pantheon in the Old Babylonian period (Renger, "Götternamen in der altbabylonischen Zeit," *HSAO*, p. 164, 143-144).

[268] *KAV* 173:12; *CT* 26, 42, i 8.

[269] For the love aspect note *ana* ^{d}*Išḫara mayyālum nadīma*, "For Išḫara the bed is laid out" (Gilgameš, Pennsylvania Tablet, rev. ii 22-23), and another passage in the Atraḫasīs Epic where a marriage is being celebrated, *9 ūmī [liššа]kin hidūtum Ištar[litta]bbû* ^{d}*Išḫara*, "Let the festival be held for nine days. Let them repeatedly call Ištar Išḫara" (*CT* 46, pl. 8:23-24; reconstruction of Lambert, cited by Finklestein, "Ana bīt emim šasû," *RA* 61 [1967], p. 133. Cf. now W. G. Lambert, *Atra-ḫasīs*, p. 155. This restoration is not sure, however, since the Gtn of *nabû* is otherwise unattested). This trait clearly goes back to Old Akkadian times, for it is found in the Old Akkadian love incantation recently published by Gelb (*MAD* 5, 8:33). For the war aspect see III *R* 43, iv 28, ^{d}*Išḫara GAŠAN-li-ti da-ad-ma ina tāḫāzi danni lā išemmīšu*, "Išḫara, the mistress of the inhabited places, will not hear him in the strong battle."

[270] Jos. Epping and J. N. Strassmaier, "Neue babylonische Planeten-Tafeln," *ZA* 6 (1891), p. 242:21.

[271] The vocalization *i-ni-ib* in the king list must be taken with a grain of salt, since while the king list gives the names of Presargonic kings, it was written in the later period.

[272] This appears to be a hypocoristic name like *Adda*.

[273] The remnants of the signs in this name support Jacobsen's reading, but the meaning of the name is odd, so perhaps the signs should be restored differently.

[274] Stamm's statement that *dāri* is not said of "eigentlichen Goettern" must be corrected on the basis of this name (*ANG*, p. 284, n. 1).

[275] This is an abbreviated form of the preceding name.

[276]For the contraction of the final *a* of the particle and the beginning *i* of *ilī* compare *I$_3$-li$_2$-mi-la-at/Ilī-ma-illat/* (*MAD* 3, p. 166). Gelb wants to connect *me-NI* to a noun *menyum*, "love " (*MAD* 3, p. 179).

[277]The interpretation of this name is difficult. There does not seem to be a good Akkadian derivation for *a-ma-an*, since one would not expect the ancient name-giver to speak of Eštar as *āmânûm*, "gossipy." One could derive it from West Semitic *'MN*--cf. the Phoenician names *'l'mn* and *['smn]'mn* (Harris, *AOS* 8, pp. 77-78)--but if *E-ma-an-Eštar* (below) is just a variant to the same name, this etymology is unlikely, since the aleph should not have caused the *a* to *e* shift in Old Akkadian (*MAD* 2, p. 119).

[278]This name could also be read as *Amur-Eštar* Look-O-Eštar (*MAD* 2, p. 181), but later names like *A-mur-i-lu-su$_2$* I-Saw-His-Divinity (*ANG*, p. 185f.) point more to the preterite interpretation.

[279]This name is open to other possibilities: *Dādī-Eštar* Eštar-Is-My-Beloved, or *Dādi-Eštar* Beloved-Of-Eštar. In the last interpretation the final *i* on *dādi* is simply the construct of a monosyllabic noun with a long vowel like *qāti* and *māri*; compare *Šar-kali-šarrī DUMU da-ti ^{d}En-lil*, "Šar-kali-šarrī, the son beloved of Enlil" (*BE* 1, 2:2).

[280]This interpretation assumes that *ūbil* is used here in abbreviated fashion for the idiom *pānī wabālum*.

[281]There is also a group of theophoric personal names from the Diyala region which may conceal the goddess Eštar under the ideogram *^{d}INANNA*, but the names could be interpreted as Sumerian, so they have not been included.

[282]It is possible that the name should actually be read as Aštar in Old Akkadian, since the first sign is just a variant of *aš* (*MAD* 2, pp. 47-48).

[283]Pope, *WM*, pp. 249-250.

[284]*Ibid.*, pp. 250-252. Eštar appears under four forms in the Presargonic Mari material: *^{d}INANNA x ZA.ZA*, *^{d}INANNA-ṣar$_x$-bat*, *Eš-dar-ra-at*, and *^{d}INANNA.UŠ* (D. O. Edzard, "Pantheon und Kult in Mari," *CRRA* XV, pp. 53-54). The last name is problematic, however, since as Jacobsen suggested, the

element *-uš* may merely represent an allomorph of the dative element *-iš* (*OIP* LVIII, p. 295). From the Old Babylonian period one also has the divine names *Eš$_4$-tar$_2$-ra-da-na* (*ARM* X, 87:5, 16-17, 26) and *Eš$_4$-tar$_2$-BI-iš$_3$-ra-(an)* (*ARM* VII, 263, i 2; X 50:15; W. von Soden has proposed the reading *Ištar-Qa$_2$-ab-ra* for this last name, *Ugarit-Forschungen* I [Neukirchen, 1969], p. 198).

[285]Pope, *WM*, p. 249. This astral interpretation has been questioned (J. Plessis, *Étude sur les texts concernant Ištar = Astarté* [Paris, 1921], p. 266; T. H. Gaster, *Thespis: Ritual, Myth and Drama in the Ancient Near East* [New York: Schuman, (1950)], pp. 126-127, n. 36), but the identification with Venus is clear in the case of the South Arabians and the Akkadians, and there is evidence for the astral nature of the West Semitic ʿAṯtar/ʿAṯtart in Ugaritic (John Gray, "The Desert God ʿAṯtr in the Literature and Religion of Canaan," *JNES* 8 [1949], pp. 72-83), in an Egyptian text from the time of Merneptah, where the goddess is called "the mistress of heaven" (W. Herrmann, "Aštart," *MIO* 15 [1969], p. 51), and in the later Greek and Roman identification (F. Cumont, "Astarte," *REA* 2, pp. 1776-1778).

[286]The feminine form occurs in Akkadian, but apart from the Presargonic Mari material it seems to be a secondary formation from the divine name Ištar. Because of the popularity of this goddess her name was made into a common noun for goddess which took the feminine ending in the plural, *ištaru(m)-ištarātu(m)*, and the feminine singular form *ištartu(m)* then developed by a backformation from the plural (*CAD* i, p. 271).

[287]This is indicated by a late Akkadian text which makes Venus female as the evening star and male as the morning star (III *R* 53, n. 2 obv.).

[288]Cf. Chapter IV.

[289]Cf. Edzard, *WM*, pp. 84-85. As Edzard correctly notes, the oft-repeated interpretation of Eštar as a mother goddess is incorrect. The name *Eštar-ummī* refers to Eštar in the role of the personal goddess, not to her divine nature.

[290]Old Akkadian preserves only faint traces of a male Eštar. The name

Eštar-mutī could be interpreted in that manner, and the use of a masculine predicate in the woman's name *Eštar-pāliq*--the name is followed by *u 1 DUMU-sa*, "and her one son" (*MAD* 1, 7, i 10)--may also point to a male Eštar. The evidence, however, is insufficient to establish this hypothesis.

[291]W. F. Albright, *Yahweh and the Gods of Canaan* (Garden City: Doubleday & Company, 1968), pp. 128-132.

[292]W. Herrmann has clearly demonstrated the war aspect for West Semitic ʿAṯtart ("Aštart," *MIO* 15 [1969], 6-51), but the sexual aspect which he apparently wants to deny (*ibid*., p. 45) is also attested. The description of Keret's future bride in Keret 146, *km tsm ʿṯtrt ts[m]h*, "her beauty is like the beauty of ʿAṯtart," has far more to do with sex than war.

[293]At Ugarit ʿAnat is "the Virgin ʿAnat" (W. P. Albright, *Yahweh and the Gods of Canaan* (Garden City: Doubleday & Company, [1968], p. 130). Egyptian representations of ʿAṯtart often picture her as a naked girl with immature breasts (*ibid*., p. 133), and Akkadian Eštar is consistently pictured as a young woman.

[294]Georg Jacob, *Studien in arabischen Dichtern* II, p. 109, III, p. 129; A. Haldar, *Association of Cult Prophets Among the Ancient Semites* (Uppsala, 1945), pp. 191-192; T. Jacobsen, "Babylonia and Assyria: V. Religion," *Encyclopaedia Britannica*, 1968, II, 975; = *Tammuz*, p. 28. Note also the presence of women at the duel between Sinuhe and the hero of Retenu (*ANET*, p. 20), and cf. Ex. 15:20, I Sam. 18:6-7, and P. C. Craige's comments on the role of Deborah ("The Song of Deborah and the Epic of Tukulti-Ninurta," *JBL* LXXXVIII [1969], pp. 259-260) for a later development of this practice.

[295]Gilgameš VI.

[296]This reading has been established by W. G. Lambert, "The Reading of the God Name *^{d}KA.DI*," *ZA* nF 25 (1969), 100-103.

[297]The name appears to be composed of the divine name *Ištar* + *-ān* (*ibid*., p. 103), but the precise grammatical function of the final element *-ān* is not clear.

[298]Ibid., p. 103. The suggestion that the deity was of Elamite origin (Edzard, WM, p. 119) was based on the erroneous reading of the divine name as Sataran (Ernst Weidner, "In aller Kürze," AfO 16 [1952], p. 24).

[299]TCS III, Temple Hymn 33: E. R. Weidner, "Die Feldzüge Samsi-Adads V. gegen Babylonien," AfO 9 (1933), p. 99.

[300]UET VIII/2, 11.

[301]Cf. footnotes 17-18 above.

[302]The author of the Erra Epic etymologizes the name as Sumerian (i = nâda and šum = ṭabāḫu) to get Išum ṭābiḫu na'du, "Išum the famous slayer," but this merely represents the author's love for etymologies, spurious and otherwise, that has been noted before (see W. G. Lambert's review of F. Gössmann's Das Era-Epos, AfO 19/2 [1958], p. 400).

[303]In CT 15, Pl. VI, vii 11, the name is even declined with case ending and mimation.

[304]The masculine occurs in Hebrew 'ēš, "fire."

[305]I 10.

[306]I 105 passim.

[307]CT 16, 49:305.

[308]CT 16, 15, v 22.

[309]Erra Epic I 21.

[310]This would seem to follow from the statement that Išum as the night watchman "gives light like the day," unammaru kīma ūmi (Erra Epic I 22).

[311]Erra Epic I 105, passim.

[312]TuL 7:16.

[313]He consistently occurs among the underworld gods in lists (MDP 6, Pl. 10, v 33-vi 4; Šurpu 8:20).

[314]See Schiller's beautiful statement of this double aspect of fire in his "Das Lied von der Glocke" Schillers Sämtliche Werke I, edited by E. von der Hellen (Stuttgart and Berlin: Gotta'sche Buchhandlung, 19??), pp. 50-52, lines 155-217.

[315] E. F. Weidner, "Altbabylonische Götterlisten," AfO 2 (1924), p. 17:24.

[316] dIšum mālikšu mukīl abbutti ētir napištim rā'im kināti, "Išum, his counselor, the intercessor, who saves life, who loves righteousness ... " (TuL 7:16).

[317] V 40-41.

[318] Erra I 2; cf. CT 16, 15, v 22; 49:305.

[319] Enlil pāšu īpušamma izzakkar ana lābatim dIštar (Inanna) ayyam aḫaki tariāt aḫaki ša ana aḫīki waldu dIšam dNinlil ana Šamaš (dUTU) ūlidma, "Enlil opened his mouth and spoke to the lioness Istar, 'Which is your brother (kinsman?) that you are tending? Your brother (kinsman?) who was born to your brother?' (Ištar replied), 'Ninlil bore Išum to Šamaš'" (CT 15, Pl. VI, vii 7-11). This text is strange because Ninlil is not the wife of the sun god, but the idiom walādu ana can hardly mean anything else except Ninlil has Samas's baby, unless it is being used as an adoption formula as in Nuzi (CAD a, p. 291), and that is very unlikely.

[320] ABRT I, 58:11.

[321] CT 25, 48:14.

[322] KAV 63, ii 42.

[323] The BIN reference mentions SAG.UB^{ki}, a site near Lagash (cf. BIN 8, 141:13-14).

[324] A connection between these writings and GAR_3 which also occurs in some other names cannot be rigorously demonstrated, but it seems probable (MAD 3, pp. 148-149).

[325] MAD 3, p. 148; von Soden suggests kārum/karrum, "quay, trade authority" (AHw, p. 452), but this is questionable as he indicates.

[326] Cf. Su'en/Eštar/Ilum/Erra/DINGIR-kar (MAD 3, pp. 148-149).

[327] It is possible that both these names are Sumerian. The Ur-Keš in MO is designated as the ancestor of Ur-Marad-da, and Ur-Marad-da is Sumerian, since the Sumerian genitive is indicated in the writing: Ur-Marad.a(k).

[328] Edzard, ZZB, p. 121, n. 625.

[329] OIP 57, p. 226, under kikk.

[330] FM 33:50; cf. ibid., p. 278.

[331] Edzard, ZZB, pp. 120-121.

[332] Selim J. Levy, "Harmal Geographical List," Sumer 3 (1947), p. 52:61, URU-Ki!-de^{ki}.

[333] Edzard, ZZB, p. 121, n. 625.

[334] DINGIR/Eštar/Nāru/Inin-Iaba (MAD 3, pp. 159-160).

[335] Cf. La-i-im (ARM V, 4:6), and Ugaritic Yrgb-l'im (Ugaritica V, p. 595, 14, B, 8).

[336] ^{d}KAL can stand for šēdum, baštum, lamassum, ^{d}Lamma, ^{d}BE ša naphari, and ^{d}Papsukkal ša lamassi (ŠL 322, 35). KAL.LA may very well stand for a different divine name.

[337] MAD 3, p. 162.

[338] It is questionable whether Malik occurs as a divine name in the Presargonic material. Two names occur which should be considered: (1) Su-ma-malik (CT 32, 8, iii a), and (2) Ilšu-malik (UET II, pl. xxxv, 308). Gelb takes malik in the second name as a divine name (MAD 3, p. 177), but this is not necessary. Indeed, the normal construction of the nominal sentence name with Il/DINGIR-su in subject position is to make the predicate an adjective or qualifying noun--aba/aḫa/dān/GAR$_3$/laba/rabi (MAD 3, p. 31). It is possible, however, that the strange word order is merely due to the freedom of writing found in the Presargonic period.

[339] AHw, pp. 595-596.

[340] The same would be true of the other Semitic languages where a god Malik is attested. Cf. P. Jensen, "Die Götter K^{e}moš und melek und die Erscheinungsformen Kammuš und Malik des assyrisch-babylonischen Gottes Nergal," ZA 42 (1934), pp. 236-237; Hoefner, WM, p. 453; Pope, WM, p. 299.

[341] Ir'am-Malik = Ir'am-Dagan, Ir'e-Malik = Ir'i-Dagan, Ūṣi-Malik = Īṣi-Dagan.

[342] In the later period Malik is identified with Nergal (KAV 63, ii 37;

E. F. Weidner, "Altbabylonische Götterlisten," *AfO* 2 [1924], p. 17:20), and in the Ur III and Old Babylonian periods *mal(i)kum* occurs in the plural to designate what appear to be underworld deities (J. Nougayrol, "Textes hépatoscopiques d'époque ancienne conservés au Musée du Louvre (III)," *RA* 44 [1950], p. 33; *OLZ* [1961], col. 604; *MAD* 3, p. 176; *ARMT* 9, p. 286). The plural is a bit strange, but it should perhaps be seen in relation to the large number of Sumerian underworld deities beginning with the element *lugal* (*PB* 1854-2004). At Mari these *malku* receive an offering in connection with the *Kispum*-offering for the dead (cf. the discussion under Dagan). Perhaps Dagan was considered the chief of these *malku* and as such the *mal(i)kum* par excellence.

[343]Dagan had a temple at Mari (*ARM* 1, 74:35), held an important place in its pantheon (Georges Dossin, "Le panthéon de Mari," *Studia Mariana* [Leiden: E. J. Brill, 1950], p. 43:5), and bore the title *šar mātim* (Georges Dossin, "Inscriptions de fondation provenant de Mari," *Syria* 21 [1940], pp. 164-168). Malik, on the other hand, is designated in a late text as *šarru (LUGAL) ša* Ma$_2$-eri$_4$^{ki}, "king of Mari" (II *R* 60, i 20). Note, however, that Itūr-Mer also bears the epithet *šar (LUGAL) Mari*^{ki} (*ARM* 10, 63:16).

[344]The doubling of the *-m-* is suggested by the onomastic material from Mari where the name is sometimes written ^{d}*Ma-am-ma* in addition to the normal orthography *Ma-ma* (*ARMT* 7, p. 347, n. 1). Note also the doubling in the Old Babylonian Zû Epic (Vincent Scheil, "Fragments de la légende du dieu Zû," *RA* 35 [1938], pp. 20-21).

[345]Edzard, *WM*, p. 105. The difference in the final vowel is only phonetic. The spelling varies in different copies of the same text (Erra Epic I 20).

[346]In addition to the evidence from the personal names, note the god list *SLT* 122, vii 11.

[347]*CT* 46, Pl. XXII, 4 iii 6, 12, 25 (= *Atra-ḫasīs* I 193, 198, 211); cf. *CH* III 28-35.

[348] CT 46, Pl. VII, 1:19-20 (= Atra-ḫasīs I 246-247); cf. CT 15, Pl. I, i 1-3.

[349] CT 46, Pl. XXVI, 13 rev. 9; CT 15, 49 iv.

[350] iltam issū išālū tabsūt ilī erištam ᵈMammi attīma šassūru bāniat awīlūti binīma lullâ lībil abšānam, "They summoned and asked the goddess, the midwife of the gods, wise Mammi, 'You are the womb, the creatress of mankind. Create man that he may bear the yoke.'" (CT 46, Pl. XXII, 4 iii 5-9 = Atra-ḫasīs I 192-195).

[351] CT 46, Pl. VI, 54-57 (= Atra ḫasīs I 223-226); Pl. XXII, 4 iii 17 (= Atra-ḫasīs I 203).

[352] I 20.

[353] E. F. Weidner, "Altbabylonische Götterlisten," AfO 2 (1924), p. 17: 19.

[354] W. G. Lambert, "The Gula Hymn of Bullutsa-rabi," Orient. NS 36 (1967), p. 119:51-53.

[355] Weidner, who wrote before the Erra text was available, pointed out that Ma-ma/Ma-mi appeared elsewhere as a form of Bēlet-ilī, so he suggested that Ma-ma in his list was just a mistake for Māmētu, who is attested as the wife of Nergal in several places ("Altbabylonische Götterlisten," AfO 2 [1924], p. 17, n. 7). Edzard, who wrote after the Erra texts made a mistake unlikely, simply stated, "Mami and Mame as the spouses of Nergal or Erra are probably identical with Māmītu (abbreviations of the name) and have nothing to do with the mother goddess Mama, Mami" (WM, p. 95). It seems rather unlikely to this writer that the Akkadian scribe would abbreviate the name of one goddess with the name of another, totally distinct goddess! It is easier to assume that we are dealing with different traditions and that Mamma is the wife of Nergal under his Akkadian name and form as Erra.

[356] G. van der Leeuw, Religion in Essence and Manifestation, translated by J. E. Turner (London: George Allen & Unwin, 1938), pp. 91-100; D. Dieterich, Mutter Erde (Leipzig, 1905). But note also the critique of O.

Pettersson, Mother Earth (Lund, 1967). The evidence for Mamma as "Mother Earth" is not clear, but an unpublished text refers to her as rabītam sabsūt rīmim qaqqarim u šamai, "the great midwife of the womb (which is) earth and heaven" (W. von Soden, "Die Hebamme in Babylonien und Assyrien," AfO 18 [1957], p. 119).

[357] Tallqvist, Götter-epitheta, p. 359.

[358] This role may explain in part why Bēlet-ilī is identified both with the mother goddess and with Gula, the great physician (SAHG, pp. 400-401, n. 60).

[359] ARMT 7, p. 171; ARMT 15, p. 164; AHw, p. 601.

[360] The personal name comes from the general area in which the month name was later current, since it is attested in the Assyrian correspondence from Mari. On the other hand, one should note that the month names are often derived from divine names, so the lack of attestation for Ma-na as a divine name is not conclusive.

[361] Cf. also the names Me-me-ti-x and Me-me-A.?GAB (UET II, p. L 49, rev. 4-5).

[362] KAV 63, ii 42.

[363] CT 25:48.

[364] V R 33, 9-10c; AS 16, p. 22:1.

[365] ^{d}Meme bānit pir'i ^{d}Meme damiqtu šāpikat erṣetim šamāmi, "Meme who creates the sprouts, favorable Meme who piles up the earth (and) heaven" (ABRT II, 16:17).

[366] Mari is not included in this list because I interpret the Presargonic name Lam-gi$_4$-Ma-ri$_2$ (F. Thureau-Dangin, "Inscriptions votives sur des statuettes de Ma'eri," RA 31 [1934], p. 140) as La-amki-Mari I-Did-Not-Neglect-Mari.

[367] TH No. 36, TCS III.

[368] A. Heidel, "The Meaning of MUMMU in Akkadian Literature," JNES 7 (1948), pp. 98-105.

[369] Ibid., p. 105.

[370] The doubling of the -n- is suggested by the orthography of some Mari names mentioned below.

[371] ARMT 13, 1, ii 3. Cf. the women's names Na-na-ak-ka (iii 4), Na-an-na (vii 28), and the probable female names Ši-Na-an-na (i 19) and Na-an-ni-ia (i 66).

[372] That she is a goddess is suggested by her popularity in women's names; cf. ^fd^Na-an-ni-šar-ra (ARMT 13, 1, v 31).

[373] Georges Dossin, "Le panthéon de Mari," Studia Mariana (Leiden: E. J. Brill, 1950), p. 43:14. Cf. also ARMT 15, p. 158; ARMT 7, pp. 194-195; Huffmon, APNMT, p. 62, 273.

[374] MAD 3, p. 202.

[375] Huffmon, APNMT, p. 62.

[376] Perhaps one should see some connection between her and the mountain ḫur.sag Na-an-ni which occurs in the curse formula of Hittite treaties, PD 1, rev. 41, and is to be located in the neighborhood of Mount Cassius (Heinrich Otten, "Die Berg- und Flusslisten im Ḫišuwa--Festritual," ZA [1969], p. 252).

[377] CAD i, p. 8.

[378] Bottéro gives several references in a note in ARMT 7, p. 346, which together with ARM 7, 163:5, ina E_2 Na-ri-im, seem to indicate that a god Nāru was known at Mari even in Old Babylonian times. Na-ru-um awīlam izear, "the river hates the man " (J. Nougayrol, "Textes hépatoscopiques d'époque ancienne conservés au musée du Louvre," RA 44 [1950], 34, 5; cf. AHw, p. 748) may also be taken as evidence for a river god Nāru(m). W. G. Lambert ("Nebuchadnezzar, King of Justice," Iraq 27 [1965], p. 11 appendix) and H. Hirsch ("Zur Lesung von $^{d}ID_2$," AfO 22 [1969], p. 38) cite other evidence for the reading Nāru(m).

[379] CAD i, p. 8; h, pp. 254-255. Ugaritic also knows a ṯpṭ nhr, "Judge River," though at Ugarit it appears to be an epithet of Yamm (UT, p. 506).

[380] TuL, p. 91:10.

[381] For the reading Nazi as a variant of Nanše see Falkenstein, AnOr 30, p. 85, n. 1, and the literature cited there. Note also the syllabic writings ^{d}Na-aš$_2$ (O. R. Gurney, "The Sultantepe Tablets [continued]; VII. The Myth of Nergal and Ereshkigal," Anatolian Studies 10 [1960], pp. 110-111:41 and the note to this passage on p. 128), Na-si (Ya-ah-wi-Na-si, ARM 7, 200:8, 10), and ^{d}Na-as-si$_2$ (Ip-qu-^{d}Na-as-si$_2$, ARM 7, 180 v' 21'), though one could question the equation of these last two names. Note also UM 55-21-295 (3-N-T 272), III-IV 51 ^{d}Nanše; na-as-[x].

[382] [ME]-Nazi (MAD 1, 72, rev. 3) should also be considered, although it might be Sumerian.

[383] T. Jacobsen, "Babylon and Assyria: V. Religion," Encyclopaedia Britannica, 1968, II, pp. 973-974; = Tammuz, p. 23; Edzard, WM, pp. 108-109; Falkenstein, AnOr 30, pp. 84-87.

[384] Edzard, WM, p. 113.

[385] A goddess identified with Nanâ, PB 2730.

[386] ME-^{d}Nisaba (CT 1, 1a:10) and Ur-^{d}Nisaba (MDP 18, 73:1) should also be considered, but they could be Sumerian as well as Akkadian.

[387] Edzard, WM, pp. 115-116; Falkenstein, AnOr 30, pp. 110-111.

[388] This assumes that Nu-ni is just a phonetic variant of Nu-nu comparable to Mamma/Mammi. One could explain the -i vowel as due to inflection in the genitive case, but the name Šu-Nūnu, unless it is to be interpreted as He-Is-Nūnu (a manifestation of Nūnu), suggests that the divine name was not normally inflected.

[389] Note Nūn, the father of Joshua (BDB, p. 630; cf. Noth, IPN, p. 230, who takes Nūn as a profane name like the many animal names occurring in Hebrew onomastica).

[390] Julius Lewy, "Ḫatta, Ḫattu, Ḫatti, Ḫattuša and 'Old Assyrian' Ḫattum," ArOr 18/3 (1950), pp. 385ff., 392.

[391] EBPN, p. 205.

[392] J. Nougayrol, "Textes et documents figurés," RA 41 (1947), p. 30:6;

cf. F. Thureau-Dangin, "Un acte de donation de Marduk-zâkir-šumi," RA 16 (1919), 154:9, where the text has ^{d}UB-na instead of ^{d}Nu-nu. The writing nu-nu also occurs in the three column syllabic vocabulary published by Sollberger, but it contributes little to the knowledge of the god, since the reference is obscure: nu-nu = a-na re-qi$_2$-tim = za-aḫ-ḫi-x ("A Three-Column Silbenvocabular A," AS 16, p. 23:58).

[393]Lugaldukuga founded Esaggil, which is in the midst of the apsū (CT 13, Pl. XXXVI). Apparently he is Enlil's father according to An-Anum (CT 24, 5:37), but he is also mentioned in the recitation of the fifty names of Marduk where Marduk replaces Enlil as Lugaldukuga's son (En.el. VII 99-100). Perhaps this displacement of Enlil by Marduk was aided by the ties that both their fathers had to the apsū.

[394]F. Thureau-Dangin, "Un acté de donation de Marduk-zâkir-šumi," RA 16 (1919), pp. 147-148.

[395]PB 2954.

[396]MAD 3, p. 212.

[397]It is used of the flames of love (Song of Solomon 8:6), of lightning (Psalm 78:48, wysgr lbrd bʿyrm wmqnyhm lršpym, "He gave over their cattle to the hail and their livestock to the flames." Some scholars correct brd to dbr to get the parallelism dbr = ršp found in Hab. 3:5, and thus translate ršpym here as pestilence (Kraus, BK XVI, pp. 537, 539), but the textual evidence for this correction is very slim, and the fact that ršpym is plural here makes the parallel with Hab. 3:5 unconvincing), and of flames of the bow, i.e., arrows (Psalm 76:4; Dahood questions the traditional rendering of the phrase, but his reinterpretation is unconvincing, Anchor Bible Psalms II, p. 218).

[398]Hab. 3:5, lpnyw ylk dbr wyṣ' ršp lrglyw, "Before him goes plague, and ršp follows at his feet." Deut. 32:24, mzy rʿb wlḥmy ršp wqṭb mryry, "sucked dry by famine and devoured by ršp and bitter qṭb-disease."

[399]He destroys one fifth of Keret's family in the Ugaritic epic, A 18-19.

[400]E. F. Weidner, "Ausgrabungen und Forschungsreisen: Neue Entdeckungen in Ugarit," AfO 18 (1957), p. 170; J. Nougayrol, Ugaritica V, p. 45:26.

[401]Pope, WM, p. 306.

[402]UET 1, 11; cf. the discussion of the passage in MAD 3, p. 243.

[403]ZU.EN-LUGAL (YOS IX, 1:1).

[404]PNC, p. 3.

[405]PB 2929.

[406]Thorkild Jacobsen, "Early Political Development in Mesopotamia," ZA nF 18 (1957), p. 93, n. 3; = Tammuz, pp. 367-368, n. 3.

[407]Ryckmans, LNPSS, p. 13, 25.

[408]By the Old Akkadian period Su'en was identified with Nanna, with Sumerian city god of Ur (TH No. 8, TCS III). UET VIII/2, 12 could be interpreted as implying a distinction between Su'en and Nanna, but this is not necessary (cf. Sollberger's comment on the problem, UET VIII/2, p. 3). In the Presargonic texts from Ur, however, Su'en does not occur in a single Sumerian and in only one or two of the extremely rare Akkadian names while Nanna is well attested. Even in the Sargonic period Su'en is scarcely attested in personal names from Ur, and when he does appear, it is only in Akkadian names. A man with the Sumerian name Ur-Su'ena(k) does occur in a number of texts in MAD 4, but the majority of these texts have the x mu x itu date formula, and hence date from the Gutian period. By Ur III the deity is much more common in personal names, but he is still primarily limited to the Akkadian names, and the same holds through the Old Babylonian period. The picture that emerges from this survey suggests that Su'en was introduced into Ur by the Akkadian and was only gradually assimilated by the Sumerians. The use of ^{d}EN.ZU in Sumerian literature from the Ur III period is no evidence against a Semitic origin, because it may be the result of this same assimilation that allowed ^{d}EN.ZU to be used in Sumerian personal names by the Ur III period.

[409]Cf. the preceding note.

[410]Edzard, WM, p. 102.

[411]The element may occur in the Presargonic name Il-ta-sa-du-um (SKL, p. 82), but the interpretation of this name is not clear.

[412]'Ayya/Addu/Eštar/Inin/Mamma/Mummu/Šamaš-šadu (MAD 3, p. 264).

[413]Edzard, WM, p. 118.

[414]The other occurrence of sa_2-lim can be explained as a verbal element, but it is very strange that the predicate should always occur in first position: Šalim-aḫu (MO C 10:23; MAD 1, several; UCP 9, 204, no. 83, iii), Šalim-bēlī (MCS 9/2, 242:4; 248:4; HSS X, 153, iv 9), Šalim-m(a)-ilī (FM 30:8), Šalim-NAR (MDP 14, 73:3).

[415]Delitzsch, HWB, p. 664.

[416]Pope, WM, p. 306.

[417]He is called a "gracious and pleasant god" (ibid.). This side of the god's character may well arise from the natural phenomenon with which he was identified, for twilight is one of the most pleasant parts of the day in the hot, arid regions of the Near East.

[418]R. Frankena, Tākultu de sacrale Maaltijd in het assyrische Ritueel (Leiden, 1954), p. 112, n. 202.

[419]One could also consider Šamaš-liddin Let-Šamaš-Give.

[420]There are other names which may belong here, but since the deity is designated by an ideogram which could also be taken as the Sumerian god Utu, I have limited the names to those which seem definitely Akkadian to avoid possible contamination.

[421]Before one could assume that the ideogram stood for the Sumerian sun god Utu, he would need examples where Utu was written out syllabically in Akkadian proper names. The pronunciation of the Old Akkadian divine name is not certain. An Ur III syllabic spelling gives the Akkadian name as Šamaš (MAD 3, p. 277), but if ^{d}Ša-mu-uš really belongs in this group of names--the use of the determinative with a syllabic spelling of an Akkadian name is strange--the variation between a/u in the second vowel suggests that it was

not a full vowel (a change šamšu > šamaš > šamāš > šamōš is not likely this early), so perhaps a vocalization Šam^{ə}š should be assumed for Old Akkadian.

[422]Gordon, *UT* p. 493.

[423]Knudtzon, *VAB* 2, 155:6, 47; 323:22 (discussed by Moran in *Biblica* 45 [1964], p. 81). Possible evidence for a feminine Šamaš at Mari is found in *ARM* I, 10:24', but see von Soden, *OLZ* (1960), p. 487.

[424]Werner Caskel, "Die alten semitischen Gottheiten in Arabien," *ADS*, p. 108.

[425]One could avoid this implication by interpreting these names on the analogy of the Ur III *Tūlid-šamšī* She-Gave-Birth-To-My-Sun, where *šamšī* refers to the new born child as in *Tūlid-dannam* She-Gave-Birth-To-A-Strong-Lad. One must seriously question, however, whether this suffixed form of the root can be expressed by the ideogram alone without a phonetic complement. The analogy with *Tūlid-Mamma* strikes this writer as more convincing. If, then, Šamaš is the subject in these names, the deity would appear to be feminine, since there are no clear examples where a masculine deity takes a feminine predicate (Edzard, "^{m}Ningal-gāmil, ^{f}Ištar-damqat. Die Genuskongruenz im akkadischen theophoren Personenamen," *ZA* nF 21 [1963], p. 127). The names where Šamaš occurs with a masculine predicate, on the other hand, say nothing about the gender of the deity, since they reflect only the gender of the person named (*ibid.*).

[426]Interestingly, *ummu* is the standard epithet applied to the Ugaritic sun goddess Šapš in a new incantation against snakebite (*Ugaritica* V, pp. 564ff.).

[427]H. Frankfort, *Cylinder Seals* (London: MacMillan & Co., 1939), pp. 95-109, pl. XVIII; but pl. XVIIIj seems to represent a sun goddess (p. 129).

[428]Edzard, *WM*, p. 126.

[429]*Špš rp'im tḥtk Špš tḥtk 'ilnym*, "Šapš will judge (?) the 'hale ones,' Šapš will judge (?) the divinities" (F. M. Cross, Jr., "The Canaanite Cuneiform Tablet from Taanach," *BASOR* 190 [1968], p. 45, n. 24).

[430]Gelb has suggested that the interchange of very similar signs for which *a priori* two different readings could be assumed forms an inherent part of the system of cuneiform writing. Thus he argues that *SA* in this name really stands for *E*$_2$ (*MAD* 2, pp. 45-46). That would certainly solve certain difficulties that he points to in his discussion, but the question is impossible to decide on the basis of copies, and I have not been able to see many of the original tablets.

[431]*PB* 2892. In the later period the name was apparently read as *ilū sibittu* The-Seven-Gods (cf. *STT* 2, 176:6': *DINGIR.MEŠ si-bit-ti*; E. Reiner, "Another Volume of Sultantepe Tablets," *JNES* 26 [1967], p. 184). The divine element may also occur in the Hebrew name *'lyšb'*, though Noth rejects this interpretation (*IPN*, p. 146).

[432]Erra Epic I 23-40.

[433]Edzard, *WM*, pp. 124-125.

[434]They take this role primarily in incantations against evil demons; cf. Edzard, *WM*, p. 125, and the material cited there under *S. als gute Daemonen*.

[435]The attempt to separate the good *DINGIR.IMIN.BI* from the bad *DINGIR.IMIN.BI* strikes me as artificial. The favorable *DINGIR.IMIN.BI* have the same warlike character as the bad ones; it is just turned to a different purpose (*KAH* 102:19; IV *R*^{2} 21, 1b rev. 12ff.; B. Meissner and P. Rost, "Die Bauinschriften Asarhaddons," *BA* III [1898], 287:12; O. R. Gurney, "Babylonian Prophylactic Figures and Their Rituals," *AAA* 22 [1935], pp. 44-47:17-'5; p. 66:21-25).

[436]*Narām-Sîn šar kibrātim arba'im īnu Ḫaršamatki bēl Aram u Am imtaḫṣuni (IN.DA.LA$_2$-ni) Tibar šadu'im šūma ušamqissu tamšīlšu ibnīma ana Enlil išruk*, "Which he fought with Ḫaršamatki, the lord of Aram and Am, Narām-Sin, the King of the four regions, personally cut him down (in) Mount Tibar, made his image and donated (it) to Enlil" (F. Thureau-Dangin, "Une inscription de Narām-Sîn," *RA* 8 [1911], p. 200, ii).

[437]As far as this writer knows, the geographical name does not appear elsewhere in the literature.

[438] *HEI*, p. 160, n. 11. Note, however, the month name at Mari (*ARMT* 15, p. 164; *ARMT* 7, p. 171) and compare with *Šu-Mana*.

[439] The verbal root here seems to be **ḏmr*, attested in Amorite, Hebrew, Ugaritic, and Arabic (*APNMT*, pp. 187-188).

[440] Edzard, *WM*, p. 130; Dhorme, *Les religions de Babylonie et d'Assyrie* (Paris, 1949), p. 109.

[441] "Babylonia and Assyria: V. Religion," *Encyclopaedia Britannica*, 1968, II, 975; = *Tammuz*, p. 34.

[442] *Ibid.*

[443] The *pitrās* form is rare with verbal roots, though attested (*GAG* § 56n); the metathesis with *š̱* as first radical is not clearly attested in Old Akkadian (*MAD* 2, p. 174), though this could be due to the scarcity of sources, since it is found in the closely related Old Assyrian dialect (*GAG* § 36a); and the infixed *ṯ* of the *pitrās* form normally has a reciprocal connotation (*itbāru*, *gitmālu*; cf. *CAD* g, p. 111. Von Soden's idea that the form puts "stress on the totality of a concept" [*GAG* § 56n] does not seem well-founded), which is not obvious in Jacobsen's translation of *Tišpāk*.

[444] The *labbû* in this myth is clearly described as a sea dragon, so the word should be related etymologically to the comparable West Semitic *lwytn* (Hebrew), contracted to *ltn* in Ugaritic, from the root *lawûm*, "to encircle." The form *labbû* could be taken as a *parras* formation and be translated, "The Twisting One," an apt name for a sea serpent.

[445] He causes the cloud to spring up [creates] the storm, and finally shoots the dragon with his arrow (*CT* 13, 34a).

[446] Alexander Heidel, *The Babylonian Genesis: The Story of the Creation* (Chicago: University of Chicago Press, [1942]), p. 121.

[447] Franz Köcher, "Der babylonische Göttertypentext," *MIO* 1 (1953), p. 78, v 52-vi 4. The term *bašmu* used here is etymologically the same as the term *bṯn* used of *ltn* in the Ugaritic material (*UT*, 67 i 1).

[448] *CT* 24, 50:11; 12, 11:34b. Storm gods are often seen as warriors.

[449]*CT* 24, 41:64.

[450]*MAD* 1, 192:1; *MAD* 3, p. 15. This title recalls the Ugaritic text which makes Baal the slave of Mot (*UT* 67, ii 12).

[451]TH No. 34, *TCS* III, pp. 42-43.

[452]Cf. *MAD* 3, p. 297.

[453]This name, written *Ša-at-^{d}Tu-tu*, is also attested as a place name (*MAD* 5, 67, rev. i 6), as is *Tu-tu^{ki}* alone (*MAD* 4, 6:5).

[454]*Tu(d)* = alādum (*ŠL* 58, 4); *^{d}Tu-tu(d)* - *mu'allid ilāni* (*PB* 3264).

[455]*En. el.*, VII 9-34.

[456]E. F. Weidner, "Altbabylonische Götterlisten," *AfO* 2 (1924), p. 74:28b.

[457]One might think of a deified city name, since the name is attested without the determinative as a city.

[458]*RLA* 2, p. 484.

[459]TH No. 40, *TCS* III, p. 47.

[460]Cf. R. Frankena, *Tākultu*, p. 117, and references cited there. *An-Anum* gives the equation *^{d}ug* = *^{d}u$_4$-mu*, *CT* 25, 22:35.

[461]In III *R*. 66, II 26-32 (=*Tākultu*, p. 6), ^{d}U$_2$-mu is listed with Sîn, Šamaš, *ṣalam* Šamaš, Ningal, Ay(y)a, Bunene, Ebiḫ, Kittu, and *^{d}Ta-am-ba-a-a* as *DINGIR.MEŠ ša$_2$ E$_2$ ^{d}XXX ^{d}UTU ša$_2$ URU.ŠA$_3$.URU*, "the gods of the temple of Sîn-Šamaš which is in Aššur"; and *KAV* 42, obv. ii 16 (=*Tākultu*, p. 124), lists Šamaš, Ay(y)a, Kittu, Bunene, and *^{d}U$_2$-mu* as *PAP 5 DINGIR.MEŠ ša$_2$ E$_2$ ^{d}UTU*, "total of five gods of the temple of Šamaš."

[462]This interpretation is not entirely free of difficulties. *CT* 25, 17 i 29, gives the equation *^{d}U$_4$-mu* = *^{d}IM*, and II *R*. 61, 1:13b, mentions a *E$_2$ ^{d}U$_4$-mi*, "temple of Ūmu," in a group of temples dedicated to underworld deities. Moreover, there may be some connection between the god *Ūmu* and the *ūmu* (= Sumerian *U$_4$*) written without the determinative for deity which according to Landsberger refers to some kind of spirit, perhaps a "storm demon" (Benno Landsberger, *Die Fauna des alten Mesopotamien nach der 14. Tafel der Serie Ḫar-ra = ḫubullu*, *ASAW* 42/6 [1934], p. 75). The other possibility is

to take the word as a designation for some kind of light phenomenon, which Sjöberg sees as the original meaning of U_4 (*TCS* III, pp. 100-101). This finds some support in the epithet of Ninazu, the god of the sun's heat-rays (Edzard, *WM*, p. 111), *UD.MEŠ GAL.MEŠ zīmu ruššutu* "great ..., shining red countenance" (W. G. Lambert, "The Gula Hymn of Bullutsa-rabi," *Orient.* NS 36 [1967], pp. 118-119:53).

[463]*Ugaritica* V, p. 248:17: *$^{d}[U]_4$ = tu-en-ni = yu-m[u]*. The reading *yu-mu* instead of Nougayrol's *ya-mu* is required by the normal phonological rules if one is going to take this word as cognate with Hebrew *yôm* and Akkadian *ūmu* as Nougayrol does. Note his comment: "Therefore it seems that by the side of a god Sea (*ym*), Ugarit may have also revered a god Day (ym)" (*ibid.*, p. 248, n. 5). It may also be found in Amorite (*APNMT*, p. 211).

[464]KAI 222, A 12. The deification of day (and night) is also found in Hittite religion; see the literature cited by Moran in *Biblica* 43 (1962), p. 319, n. 5.

[465]The day involved is the day on which an oath was taken: *Ištar, Il-aba, Šullat u Ḫanīš, Šamaš u_3 u_4-mu-um šu-u Kiš^{ki} lā nakār a-ḫu-tum [...]*, "by Ištar, Il-aba, Šullat and Ḫanīš, Šamaš, and that day Kiš had [sworn] unalterable (?) friendship (A. Poebel, *AS* 14, p. 24:21-23). Behind such a practice lay the ancient sense of qualitative time amply attested in the hemerologies and menologies. A day was responsible for what it brought forth.

[466]Cf. below, pp. 269-270.

[467]*KAV* 46:9.

[468]Frankena, *Tākultu*, p. 118; Ungnad, *OLZ* 40 (1937), 733, n. 1. Ungnad also explains the Assyrian writing *$^{d}KU_3$-KA_2* (= *^{d}Ellu-bāba*) as reflecting this divine name.

[469]3N-T 408:5.

[470]*AfO* 2, p. 13, n. 7.

[471]R. D. Biggs, "The Abū Ṣalābīkh Tablets: A Preliminary Survey," *JCS* 20 (1966), p. 80.

[472]Falkenstein, *SGL*, p. 113.

[473]A good Akkadian etymology seems to be lacking--the G stem of **zabābum*, "to be in a frenzy," is not attested (*CAD* z, p. 1)--but one should consider a possible connection with the West Semitic deity *Baʿal* Z^{e}*būb* (2 Kings 1:2), particularly since the Ugaritic reference *klt . bt . 'il . ḏbb*, "I have destroyed the house/daughter of 'Il *ḏbb*" (*CTA* 3, iii 43; *UT*, p. 388), makes it impossible to simply dismiss Z^{e}*būb* as a vulgarization of Z^{e}*būl*.

[474]*CT* 24, 50, K 47406, obv. 5.

[475]*CH* R XXVII 81-91.

[476]"Keilschrifttexte nach Kopien von T. G. Pinches," *AfO* 13 (1939), p. 46, ii 5. He is described as having sharp horns in this passage (W. von Soden, "Status Rectus-Formen vor dem Genitiv im Akkadischen und die sogenannte uneigentliche Annexion im Arabischen," *JNES* 19 [1960], p. 164), which corresponds to the picture of him in the older Abū Ṣalābīkh material as *gu$_4$.du$_7$ Kiš ^{d}Za.ba$_4$.ba$_4$*, "the goring ox of Kish" (R. D. Biggs, "The Abū Ṣalābīkh Tablets: A Preliminary Survey," *JCS* 20 [1966], p. 80).

[477]*PB* 1310. Like Ninurta and Ningirsu he can be pictured as a storm (*SAHG*, p. 132, no. 30).

[478]*PB* 1310.

[479]*Ibid.*

[480]The interpretation of this name is not sure. Gelb has suggested that it might be a mistake for *Ga-zu-a-lum* (*MAD* 1, p. 227).

[481]*Ibbi-DINGIR/'Ayya/Enlil/Su'en/ilum/Ištarān/Lulu/Nanše/Šamaš/Zababa* (*MAD* 3, pp. 194-195); *I-mi-Durul/DINGIR/Su'en/ilum/Erra/Šamaš* (*MAD* 3, p. 44); *Iddi(n)-Erra/Dagan/DINGIR/'Ayya/Eštar/Nāru* (*MAD* 3, p. 198); *Puzur-Ayya/'Ayya/Enlil/Su'en/Eštar/Ḫarīm/Nāru/Adad/Erra*/etc. (*MAD* 3, pp. 220-221).

[482]Benno Landsberger, "Einige unerkannt gebliebene oder verkannte Nomina des Akkadischen," *WZKM* 57 (1961), 1-23. Lambert's arguments for retaining the traditional reading cannot be dismissed out of hand, but they do not seem sufficient to refute Landsberger's case ("The Gula Hymn of Bullutsa-rabi,"

Orient. NS 36 [1967], p. 130, n. 13).

483 Even if it is argued that the name Su'en is not originally Semitic, the part played by the moon god under other names in the Semitic world makes it clear that the moon god was important in the Proto-Semitic period.

484 Jacobsen has pointed out that the astral aspect in the Sumerian pantheon comes from the areas where cattle or sheep herding is the main occupation ("Babylonia and Assyria: V. Religion," Encyclopaedia Britannica, 1968, II, 974; = Tammuz, p. 27); D. Nielson has emphasized the role of the astral deities among the Arabs of the desert (Der dreieinige Gott in religionshistorischer Beleuchtung II [Copenhagen, 1942], pp. 20ff.); and Gray, following Nielsen, has pointed to the decline in importance of the astral deities among the Semites settled in Canaan ("The Desert God ʿAṯtr in the Literature and Religion of Canaan," JNES 8 [1949], pp. 72-83).

485 The writer hopes to publish a more thorough study on the deification of mountains in the Ancient Near East in the near future. For the time being the best treatment of the subject is E. Douglas van Buren's article, "Mountain-Gods," Orient. NS 12 (1943), pp. 76-84.

486 Perhaps this emotional response finds its clearest expression in Sargon II's graphic descriptions of the wild mountain country through which he led his troops on his eighth campaign (F. Thureau-Dangin, Une relation de la huitième campagne de Sargon [Paris, 1912], especially lines 15-30, 96-101, 324-333). One can also detect a trace of the same response in the recurrent motif of the king who travels closed roads where his forefathers have never gone.

487 Cf. MAD 3, p. 27.

488 CAD a, pp. 383f.

489 See now the comments of Moran in JAOS 90 (1970), p. 530b.

CHAPTER III

ILUM AND THE PERSONAL DEITY

The different forms of the element ilum are far more common in the Old Semitic names than any of the proper divine names so far discussed. This chapter will discuss these different forms under their various orthographies.[1]

The Simple Form

1. I_3-lum

Presargonic: Ālu-ilum The God-Is-The-City (A-lu-i_3-lum, JRAS [1930], p. 602),[2] A-LUM-i_3-lum (Orient. NS 36, p. 62),[3] Dāda-ilum The-God-Is-Beloved (Da-da-i_3-lum, UET 1, 11:1),[4] ḪI-la-i_3-lum (Orient. NS 36, p. 65), Ibbi-ilum The God-Named (I-pi-i_3-lum, TMH V, 11, iv 10),[5] Īda-ilum The-God-Knew (I-da-i_3-lum, TMH V, 31, ii 3), I-gi/gi_4-i_3-lum (Orient. NS 36, p. 62),[6] Išma/e-ilum The-God-Heard (Iš-ma_2-i_3-lum, BIN 8, 11:16, 38; Iš-me-i_3-lum, MAD 3, p. 275; Iš-me-lum, TMH V, 11, v 2; BIN 8, 15:21),[7] Išni-ilum The-God-Repeated (Iš-ni-lum, TMH V, 97, ii 5),[8] RA-i_3-lum (RTC 75, iii 5), Rabi-ilum The-God-Is-Great (Ra-bi_2-i_3-lum, CT 32, 8, rev. ia:7; BIN 2, 2, iv 8), Šar-ilum-ma Only-The-God-Is-King (Sar-i_3-lum-ma, OIP LIII, p. 148, no. 5:1),[9] Su-tu-i_3-lum (OIP 14, 51, v 3), Ilum-aḫa The-God-Is-The-Brother (I_3-lum-a-ḫa, BIN 8, 11:30),[10] Ilum-bānī The-God-Is-My-Creator (I_3-lum-ba-ni, TMH V, 104, iii 6), I_3-lum-GAR_3 (Orient. NS 36, p. 62; NTSŠ 140, i 2; DP I, 2, i 3), Ilum-malik The-God-Is-The-Prince (I_3-lum-ma-lik, Orient. NS 36, p. 62),[11] I_3-lum-i-pi (TMH V, 170, i 4),[12] Ilum-qurād The-God-Is-A-Warrior (I_3-lum-gur-ad, UET II, Pl. XLVII, 19, i 2), I_3-lum-LA (MAD 3, p. 27), Ilum-rabi The-God-Is-Great (I_3-lum-ra-bi_2, BIN 8, 11:28, 42), Ilum-šā'ir The-God-Is-A-Fighter (I_3-lum-$ša_x$(SAG)-ir, EK IV, Pl. XL).

Sargonic: Abu-ilum The-Father-Is-The-God(?) (A-bu_3-i_3-lum, RSO 32, p. 90; A-bu-lum, HSS X, 158, iii 10; 109:9; 142:14), Aḫu-ilum The-Brother-Is-

The-God(?) (*A-hǔ-i$_3$-lum*, *RSO* 32, p. 90), *Akū(n)-ilum* I-Proved-True-O-God (*A-ku-i$_3$-lum*, *MO* D 14:11),[13] *BALA-i$_3$-lum* (*RSO* 32, p. 89), *Damiq-ilum* The-God-Is-Gracious (*SIG$_5$-i$_3$-lum*, *MO* C 18:27), *Ennī-ilum* Mercy-For-Me-O-God (*En-ni-lum*, *MAD* 3, p. 52),[14] *Ēpir-ilum* The-God-Provided (*E-pi$_2$-ir-i$_3$-lum*, *MO* A 3:7),[15] *Gu-NI-lum* (*HSS* X, 207:2),[16] *Ibbi-ilum* The-God-Named (*I-bi$_2$-i$_3$-lum*, *MO* D 14:18), *Iddi(n)-ilum* The-God-Gave (*I-ti-lum*, *MAD* 1, 251:9; *ITT* I, p. 22, 1344), *I-ki-lum* (*MO* C 3:6; 6:1, 18, 23; 15:13; D 12:3),[17] *I-mi-i$_3$-lum*, (*RSO* 32, p. 87),[18] *Išma-ilum* The-God-Heard (*Iš-ma$_2$-i$_3$-lum*, *RSO* 32, p. 87), *Īṣi-ilum* The-God-Went-Forth (*I-zi-lum*, *MAD* 1, 42, ii 2; 1:1; 163, ix 23; 255, ii 2; 232, ii 8), [*I$_3$?-t*]*um-i$_3$-lum* (*MAD* 5, 80:11), *Mēṣi-ilum* The-God-Is-The-One-Who-Causes-To-Go-Forth (*Me-ṣi-i$_3$-lum*, *MO* A 5:11),[19] *Rabi-ilum* The-God-Is-Great (*Ra-bi$_2$-i$_3$-lum*, *RSO* 32, p. 89; *Ra-bi$_2$-lum*, *BIN* 8, 324:4), *Šadu-ilum* The-God-Is-The-Mountain (*Sa-tu-i$_3$-lum*, *MAD* 5, 38, ii 3), *Ūlid-ilum* The-God-Begat (*U-li-id-i$_3$-lum*, *MO* D 5:8), *Ilum-asû* The-God-Is-A-Doctor (*I$_3$-lum-a-zu*, *RSO* 32, p. 90), *Ilum-dān* The-God-Is-Strong (*I$_3$-lum-dan*, *RSO* 32, p. 93), *I$_3$-lum-GAR$_3$* (*RSO* 32, p. 88), *I$_3$-lum-GIŠ.RIN$_2$* (*RSO* 32, pp. 91-92), *Ilum-šar* The-God-Is-King (*I$_3$-lum-sar*, *RSO* 32, p. 92).

Where the writing *i$_3$-lum* occurs in the Old Semitic names, *ilum* appears to designate a specific, though unnamed deity. The writing occurs in positions usually occupied by a proper divine name and is significantly lacking in names composed of a proper divine name and the generic word for god, that is to say: *DN-i$_3$-lum* does not occur. One could argue on this basis that *i$_3$-lum* should be interpreted as a proper divine name, but there are several considerations which tell against such an interpretation: (1) it is rare for the genuine Akkadian proper divine names to take case endings, and mimation is even rarer; (2) the formal distinction between *Il*, which is clearly used as a divine name, and *ilum* probably corresponds to a difference in usage; and (3) *ilum* is used fairly consistently in the later periods as a generic term for god. Therefore, one should probably translate *i$_3$-lum* in these names as "the god."

2. DINGIR

Presargonic: Ibni-ilum The-God-Created (Ib-ni-DINGIR, CT 5, 3, 4), Ūbil-ilum The-God-Pardoned (U$_2$-bil-DINGIR, TSA 12, rev. ii), Rêṣ-ilum The-God-Is-A-Helper (Ri$_2$-is-DINGIR, PSBA 20, Pl. I, ii 12), Ilum-ennī The-God-Is-My-Grace (DINGIR-en-ni, MAD 3, p. 32).

Sargonic: Ayyar-ilim Man-Of-The-God (A-ar-DINGIR, MO A 4:14, 18), Aba-ilum The-God-Is-The-Father (A-ba-DINGIR, MDP 14, 6, iii 1; ITT V, p. 39, 9450), Abu(m)-ilum The-Father-Is-The-God(?) (A-bum-DINGIR, HSS X, 153, iv 3; 155, v 5; MDP 14, 8:5; ITT I, 1378:3; BIN 8, 121:29),[20] Aḫu-ilum The-Brother-Is-The-God(?) (A-ḫu-DINGIR, MAD 1, 319:24; MAD 5, index; ITT I, p. 16, 1247; HSS X, 36, v 13; 72, ii 7; 153, x 8), Akū(n)-ilum I-Proved-True-O-God (A-ku-DINGIR, MAD 5, 62:13, 26),[21] Āmur-ilam I-Saw-The-God (A-mur-DINGIR, JCS X, 26, v 2; MAD 5, index; FM 44:15; MAD 1, 250, iii 7; 302:2), Addī-ilum The-God-Is-My-Father (A-ti-DINGIR, MAD 5, 22:1; CT 1, 1c:11), Asû-ilum The-God-Is-A-Doctor (A-zu-DINGIR, MAD 1, 215:9; 320:7), Bēlī-ilum The-God-Is-My-Lord (Be-li$_2$-DINGIR, HSS X, 51:8; 188, iii 14; iv 1; 199:8; MDP 14, 74:13),[22] Bi$_2$-bi$_2$-DINGIR (MAD 1, 206:8; 265:10), Dāda-ilum The-God-Is-Beloved (Da-da-DINGIR, CT 44, 48:13), Damiq-ilum The-God-Is-Favorable (SIG$_5$-DINGIR, MAD 4, index; MAD 5, index; MAD 1, 203:1-2, 234:20; 215:10, 14; 317, ii 6), E-ar-DINGIR (MAD 1, 163, vii 38),[23] Ela-il(um) Il(um)-Is-God (E-la-DINGIR, MAD 5, 71:2; ZA 12, p. 334), Enbu-ilim Fruit-Of-The-God (En-bu-DINGIR, MO A 9:24; 13:17; MAD 5, index; MAD 1, 33:2; 88:3; 158:5; 179:4; 303:10; 319:17; MDP 14, 72, iv 10; RSO 32, p. 87; HSS X, 155, iv 5; 39:3; 153, vi 21; 154, ii 6; 157, ii 2; 146:15; 154, iv 16; 143:13; 153, iv 24; vii 22; 158, iv 8; BIN 8, 121:38), Enna-il(um) Mercy-O-God (En-na-DINGIR, MAD 5, index; HSS X, 55:8; 130:15; 211:13; RTC 91, obv. iii 10; MCS 9/1, 245:28), Gu-Ni-DINGIR (HSS X, 153, vii 11; 187, vi 4), Ḫusus-il(um) Remember-O-God (Ḫu-zu-us-DINGIR, MAD 3, p. 33),[24] Ibbi-ilum The-God-Named (I-bi$_2$-DINGIR, MAD 1, 163, vi 11; MAD 5, index; MDP 14, 6, ii 8), Iblul-ilum The-God-Mixed (Ib-lul-DINGIR, MO C 14:6; 17:29), Iblul-napištam-ilum The-God-Mixed-Life (Ib-lul-ZI-DINGIR, HSS X, 188, iii

21),[25] Ibni-ilum The-God-Created (Ib-ni-DINGIR, MAD 1, 5, i 1; 232, iii 5; MAD 5, index; HSS X, 72, iii 2; MDP 14, 2, iii 7; 24, i 3), Īda-ilum The-God-Knew (I-da-DINGIR, MO A 11:10; C 15:27; 17:28; 19:10; HSS X, 172:10; 201:3; MAD 1, 4, ii 4; 135:3; 161, ii 2; 240:4; 255, v 16; 283, rev. 3; 285:4; 301:4; 322:2; An.Or 7, 372:13; MAD 4,index; MAD 5, index), Iddi(n)-ilum The-God-Gave (I-din-DINGIR, MAD 1, 53, rev. 5; I-ti-DINGIR, MO A 2:15; 3:15; B 2:7; C 10:3; 18:20; MAD 5, index; MAD 1, 163, x 9; MDP 14, 13:6), Idī-ilum The-God-Is-My-Arm (I$_3$-ti-DINGIR, MDP 14, 72, ii 16),[26] Idlul-ilam He-Praised-The-God (Id-lul-DINGIR, BIN 8, 256:6), I-ki-DINGIR (HSS X, 55:12), Ikrub-ilum The-God-Blessed (Ik-ru-ub-DINGIR, MO A 14:22; C 16:23; 18:17; MAD 1, p. 201), Ilū-il/ilum Ilū-Is-The-God (I-lu-DINGIR, JCS X, 26, vi 13), Ilul-ilum The-God-Acclaimed (I-lul-DINGIR, RA 24, p. 96, 1:6; MAD 5, index; MAD 1, 35:4; 46, ii 18; 90:3; 97, iii 1; ITT I, 1096:1, HSS X, 135:2; 155, v 12),[27] I-mi-DINGIR (RA 24, p. 96, 1:5; MO C 15:6; 17:14; MDP 14, 6, ii 12; HSS X, 13, iii 7; 135:6; 153, vii 29; ix 2; 155, iii 9; 154, i 19; MAD 5, index; MAD 1, 45:9; 163, vii 4; 208:5; 233, ii 4; 232, iv 13; 317, iv 6), Ipti-ilum The-God-Opened (Ip-ti-DINGIR, MAD 1, 118:3; 137:1), Ire-ilum The-God-Shepherded (I-re$_2$-DINGIR, HSS X, 107:9), Išīm-ilum The-God-Determined (I-si-im-DINGIR, MO C 11:13), Išku(n)-ilum The-God-Placed (Iš-kun$_3$-DINGIR, MO A 14:12; Iš-ku-DINGIR, MAD 5, 48:5'), Išlul-ilum The-God-Drew-Out (Iš-lul-DINGIR, MO C 17:12; BIN 8, 148:16, 42; MDP 14, 6, i 11; MAD 1, 79:8; 216:5; MAD 5, index; HSS X, 153, ii 23; 155, iii 10), Išma-ilum The-God-Heard (Iš-ma$_2$-DINGIR, MO B 2:5; C 6:4; 12:27; 18:18; MDP 14, 7:5; 18, 72:6-7; 24, 342:21; MAD 1, 66:1; 51, rev. i 12; 163, ix 15; x 6; MAD 5, index; ITT I, 1475:10; CT 44, 48:35; HSS X, 9:3, passim; Iš-me-DINGIR, MAD 3, p. 34), Iš-ri$_2$-DINGIR (RA 13, p. 6),[28] Ištup-ilum The-God-Preserved (Iš-dup-DINGIR, Syria 17, pl. vii, opp. p. 24; MAD 5, index; MO A 6:21; C 5:4; 15:8; 16:2; 17:13; JCS X, p. 26, vi 12), Išu-ilum The-God-Exists (I-su-DINGIR, MO A 15:22; MDP 14, 6, i 3), Īwu-ilum The-God-Spoke (I-wu-DINGIR, MDP 28, 524:2), Pu-ma-ilim The-Mouth-Of-The-God (KA-ma-DINGIR, MAD 4, index; ITT I, 1448, i 10, 1365:4; RTC 98, rev. 4; BIN 8, 122:3; 123:2),[29] KIL-DINGIR

(MAD 1, 225:2; 246:1), Ku-NI-DINGIR (MDP 14, 72, iv 6), Ku-ru-DINGIR? (MAD 5, 71:6; 103, rev. 6'), Laba-ilum The-God-Is-A-Lion (La-ba-DINGIR, ZA 12, p. 332), ME-DINGIR (MAD 1, 255, i 3; MAD 5, index), Me-ra-DINGIR (MAD 3, p. 34), [Na?-ḫ]a-DINGIR? (MAD 5, 14:3), NAR-DINGIR (UCP 9, p. 204, No. 83-37), Nir-ra-DINGIR, MAD 3, p. 34), Paluḫ-ilum The-God-Is-Awe-Inspiring (TE.NA-DINGIR, FM 18:17; MAD 1, 7, ii 6; 12, ii 1), Pašaḫ-ilum Become-Tranquil-O-God (Ba-sa-aḫ-DINGIR, MDP 14, 10, rev. ii 10; 4:8; 28, 523:2; MO C 14:1; 17:10; MAD 5, index; MAD 3, p. 218),[30] Pu-ilim Mouth-Of-The-God (Pu$_{3}$-DINGIR, MAD 4, 3:5; 7:2), Qīpā-ilam Trust-The-God (Gi-ba-DINGIR, MAD 1, 255, iii 13), Rabi-ilum The-God-Is-Great (Ra-bi$_{2}$-DINGIR, MO A 8:18; 13:13; C 5:7; 10:26; 18:15; 16: 20; 18:28; 19:2, 7; D 12:12; MAD 5, index; FM 2:13; MDP 14, 7:4; 10, iii 8; HSS X, 27:14; 88:4; 132:6; 161:11; 179:8; 181:5), Rêṣ-ilum The-God-Is-A-Helper (Ri$_{2}$-is-DINGIR, MAD 5, 66, rev. iii 9), Ša-ilim He-Of-The-God (Ša-DINGIR, MAD 1, 320:2), Ša-ki-DINGIR (MDP 14, 6, i 6), Ša-ri$_{2}$-DINGIR (HSS X, 108:12, 24),[31] Šadu-ilum The-God-Is-A-Mountain (Sa-tu-DINGIR, MAD 5, index; HSS X, 108:15; 146:3; 154, iv 4; 155, iii 6; 157, i 11), Šaṭpe-ilim The-Preserved-Of-The-God (Sa-at-be-DINGIR, MDP 14, 10, rev. ii 7; 6, i 3; FM 14:5; MAD 1, 101:7; 5, ii 4; 233, iii 7; Sa-at-pi-DINGIR, RTC 78:2), Šēp-ilim Foot-Of-The-God (DU-DINGIR, MDP 14, 66:8), Šu-ma-ilum He-Himself-Is-The-God (Su$_{4}$-ma-DINGIR, MAD 5, index; HSS X, 6:2; 135:4; 201:1; 153, vi 29; 154, ii 2; 155, iv 10; 161:28; MAD 1, 163, ix 11),[32] Šumu-ilim Name-Of-The-God (Su-mu-DINGIR, MAD 5, 45, rev. i 3; 64, iii 3), Tarpa-iltum The-Goddess-Healed (Dar-ba-DINGIR, MDP 14, 66:8),[33] Ulli-ilum The-God-Elevated (U-li-DINGIR, JCS X, p. 26, vi 3), Urra-ilum The-God-Is-The-Light (Ur$_{2}$-ra-DINGIR, RTC 96, ii 8; 98:5; 101:3), U$_{2}$-si-DINGIR (MDP, 14, 7), Ṣābi-ilim Soldier-Of-The-God (Za-ba-DINGIR, MAD 1, 163, ix 38), DINGIR-AB (JCS X, 26, iv 6), Ilum-aba The-God-Is-The-Father (DINGIR-a-ba, MAD 1, 188, i 13; ii 26; MDP 14, 47: 14; HSS X, 153, viii 11; 185, i 17), DINGIR-AB.GU (MAD 3, p. 32), Ilum-aḫa The-God-Is-A-Brother (DINGIR-a-ḫa, MAD 5, index; MAD 1, 188, i 11; ii 24; BIN 8, 129:2; 142:9; MO A 4:8; 16:2; C 18:1; D 7:4; 10:3, 13; 11:2), Ilum-ālšu

The-God-Is-His-City (DINGIR-al-su, HSS X, 169:4; FM 53:3; 7:27; CT 44, 48:6; MAD 1, 232, iv 16; 255, rev. ii 13; 5, ii 7; 335:20), Ilum-amma The-God-Is-A-Paternal-Uncle (DINGIR-a-ma, MAD 1, 37, iv 5),[34] Ilum-andul The-God-Is-Protection (DINGIR-an-dul_3, MAD 4, 68:6), Ilum-asû The-God-Is-A-Doctor (DINGIR-a-zu, MO A 5:6; B 5:8; C 14:22; MAD 1, 163, ix 25; 188:7, 20; 250, iii 16; 232, iii 13; 326, iii 11; FM 1:11; 16:4; MAD 4, index; MAD 5, index; HSS X, 72, iii 10; 157, ii 4; JCS X, 26, iii 9), Ilam-ba'ā Meet-The-God (DINGIR-ba-a, MAD 5, 66, ii 6), DINGIR-BALA (MAD 1, 272:7; MDP 18, 72:8), Ilum-balāṭ The-God-Is-Life (DINGIR-TI.LA, HSS X, 30, iv 8), Ilum-banâ The-God-Is-Friendly (DINGIR-ba-na, MO C 14:28), Ilum-bānī The-God-Is-My Creator (DINGIR-ba-ni, HSS X, 158, ii 14; 185, ii 4; 186:3; 157, iii 3; FM 14; 29; MDP 14, 85:9, 47:8; MAD 1, 187, i 2; 188:3, 16; 203:3; 250, iii 3; 252:6; 254, i 2; 307:5; MAD 4, index; MAD 5, index; RTC 80:19; MO A 8:17; C 15:23; 16:4; D 11:11), Ilum-dān The-God-Is-Strong (DINGIR-dan, MO A 15:18; B 5:1; FM 4:3; 5:4; 7:28; 33:44; MAD 1, 46, ii 1, 5, 7; 47, i 7; 84:3; 195:3; 5, i 4; 233, ii 5; 234:3; 232, ii 9; 241:17; 289:4; 319:20; MAD 5, index; MDP 14, 47:11; HSS X 71:2; 107:13; 129:8; MCS 9/1, 246:3), Ilum-dādī The-God-Is-My-Beloved (DINGIR-da-ti, ZA 12, p. 332), Ilum-ṭāb The-God-Is-Good (DINGIR-DUG_3, MAD 1, 322:14), Ilum-bīt The-God-Is-The-Household (DINGIR-E_2, MAD 1, 144, i 5; MDP 14, 6, ii 9; BIN 8, 129:9; JCS X, 26, v 4), Ilum-damiq The-God-Is-Gracious (DINGIR-SIG_5, MAD 1, 187, iv 44; BIN 8, 121:15; MDP 14, 6, iv 13), Ilam-ēriš He-Asked-The-God (DINGIR-e-ri-iš, MDP 14, 50:1),[35] DINGIR-GAR_3 (MO B 2:9; C 10:16, 21; 16:21; MAD 1, 58:6; MAD 5, index; FM 8:1; MDP 14, 72, rev. ii 12; BIN 8, 256:6), DINGIR-KAR_2 (MAD 3, p. 32), Ilum-kīn The-God-Is-Reliable (DINGIR-GI, FM 12:12; 39:7; MO C 17:16), Ilum-kimat The-God-Is-The-Family (DINGIR-gi-ma-at, MAD 1, 1:6; 153:2; 296:9), DINGIR-GIŠ.RIN_2 (HSS X, 155, iv 7), DINGIR-GU_2 (MO C 15:28; MAD 5, index; MAD 1, 179:18; 188:5, 18; 215:9; 232, iv 15),[36] Ilum-kalī The-God-Is-My-All (DINGIR-ga-li_2, MAD 4, index; MAD 5, index; MO B 5:15), DINGIR-gu-NI (HSS X, 97, ii 1), DINGIR-ku-NI (MAD 1, 219:11), Ilum-illat The-God-Is-The-Clan (DINGIR-il-la-at, CST 17:14), Ilum-illassu The-God-

Is-His-Clan (DINGIR-il-la-zu, MAD 1, 326, ii 4; 114:2), Ilum-išar The-God-Is-Just (DINGIR-i-sar, RA 33, p. 178), Ilum-laba The-God-Is-A-Lion (DINGIR-la-ba, CST 17:5; HSS X, 172:13), Ilum-lala The-God-Is-A-Billy-Goat (DINGIR-la-la, MAD 1, 11:2),[37] Ilum-ma He-Is-The-God (DINGIR-ma, MAD 3, p. 32), DINGIR-ma-LU_2 (MAD 4, 47:8), Ilum-mūda The-God-Is-Wise (MO C 16:25; D 6:7; MCS 9/1, 235:15; HSS X, 154, iii 15; 155, iv 9; 157, ii 1; 199:6; BIN 8, 196:20; MAD 5, index; MAD 1, 129:6; 187, iv 41; 188:9, 22; 9, i 4; 232, iv 1; 255, iii 12), Ilum-nāṣir The-God-Is-A-Protector (DINGIR-na-zi-ir, MDP 14, 10, ii 9; FM 9:3; 28:3; MAD 5, index; MAD 1, 3, vi 6; 57, rev. 16; 97, iii 3; 47, iii 4; 292:14; 319:28; 320:4), Ila(m)-nu''id Praise-The-God (DINGIR-nu-id, MAD 5, index; MO C 11:8; BIN 8, 160:38; cf. I_3-la-nu-id, MAD 5, 4:7; 9, rev. i 10),[38] Ilum-pālil The-God-Is-A-Scout (DINGIR-IGI.DU, BIN 8, 249:10; 314:1; MAD 1 120:7), Ilum-rabi The-God-Is-Great (DINGIR-ra-bi_2, RTC 98:8; MAD 5, 50:4), Ilum-rē'i The-God-Is-A-Shepherd (DINGIR-SIPA, FM 13:1; MAD 1, 232, iv 14; MAD 5, index; MDP 14, 47:3; HSS X, 70:2; 155, v 14; 188, iv 16), Ilum-sukkal The-God-Is-Vizier (DINGIR-SUKKAL, BIN 8, 53:6; 149:7; 293:12, 15, 18, 21; 133:13; 249:4; 265:3; 268:4; RTC 95:15),[39] Ilum-šar The-God-Is-King (DINGIR-sar, MAD 1, 232, ii 13), DINGIR-ŠUM (HSS X, 138:1), DINGIR-su-su (RTC 122:13; MO A 12:15), Ilum-tappā The-God-Is-A-Companion (DINGIR-tab-ba, MAD 5, index; MAD 1, 46:12; 163, ix 6; 187:38; 277:4),[40] Ilum-qarrād The-God-Is-A-Warrior (DINGIR-UR.SAG, MDP 24, 342:28; FM 12:8; MDP 14, 72, rev. iv 18; MAD 1, 335:14; BIN 8, 160:33; JCS X, 26, iv 7), DINGIR-zu-zu (MAD 1, 135:2).

In contrast to the more limited i_3-lum, the ideogram DINGIR can represent any syntactically determined, singular form of ilum, i.e., ilum, ilam, ilim, and il, and perhaps iltum. The ideogram alone, however, does not seem to suffice to indicate suffixed forms of ilum. As one will observe in the next section, these apparently had to be indicated either by the addition of phonetic complements to the ideogram or by the choice of the other, completely phonetic orthography. In terms of meaning it is very difficult to distinguish between DINGIR and i_3-lum. Both seem to refer basically to a specific though unnamed deity, but it is possible that the divine name Il is sometimes hidden under the ideogram.

The Predicate in -a

1. Ela

Sargonic: Ela-il(um) Il(um)-Is-The-God (E-la-DINGIR, MAD 5, 71:2; ZA 12, p. 334), Ela-Illat Illat-Is-The-God (E-la-^{d}Il-at, ITT I, 1460:7).[41]

Neither of these names is absolutely clear. Since Ela has first position, one might be tempted to take it as the subject and regard it as an Old Amorite form of Il.[42] This, however, does not work well with the second name, since Il-at, if it were not a divine name, should be inflected. Moreover, the predicate in -a often takes first position, so the above interpretation seems the most probable.

Forms with the Dative Ending -iš

1. Il-iš

Sargonic: Il-iš-takal Trust-In-(The)-God (I_3-li_2-iš-da-gal, MAD 1, index; MAD 4, index; MAD 5, index; HSS X, 10:7; 155, v 9; BIN 8, 121:1, 44; MDP 14, 30, iii; 80; FM 4:11; MDP 28, 44; Iraq 7, p. 42).

One could consider the possibility that some of these names belong under Il used as a proper name, but the more general use of the word il(um) appears more probable.

Suffixed Forms of Ilum

1. Ilī

Presargonic: Al-ilī Where-Is-My-God (Al-i_3-li, BIN 8, 46, i 5), Ikū(n)-ilī My-God-Proved-True (I-gu-i_3-li_2, MAD 3, p. 29), Ūmu-ilī Ūmu-Is-My-God (U_3-mu-i_3-li_2, OIP 14, 51, iv 6), Ilī-aḫī My-God-Is-My-Brother (I_3-li_2-a-ḫi, TMH V, 79, ii 2; BIN 8, 11:23), I_3-li-ASAL (TMH V, 35, ii 6),[43] Ilī-bēlī My-God-Is-My-Lord (I_3-li_2-pi-li_2, BIN 8, 347:98; 349:8; 354:63; 391:49; TMH V, 163, i 2; TSA index), Il-ilī Il-Is-My-God (I_3-li_2-li_2, BIN 8, 16:8), Ilī-ṭāb My-God-Is-Good (I_3-li_2-DUG_3, TMH V, 174, i 5).

Sargonic: Abī-ilī My-God-Is-My-Father (A-bi_2-i_3-li_2, MAD 1, 77:3; A-bi-i$_3$-li$_2$, ITT II/2, p. 20, 4360), Abu-(i)lī My-God-Is-The-Father (A-bu-li, HSS X 136:9), 'Ayya-ilī 'Ayya-Is-My-God (E$_2$-a-i$_3$-li, MAD 5, index; FM 1:7), Al(i)-ilī Where-Is-My-God (Al-i$_3$-li$_2$, FM 8:2; A-li-li, FM 15:4; 30:6; 33:30; RSO 32, p. 87; MAD 1, 91:4; 163, iii 22, x 17; MAD 5, index; MDP 14, 75:2; BIN 8, 161: 6; A-li$_2$-li$_2$, MAD 5, 33:6), Arik-ilī My-God-Is-Patient (?) (A-ri$_2$-ik-i$_3$-li, ITT II/2, p. 14, 3072),[44] Bēlī-ilī My-God-Is-My-Lord (Be-li$_2$-li$_2$, MO A 11:16; MAD 1, 326, iii 9; MAD 5, index; HSS X, 151, ii 12; 153, x 20; 132:3, 13; RSO 32, p. 89; CT 44, 48:34),[45] Dān-ilī My-God-Is-Strong (Dan-i$_3$-li$_2$, FM 1:8, 8:10, 20; Dan-i$_3$-li, MAD 4, index; MO A 14:4; Da-ni-li$_2$, ITT II/2, p. 16, 3117), Dayyān-ilī My-God-Is-A-Judge (DI.TAR-i$_3$-li, MAD 3, p. 29), Ennī-ilī My-God-Is-My-(Source-Of)-Mercy (En-ni-li$_2$, MAD 1, 73, ii 5; HSS X, 16:6; FM 33:60), Ennam-ilī Mercy-O-My-God (En-nam-i$_3$-li$_2$, CT 44, 48:25; MDP 14, 50:4), Kalî-ilī My-God-Is-My-All (Ga-li$_2$-i$_3$-li, MO A 14:24; Ga-li-li, HSS X, 157, ii 14; 42:5; MAD 1, 128, i 11; MAD 5, index; Ga-li$_2$-li$_2$, HSS X, 187, iv 5; 188, i 16), GAR$_3$-i$_3$-li (MDP 14, 76:2), GAR$_3$-i$_3$-li$_2$ (JAOS 52, 113, F 974:7), I-da-bi$_2$-i$_3$-li (FM 2:2; 12:17; MAD 1, 72:2; BIN 8, 139:7), Imittī-ilī My-God-Is-My-Support (ZAG.MU-i$_3$-li$_2$, PBS 9, 98:5), Išar-ilī My-God-Is-Just (I-sar-i$_3$-li$_2$, MCS 4, p. 13, 3:10), Ku-li-li (HSS X, 51, i 4; 52, i 5; Gu-li$_2$-li$_2$, MAD 5, 65:11),[46] Lipit-ilī Creation-Of-My-God (Li-bi$_2$-it-i$_3$-li, YOS 1, 10:20), Mani-(i)lī Beloved-Of-My-God (Ma-ni-li$_2$, ITT I, 1462:2; RTC 127, rev. iii 17; HSS X, 105, i 7; 106:3), Narām-ilī Beloved-Of-My-God (Na-ra-me-i$_3$-li, RTC 127, rev. iv 18), Narām-Su'en-ilī Narām-Sîn-Is-My-God (^{d}Na-ra-am-^{d}EN.ZU-i$_3$-li$_2$, MCS 9/1, 235), Naṣib-ilī Suckled-Of-My-God (Na-zi-ib-i$_3$-li, MDP 14, 47:16), Naṣir-ilī Guarded-Of-My-God (Na-zi-ir-i$_3$-li$_2$, FM 6:9), Pu-ilī Mouth-Of-My-God (Pu$_3$-i$_3$-li$_2$, FM 8:1; MAD 1, 50, i 11; 152:6; 42, ii 3; 233, ii 6; 335:19; HSS X, 103:4), Puzur-ilī Protection-Of-My-God (PU$_3$.ŠA-i$_3$-li, MO A 12:3; PU$_3$.ŠA-i$_3$-li$_2$, SKL, p. 114), Qurādī-ilī My-God-Is-My-Warrior (Qu$_2$-ra-ti-i$_3$-li$_2$, Coll. de Clercq, I 105), Šarru-ilī The-King-Is-My-God (Sar-ru-i$_3$-li$_2$, RTC 131:5; 121: 4; MO A 15:25; ITT I, 1106:2), Ša-ri$_2$-DINGIR-li$_2$ (UET II, Pl. XLVIII, 33:2), Šarru-kīn-ilī Sargon-Is-My-God (Sar-ru-GI-i$_3$-li$_2$, MO A 12), Šu-ilī He-Of-My-

God (*Šu-i$_3$-li$_2$*, *ITT* II/2, p. 5, 2899; *Šu-i$_3$-li*, *MO* A 13:1; C 6:11; *MDP* 14, 86, rev. ii 8; *ITT* I, p. 20, 1317), *Ṭāb-ilī* My-God-Is-Good (*Tab-i$_3$-li$_2$*, *FM* 35:6), *Tamkār-ilī* Merchant-Of-My-God (*Dam-qar-i$_3$-li$_2$*, *MDP* 28, 526:20), *Tu-li-li* (*MDP* 14, 75:10), *U$_3$-i$_3$-li$_2$* (*MDP* 24, 324:26; *BIN* 8, 143:14; 144:22, 29, 38; *MAD* 5, index; *MO* D 12:8), *Watar-ilī* My-God-Is-Surpassing (*Wa-dar-i$_3$-li*, *MAD* 4, 4:14), *Ilī-abī* My-God-Is-My-Father (*I$_3$-li$_2$-a-bi$_2$*, *MAD* 5, index; *FM* 50:10), *Ilī-aḫī* My-God-Is-My-Brother (*I$_3$-li$_2$-a-ḫi*, *FM* 8:11, 19; 27:2; 52:3; *MO* A 13:10; 16:1; C 5:2; 15:18; *RSO* 32, p. 91; *CST* 2:6; *MCS* 9/1, 254:4; 256:13; *MDP* 14, 72, iii 5; *ITT* I, 1475:7; *MAD* 1, 250, iv 3; 242:5; 195:6; 302:11; *MAD* 5, index; *CT* 44, 48:10), *I$_3$-li$_2$-BALA* (*MAD* 5, 143:22), *Ilī-bānī* My-God-Is-My-Creator (*I$_3$-li$_2$-ba-ni*, *FM* 51:4), *Ilī-bēlī* My-God-Is-My-Lord (*I$_3$-li$_2$-be-li$_2$*, *MAD* 5, index; *BIN* 8, 336:2; *HSS* X, 11:7, 146:2; 187, ii 15; 153, v 11; *MCS* 9/1, 247:23; *CST* 27, iii 7; *I$_3$-li$_2$-EN*, *HSS* X, 188, iv 9; *I$_3$-li$_2$-pi-li$_2$*, Nikolski, *Dok*. II 14, i 2), *I$_3$-li$_2$-bi$_2$* (*MAD* 1, 215:22; 206:11; *MAD* 5, index; *MDP* 14, 71, rev. iv 2), *Ilī-bilanni* O-My-God-Pardon-Me (*I$_3$-li$_2$-bi-la-ni*, *MAD* 1, 163, iii 18; 320:9; *MAD* 5, index; *MDP* 14, 72, v 11; *CT* 44, 48:24; *I$_3$-li$_2$-bi$_2$-la-ni*, *RTC* 245:11), *Ilī-dān* My-God-Is-Strong (*I$_3$-li$_2$-dan*, *MO* A 7:9; *FM* 28:6; *AnOr* 7, 372:11; *MAD* 1, 86, iv 4, 6; 99, rev. 3; 157:6; 190, rev. 2; 2, vi 13; 57, rev. 14; 179:16; 252:4, 15; 254, ii 11; 289:7; 297:3; 327, rev. 3; 335:3; *MAD* 5, index; *HSS* X, 36, iii 11; 145, iv 18), *Ilī-dumqī* My-God-Is-My-Good-Fortune (*I$_3$-li$_2$-dum-ki*, *MAD* 1, 326, i 7), *Ilī-ennu(m)* O-My-God-Mercy (*I$_3$-li$_2$-en-num$_2$*, *MAD* 1, 53, i 3; 163, k 8; 5, iv 2; 319:10; 336:13; *I$_3$-li$_2$-en-nu*, *MAD* 5, 57, i 12), *Ilī-Eštar* My-God-Is-Eštar (*I$_3$-li$_2$-Eš$_4$-dar*, *Iraq*, 1, pl. IIIa; = Ward, *SCWA*, no. 387), *Il-ilī* Il-Is-My-God (*I$_3$-li$_2$-li$_2$*, *MO* A 16:13; *FM* 37:12; *MAD* 1, 212:6; *CT* 44, 48:21; *HSS* X, 188, ii 25; 216:5; *BIN* 8, 142:4; *MAD* 5, 56, i 15; 9, i 16; *I-li$_2$-li$_2$*, *HSS* X, 205:6; 115:8; *MAD* 5, 5:8; 9, rev. i 15; 18:8; 28:2; 29:1'; *E-li$_2$-li$_2$*, *MAD* 5, 15, rev. 2; *E$_2$-li-li*, *MAD* 5, 106:13), *Ilī-illat* My-God-Is-The-Clan (*I$_3$-li$_2$-il-la-at*, *MDP* 14, 72, iv 23; *I$_3$-li-il-la-at*, *ITT* II/2, p. 15, 3093), *Ilī-išma/ênni* My-God-Heard-Me (*I$_3$-li$_2$-iš-me-ni*, *ITT* II/2, p. 5, 2899; *I$_3$-li$_2$-iš-ma-ni*, *MAD* 1, 219:5; 234:9; 256:5), *Ilī-karābī* My-God-Is-My-

Blessing (I$_3$-li$_2$-kara$_2$-bi$_2$, FM 16:1), Ilī-maḫrī My-God-Is-Before-Me (I$_3$-li$_2$-maḫ-ri$_2$, MAD 1, 38:2; 277:2; 314:2),[47] I$_3$-li$_2$-me-šum (HSS X, 15:2; I-lim-me-šum, MAD 3, p. 164), I-li-mu-bi$_2$ (MAD 5, 99, rev. 6'), Ilī-nuḫšī My-God-Is-My-Wealth (I$_3$-li$_2$-nu-uḫ-si, MAD 1, 163, vii 5), I$_3$-li$_2$-pa$_2$-lik (BIN 8, 249: 9), Ilī-rabi My-God-Is-Great (I$_3$-li$_2$-GAL, MDP 14, 21; FM 1:1; 18:19; MAD 5, index), Ilī-Rīmuš My-God-Is-Rīmuš (I$_3$-li-Ri$_2$-mu-uš, ITT I, 1096), Ilī-Su'en Su'en-Is-My-God (I$_3$-li$_2$-^{d}EN.ZU, MAD 3, p. 29), I$_3$-li$_2$-sa-lik (MO A 7:16; FM 5:6; MAD 1, 15:47, ii 8; 86, iv 8; 233, iv 8; 250, iii 23; 215:6, 33; 255, iii 10; MAD 4, index; MAD 5, index; MDP 14, 72, ii 5; CT 44, 48:20; I$_3$-li-sa-lik, MO A 14:27), Ilī-šarru The-King-Is-My-God (I-li$_2$-sar-ru, MO A 12:11), Ilī-šūr My-God-Is-A-Bull (I$_3$-li$_2$-su-ur, ITT II/2, p. 45, 5769), Ilī-sukkal My-God-Is-A-Vizier (I$_3$-li$_2$-SUKKAL, MAD 1, 225:3; 323:4), Ilī-tappā My-God-Is-A-Companion (I$_3$-li$_2$-tab-ba, MAD 1, 215:12; MAD 5, index; HSS X, 147:10; 296: 13; 153, i 14; 159, iv 2; MCS 9/1, 243:16; MDP 14, 2, ii 8; RTC 90, ii 8), Ilī-tukultī My-God-Is-My-Trust (I$_3$-li$_2$-tu-gul-ti, RTC 127, v 6; I$_3$-li$_2$-du-gul-ti, MAD 5, 4:8; 20:4), Ilī-water My-God-Is-Surpassing (I$_3$-li$_2$-DIRIG, FM 11:15).

2. Ilak[48]

Sargonic: Ilak-kur[ub] Worship-Your-God (I$_3$-la-ag-ku-r[u-ub], MAD 1, 232, ii 5),[49] Ilak-nu''id Praise-Your-God (I$_3$-la-ag-nu-id, MAD 1, 326, iii 16; 133:2; MAD 5, index; HSS X, 108:10; I-la-ag-nu-id, MAD 5, 68, i 3; DINGIR-ag-nu-id, MAD 5, 66, iii 6; DINGIR-la-ag-nu-id, MAD 5, 66, rev. i 7), Kurub-ilak Worship-Your-God (Ku-ru-ub-I$_3$-la-ag, MAD 5, 34:5; 45, ii 5; Ku-ru-ub-i$_3$-la-ag, MAD 1, 265:18), Nu''id-ilak Praise-Your-God (Nu-id-i$_3$-la-ag, MAD 1, 251:5; 232, iii 16).

3. Il-su

Presargonic: Il-su$_x$(BU) (Orient. NS 36, p. 63), Ilšu-aḫa His-God-Is-A-Brother (Il-su-a-ḫa, Orient. NS 36, p. 63; Il$_2$-su(d)-a-ḫa, MAD 5, 90:2), Il-su$_3$-ERIM+X (Orient. NS 36, p. 63), Il-su$_3$-GAR$_3$ (Orient. NS 36, p. 64; BIN 8, 11:13), Ilšu-malik His-God-Is-A-Prince (Il-su-ma-lik, Orient. NS 36, p. 61, n. 2).

4. DINGIR-su

Sargonic: Ilšu-aba His-God-Is-A-Father (DINGIR-su-a-ba, HSS X, 143:9; 153, vii 17), Ilšu-aḫa His-God-Is-A-Brother (DINGIR-su-a-ḫa, HSS X, 172:4; MO C 19:8; MAD 4, index; MAD 5, index; MAD 1, 212:7), Ilšu-dān His-God-Is-Strong (DINGIR-su-dan, AnOr 7, 372:39; MAD 1, 5:3; 17:3; 21:2; 57, rev. 6; 163, viii 3, 6; 250, iii 5; 232, iv 2; 289:8; 297:4; MAD 5, index; MDP 14, 10, ii 8; 14, 72, iv 21; HSS X, 67:2; 205:17; OIP 14, 179:3), DINGIR-su-Gar$_3$ (MDP 14, 24, i 9; MO C 10:4; B 4:14), Ilšu-laba His-God-Is-A-Lion (DINGIR-su-la-ba, MO C 5:16), Ilšu-rabi His-God-Is-Great (DINGIR-su-ra-bi$_2$, RTC 127, rev. iv 23; MAD 1, p. 193; MAD 5, index; MO A 14:15), Ilšu-ṭāb His-God-Is-Good (DINGIR-su-[DU]G$_3$, ITT I, 1372:10), Dagan-ilšu Dagan-Is-His-God (Da-gan-DINGIR-su, RTC 127, rev. ii).

5. Ilīšu

Sargonic: Apil-ilīšu Son-Of-His-God (A-pil-DINGIR-su, RTC 230:8), Ḫadi-ilīšu Welcomed-Of-His-God (Ḫa-ti-i$_3$-li$_2$-su, MAD 1, 163, ii 4; 53, ii 6), Šu-ilīšu He-Of-His-God (Šu-i$_3$-li$_2$-su, MO A 10:8; FM 17:6; 27:5; MAD 1, 183:10; 145:4; 31:4; 179:14; 219:18; 234:23; passim ; MAD 5, index, MDP 14, 72, ii 22; RTC 80:9; RSO 32, p. 93; HSS X, 49:2; 104:4; 108:9; passim ; CST 5:10; MCS 9/1, 242:13), Warad-ilīšu Slave-Of-His-God (ARAD$_2$-i$_3$-li$_2$-[su], MAD 5, 45, rev. i 12).

6. Elī

Sargonic: Baba-elī Baba-Is-My-God (Ba-ba-e-li$_2$, MAD 1, 41, rev. 2), Šu-elī He-Of-My-God (Šu-e-li, RTC 143), Elī-išmanni My-God-Heard-He (E-li-iš-ma-ni, OIP 14, 102).

There can be little doubt that these suffixed forms of ilum represent the personal deity of the person designated by the suffix. The content of the names largely fits with the role of the personal god as attested elsewhere. Names like Ilī-abī, Ilī-bānī, Šu-ilīšu, Lipit-ilī, Ilšu-aba, and Apil-ilīšu all refer to the creative role of the personal god in bringing his ward into existence. The love, care, and sustenance that the personal god provided find expression in *Mani-ilī*, *Naṣib-ilī*, *Ṭāb-ilī*, *Ilšu-ṭāb*, and *Ḫadi-ilīšu*. *Imittī-ilī*, *Ilī-dumqī*, *Ilī-karābī*, *Ilī-nuḫšī*, *Ilī-tukultī*, *Kalî-ilī*, and *Ilī-illat* attest the ancient Mesopotamian belief that success in life is largely dependent on the good favor of the personal god, who therefore must be valued above riches or any human support.[50] Finally the intimate nature of the relationship between the personal god and his ward is brought out in the name *Ilī-tappā*.

Apart from royal personages and the problematic element $\underline{U}_3$, the deities which occur in the personal names composed with a suffixed form of *ilum* are 'Ayya, Baba, Eštar, Dagan, Il, Su'en, and Ūmu. There is other evidence, however, to show that other deities also functioned as personal gods during the Old Akkadian period. Il-aba is specifically referred to as the god of Sargon and Narām-Sîn,[51] and such names as *Ḫarim-bēlī*, *Abī-Tišpāk*, *Bēlī-Baliḫ*, *Ummī-Gazur*, and *Malik-ṣīnšu* are most easily explained by assuming that the theophoric element represents the personal deity or its equivalent. A quick glance at these divine names makes it quite obvious that, at least in the Old Akkadian period, the personal deity could be a high god. In fact, there seems to be very little evidence from any period for the conception that the personal deity was usually a minor god or goddess.

In this connection it is worthwhile to note the significant parallels between certain names composed with Eštar and those composed with suffixed forms of ilum: *Eštar-illat* = *Ilī-illat*, *Eštar-nu''id* = *Illak-nu''id*, *Eštar-imittī* = *Imittī-ilī*, *Eštar-nuḫšī* = *Ilī-tukultī*, and the similar formations *Eštar-nūrī* and *Eštar-rēṣī*. As is well known the divine name Ištar functions in the later periods as the generic term for goddess and is often used in parallel with *ilum* in precisely those passages that speak of the personal god and goddess of a person.[52] In the Old Semitic names Eštar probably still refers to the specific goddess Eštar--the word never takes a suffix as in the later material--but the Old Semitic usage does give a clue to why this particular goddess gained the distinction of this generic meaning. One of the reasons why references to the personal goddess are less numerous than references to the personal god may be that the goddess was normally overshadowed by her spouse. The most notable exception to this rule is the Eštar figure, whose spouse, Il-aba, is a pale shadow compared to the goddess. Thus if Eštar were a person's goddess, this would stand a greater chance of finding expression in a name than, say, Šala, for if Šala were the personal goddess, one would think more readily of the personal god, Adad. The comparatively frequent usage of Ištar, in turn, would make her the obvious choice as a generic term for goddess.

The Plural of Ilum

1. *I_3-lu*

Sargonic: *Ennī-ilū* Mercy-For-Me-O-Ilū (*En-ni-lu*, *ITT* I, 1156:7; *En-ni-lu_2*, *ITT* II/2, p. 48, 1812), *Ilū-dalil* Ilū-Is-Praised (*I_3-lu-da-lil_2*, Nikolsky, *Dok*. II, 13:6), *Ilū-damqū* The-Gods-Are-Gracious (*I_3-lu-dam-ku*, *FM* 49:12; *MAD* 1, 100:2; 183:5), *Ilū-dannū* The-Gods-Are-Strong (*I_3-lu-da-nu*, *MAD* 1, 15:57, rev. 7; 297:5), *Ilū-il/ilum* Ilū-Is-The-God (*I-lu-DINGIR*, *JCS* X, 26, vi 13), *Ilū-kašad* O-Ilū-He-Had-Arrived (*I_3-lu-ga-sa-at*, *RA* 8, p. 158, AO 5659:3).[53]

2. *DINGIR.DINGIR*

Presargonic: *Išṭup-ilū* Ilū-Preserved (*Iš-dup-DINGIR.DINGIR*, *CT* 32, 8, la:9).

Sargonic: *Iddi(n)-ilū* Ilū-Gave (*I-ti-DINGIR.DINGIR*, *MO* A 13:21), *Kurub-I/ilī* Bless-The-Gods/Ilū (*Ku-ru-ub-DINGIR.DINGIR*, *MAD* 1, 1:4; 117:3; 273:4; 284:5; 293:2, 295:4; 330:6; 335:16), *Megir-I/ilī* Favorite-Of-Ilū/The-Gods (*Me-gir-DINGIR.DINGIR*, *MAD* 1, 296:10).

In *Ilū-damqū*, *Ilū-dannū*, and perhaps some of the other names *ilū* is a simple plural, "the gods," but this explanation will not work for *Išṭup-ilū*, since one does not expect a singular verb with a plural subject. Because of this disagreement in number Gelb suggested that one read the ideogram *DINGIR.DINGIR* as Anum.[54] Anum is extremely rare in the Old Akkadian personal names, however, and there is no real evidence for attaching this ideogram to him in this period. The writing is a standard way of indicating the plural, so one should not give up on the attempt to explain the underlying form as a plural until all avenues have been explored. Moreover, the same disagreement in number appears to exist in the name <u>Ilū-dalil</u>, where the word is spelled syllabically, and the lack of mimation makes a singular interpretation of <u>i_3-lu</u> improbable.

This suggests that one may be dealing here with a phenomenon similar to the so-called plural of majesty known from Hebrew and the Amarna material.[55] If this is the case, one should probably interpret these names as containing the divine name Il on the analogy of Ugaritic where the divine name 'El is sometimes written with a plural ending.[56] Whether one should regard the formation as a plural to incorporate the totality of Il's manifestations, however, is not clear.

[1]Since this chapter was already in manuscript form when the writer obtained MAD 4-5, they are cited only by their indices unless they offer a name or orthography not attested in the other sources.

[2]It is very difficult to see the element a-lu as anything but ālum, "city" (MAD 3, pp. 3-4). If a-lu is the subject, it would appear to mean that the city fulfills the function of the (personal?) god for the individual. If the name contains inverted order as assumed above, it would mean that the god offered man the protection, community, etc., that was to be found in the ancient city.

The lack of mimation on a-lu should be noted. Von Soden stated that this lack of mimation was used in Old Akkadian to give a noun qualitative determination (GAG % 63d), so he would presumably render a-lu as "the (true) city." This interpretation of the use or nonuse of mimation in the Old Semitic proper names, however, is difficult to support. It is possible that the loss of mimation is merely due to assimilation with the following consonant.

[3]The sign LUM is ambiguous. It may be read as lum or ḫum, hence the name could be rendered either Aḫum-ilum The-Brother-Is-The-God or Ālum-ilum The-City-Is-The-God.

[4]One could take Dāda as a divine name here, but only if there were other evidence that Dāda were in fact the name of a deity. The final a on Dāda, however, makes it impossible to render the name as The-Beloved-Is-The-God, since the subject of the nominal sentence should be in the nominative case. It seems best, therefore, to consider Dāda as an example of the predicate state in -a.

[5]One should also consider the possibility of reading PI as wu, and interpreting the name as Īwu-ilum The-God-Spoke.

[6]The interpretation of this name is very unsure. The initial element is probably verbal, but it could be from egûm or naqûm, and neither of these

verbal forms provide a very convincing meaning for the name. *Ilum* would have to be the subject or vocative. The-God-Was-Negligent or The-God-Sacrificed do not seem very appropriate names. Reading *ilum* as vocative one would get He-Was-Negligent-O-God or He-Sacrificed-O-God. The latter would perhaps be interpreted as a reference to the fulfilling of a vow following the birth of the child. One should also consider taking the first element as nominal from the Sumerian loan word *igu* and reading *Igī-ilum* The-God-Is-My-Prince.

[7]The variation in the writing of this one name probably reflects the tendency to lose the consonant *'4* that was not fully realized until after the Old Akkadian period. In the first form the *'4* remains a strong consonant. In the second form *'4* has quiesced, causing the preceding vowel to be lengthened and "colored" as a reflex, and this reflex is strong enough to prevent the *-ē* from contracting with the initial *i* of *ilum*. In the last form the reflex is left, but it is no longer sufficient to prevent contraction.

[8]*I.e.*, the god gave a second child. For this meaning of *šanû*, "to do something for a second time," see *MAD* 3, p. 278.

[9]Cf. the other possibilities cited by Jacobsen (*OIP* LIII, p. 148). It is difficult to take *šar* as the subject, since there is no reason for it to be in the *status indeterminatus*.

[10]The interpretation of this name is probably to be sought along the lines suggested by the Ur III name *I$_3$-li$_2$-ki-aḫ* My-God-Is-Like-A-Brother (*MAD* 3, p. 23). *Aḫum* is very rarely used in the literature as a metaphor for the deity, but the Ur III name makes it clear that it could be used. It would imply that the god felt the close concern for his ward that one would expect a human brother to show.

[11]One could also read *mālik*, "counselor," in this name, but the above interpretation which takes *ma-lik* as the predicate state of *malkum*, "prince," is more likely, since the feminine counterpart occurs in an Eštar name as *-ma-al-ga-at* (*MAD* 3, p. 177), which could hardly be a participle else the *i* should have been preserved. One also has the Ur III name *Ilī-ma-al-ki* (*MAD*

3, p. 176), where there can be no room for doubt.

[12]It is difficult to take *i-pi* in this name as *ibbi*, since it is rather strange for the preterite to occur after the subject in the Old Semitic names. One could read the element as an imperative of *nabûm* and translate, O-God-Name! If the stative prima w verbs follow the analogy of the prima y verbs in the formation of the imperative, as is probable though unprovable, since a clear G imperative of a stative prima w is still unattested (*GAG* & 103m), one could also translate, Appear-O-God!

[13]Cf. above, p. 77, n. 109.

[14]One could also interpret this name as God-Is-My-(Source-Of)-Mercy.

[15]This interpretation of the name fits best with the phonetic rules operative in Old Akkadian. **I'3-5pir* would either remain *Īpir* or change to *ēpir*, so the preterite is possible (*MAD* 2, p. 125). The participle **'3-5āpirum* and the imperative **'3-5apir* would be expected to remain *āpirum* and *apir* (*MAD* 2, p. 124), though the change to *e* is possible. This assumes that Gelb is correct in identifying the first consonant as *'3-5*, but even if von Soden's etymology from *YPR/WPR* is correct, the situation is no different. **Iypir* could have given *ēpir* (*MAD* 2, p. 125), whereas **yapir* or **yāpirum* would hardly have caused the change from *a* to *e*.

[16]Gelb wants to interpret this name as containing the element *kullûm*, "all," but this is not clearly attested in Akkadian. One could read the name as an imperative formation, *Kunni'-(i)lum* Care-For-O-God.

[17]Cf. the discussion under *I-gi-i$_3$-lum* above. Interpreted in the light of *I-ki-DINGIR* this name would merely presuppose the assimilation of the final vowel of the first element with the first vowel of the final element. One should also consider the possibility that the name is really composed of only one element, *Ikkillum* It-Is-The-Cry. One could interpret this as an exclamation referring to the first cry of the new baby or as the cry of the mother in labor (cf. *CAD* i, p. 58).

[18]Cf. above, p. 81, n. 106.

[19]The interpretation of this name is not sure. The above treatment assumes that me-ṣi is an Amorite causative participle of the meqtil pattern from the root waṣā'um. Huffmon (APNMT, pp. 148-150) following Gelb ("Lingua," 3.3.7.6.2), has pointed out that this formation is the most common form of the causative participle among the Mari names and is also found elsewhere. He even lists a Me-ṣi-tum which would appear to be the feminine hypocoristic counterpart of the Old Akkadian name being discussed (APNMT, p. 184). See also Buccellati, AUP, pp. 171-172.

[20]The writing leaves an ambiguity whether the second sign should be read bu_3 or bum, so one cannot be sure about the mimation on the element abu(m).

[21]Cf. p. 77, n. 109.

[22]Or one could read My-(Earthly)-Lord-Is-A-God-(To-Me).

[23]Perhaps this name should be regarded as a simple phonetic variant of Ayyar-ilim resulting either from the loss of the 'x as a strong consonant and the consequent reflex on the following vowel or from a simple contraction of the diphthong ay, i.e., ayyar > êyar.

[24]The interpretation of DINGIR as vocative instead of accusative is based on the comparison with the names DN-ḫussanni, "DN-Remember-Me" (ANG, p. 167) and DN-ḫasīs, "DN-Is-Wise" (ANG, p. 220).

[25]The reading of ZI as an ideogram is not sure. Meek suggested ZI could be a scribal error (HSS X, p. xxxii, n. 34).

[26]The use of the sign i_3 rather than i, which is normal for the 3ms prefix of G stem verbs, makes it unlikely that i_3-ti is to be taken as the verb form iddi(n).

[27]This interpretation assumes a simple G of alālum B that the CAD does not recognize (a, p. 331).

[28]The element iš-ri_2 appears to be a G preterite of a verbal stem šarûm, but whether it should be connected to *t̲arûm, "to be rich," is questionable. The similarity with the Hebrew Yiśra-'el suggests one might be dealing with a West Semitic root. Cf. above, p. 92, note 213.

[29]There could be some doubt about this name, but if the name is Semitic, the use of the enclitic suggests Amorite (Buccellati, *AUP*, p. 177).

[30]The reading *ilum* for the ideogram in this name is suggested by analogy with the Ur III name *Bi$_2$-sa-ḫi-lum* (*MAD* 3, p. 218). On *pašāḫum* see *ANG*, p. 168, n. 4.

[31]The element *sa-ri$_2$* appears to be related to the verbal root apparently attested in *Iš-ri$_2$-DINGIR*. One should probably not render it as *šarrī*, "my king," because that would normally be written in Old Akkadian as *sar-ri$_2$*.

[32]This is probably to be taken as a replacement name with the *ilum* in this case meaning the spirit of a dead relative. One could also take the *ma* as enclitic and read *Šu-ma-ilim* He-Of-The-God.

[33]This interpretation assumes that the name is Old Amorite and is supported by such Amorite names as *Ya-ar-pa-^{d}IM* (Huffmon, *APNMT*, pp. 263-264). The reading of the ideogram as *iltum* is attested in the later period (*CAD* i, p. 89), but *Tarpa-il* You-Healed-O-God would also be possible.

[34]The translation of **'ammum* as paternal uncle following Old South Arabic rather than as "clan, people," following Hebrew, Aramaic, and Ugaritic is probably correct, since the parallel use of *ḫālum*, "maternal uncle," in Akkadian (*CAD* h, p. 54) supports this interpretation. So Gelb (*MAD* 3, p. 43), but cf. Huffmon's discussion of the element in Amorite (*APNMT*, pp. 196ff.).

[35]It is possible that this text is as late as Ur III as the original editor suggested with reservation, but Gelb treats it as Sargonic (*MAD* 3, p. 32), and I see no compelling reason to date it any later.

The etymology of the verbal element must be seen with von Soden (*AHw*, p. 239) on the basis of Hebrew and Ugaritic as *'$_1$RŠ* against Gelb who gives *'4-5RŠ* (*MAD* 2, p. 183). The 3ms would work best, as *i'riš* to *ēriš* can be seen as analogous to the *i'mur* to *ēmur* change (*MAD* 2, p. 182), and it is in fact attested for the 3mpl of our root: *e$_3$-ri-su!-ga* (*MAD* 3, p. 67). The 1cs is out since **'a'riš* is written *a-ri$_2$-iš* (*MAD* 2, p. 183). The imperative and stative are also suspect, since they should follow the pattern *'ariš*.

The reason for 'arāšum becoming erēšum in the later language is probably due to the ē form of the prefix in the 3ms/pl and the i-i pattern, which caused it to be taken over into the verb class with etymological prima '4-5 by analogy.

[36]This could be a Sumerian name, but the patrinomics involved and the occurrence in the Diyala region, where the Sumerian names are a very small minority, would point to GU_2 being an ideogram. Ilum-ašarid The-God-Is-A-Hero is perhaps the most attractive possibility (ŠL 106, 8), but one could also consider Ilum-idum The-God-Is-The-Strength/Arm (ŠL 106, 3) or Ilum-emūqum The-God-Is-The-Strength (ŠL 106, 5), and perhaps others.

[37]This interpretation takes la-la as the predicate state of lalā'um (AHw, pp. 529-530) and regards the name as parallel in meaning to other names where the god is metaphorically described as some kind of animal.

[38]See the discussion under Ilak-nu''id.

[39]This name is read as Akkadian on the analogy of I_3-li_2-SUKKAL (MAD 1, 225:3; 323:4).

[40]Tab-ba should possibly be taken as ideographic since this writing occurs in Šu-TAB.BA, which is probably to be rendered as Šu-tappā'im.

[41]Cf. the discussion of this name in chapter II under Illat.

[42]In support of this one could cite the name [E]-la-ga-li_2/[E]la-kalî [E]la-Is-My-All (MAD 5, 59:2'), but the break at the beginning of the name makes the reading of the crucial e vowel less than certain.

[43]The interpretation of this name is dependent on the correct reading of the sign ASAL. As an ideogram with the Sumerian reading silig it can stand for šagapurum, "the very strong one, leader" (ŠL 44, 2), x-ul-ḫu-um, šapāšum, kâdum, "to hold fast," or petûm, "to open" (MSL 2, p. 145, 30-33). Moreover, ^{d}ASAL can stand for ^{d}I-lu-me-er, ^{d}Nu-ur-DINGIR.MEŠ, or ^{d}Iš-ḫu-ru (ŠL 44, 5). It also occurs as a divine name in the Fara texts (ŠL 44, 5).

[44]The interpretation of this name is doubtful. The suggestion made above is based on the idiom ikkum arākum. One could also consider the interpre-

tation My-God-Is-Late, which would refer to the child who was born overdue. The actual writing of the name is questionable. Gelb gives it as above (*MAD* 3, p. 29) and as *A-ri-ik-i$_3$-li* (*MAD* 3, p. 64), while Genouillac gives an obviously incorrect *Ari-ik-i$_3$-li*. Since I have not been able to see the text, I do not know which of Gelb's readings is correct.

[45]One could also interpret this name by analogy with such names as Narām-Suen-ilī and Rīmuš-ilī as My-(Earthly)-Lord-Is-My-God, which would have the advantage of preserving the normal order of subject and predicate in the nominal-sentence name.

[46]Whether this name actually contains the element *ilī* may be doubted. One could read it as a simple name of endearment, *Kulīlī* My-Little-Crown or My-Dragon-Fly.

[47]This name is probably to be regarded as a thanksgiving name for the effective interceding of the personal god. Cf. *šēdu damqa ilu muttamû nanzaza maḫrīya*, "the favorable *šēdu*-demon, the interceding god, who stands before me" (*CAD* i, p. 99).

[48]Morphologically the element *I$_3$-la-ag* is probably best analyzed as the accusative case of *ilum* + the clipped 2ms suffix, *ila(m)* + *k(a)* (*AHw*, p. 374). Gelb objects to this analysis on the grounds that (1) *-ka* is never abbreviated to *-k* in Old Akkadian, (2) the form *ila* before the pronominal suffix is unknown in Akkadian, and (3) the phonetic variant *Elag* in *Kur-ru-ub-e-la$_2$-ag* is written with the *LA$_2$* sign, never attested in the hundreds of Sargonic and Ur III names with *ilum* (*MAD* 2, p. 215). The first objection is not too impressive, since we have very little, if any, hymnic material from the Old Akkadian period, and by analogy with the later usage, it is precisely in this type of material that one would expect to find such clipped forms. Moreover, the meaning of the names themselves point to their origin in the hymnic tradition. The second objection is more significant, but not decisive. There is at least one example where *ilum* preserves the nominative case ending with the clipped pronominal suffix, *la nanzaz i-lu-uš*, "his god does not stand

by him" (*CAD* i, p. 96; *PBS* 1/1, 2 ii 25). The last objection carries very little if any weight, since it can be attributed to the caprice of a single scribe. On the positive side of the ledger, Gelb pointed to the correspondence *I-la-ka-šu-ki-ir* (*ARM* 8, 32a:8) = *DINGIR-ka-šu-ki-ir* (*ARM* 8, 32b:8) = *I-la-ak-šu-kir* (*ARM* 8, 28:7) as strong support for von Soden's view (*MAD* 2, p. 215). One should also note the variant spellings of the Old Semitic name *Ilak-nu''id* in texts that seem to be referring to the same man, the son of *'Ayya-dān* (*I-la-ag-nu-id*, *MAD* 5, 68, i 3-4; *DINGIR-la-ag-nu-id*, *MAD* 5, 66, rev. i 7-9; *DINGIR-ag-nu-id*, *MAD* 5, iii 6-7; *DINGIR-nu-id*, *MAD* 5, 66, rev. i 2). It is not absolutely certain that the last orthography refers to the same man, but Gelb assumes it does (*MAD* 5, p. 103), and he is probably right. But, if he is right, this is an extremely strange writing for a proper divine name I/Elag! Unless one wants to assume a mistake - <ag> -, the orthography would imply that *Ilak-nu''id* was occasionally shortened to *Ila(m)-nu''id*--a change that is explicable if *-k* is a simple suffix defining the first element as the personal deity, but inexplicable if *I/Elag* is a proper divine name.

[49]*Karābu* can be transitive, as the expression *ūmišamma ilka kitrab*, "everyday worship your God" (*BWL* 104, 135), indicates.

[50]Note the following passages: *rēṣuka ul mašrû ilumma*, "It is not wealth that is your support. It is (your) god" (*BWL* 227:42-43); *gīš mašrê bēl pānī ša gurrunu makkūru girriš ina ūm lā šīmate iqammêšu malku girrī annûtū īkušū alāka taḫšiḫ gimil dumqi ša ili dārâ šite'e*, "The socially prominent, endowed with wealth, who has piled up possessions, the king will burn in the fire before his time. Do you wish to go the way these have gone? Rather seek the lasting reward of (your) god!" (*BWL* 74:63-66); *ana ramānīšu lā ikarrab ana ilīšu likrub ilšu ana amēli šu'āti ikarrab*, "He will not bless himself. Let him bless his god, and his god will bless that man" (*KAR* 178, iii 34f.).

[51]*PBS* V, Pl. XX, vi; *UET* 1, 275, ii 20f.

[52]*CAD* i, p. 273.

[53]The form *kašad* is unusual since the stative normally takes the *i* vowel, *kašid*. One could also consider the interpretation Ilū-Arrived.

[54]*MAD* 3, p. 34.

[55]Brockelmann, *GVGSS* II, pp. 60-61. A similar phenomenon occurs in "good" Akkadian where the scribes sometimes write *DINGIR.DINGIR* or *DINGIR.MEŠ* when the context, singular suffixes, or a parallel, "goddess," shows that a singular is meant (*BWL*, p. 67; W. G. Lambert, "The Gula Hymn of Bulluṭsa-rabi," *Orient*. NS [1967], p. 132, note on line 157; cf. A. Jirku, *Altorientalischer Kommentar zum alten Testament*, pp. 18-19).

[56]Note especially the common epithet of Mot, *bn ilm*, "son of 'El" (*UT* 49 II 13, 25, 31, *passim*). The explanation of the *m* as the enclitic is not convincing.

CHAPTER IV

THE IMPERIAL PANTHEON AND SUMERIAN-SEMITIC SYNCRETISM

The Imperial Pantheon

Next to the theophoric personal names, the royal inscriptions of the Sargonic dynasty represent the major source for our knowledge of the Semitic deities worshipped in the period before Ur III.[1] One can discover in these inscriptions not only the names of the most important Semitic deities, but some of the earliest indications of their character as well. Enḫeduanna's collection of temple hymns,[2] which reflects the situation after Sargon's conquests, provides the most comprehensive picture of the deities worshipped in the empire, since it lists forty-one of the major deities together with their cities and temples.[3] Its usefulness for this study is somewhat impaired, however, because of its decidedly Sumerian orientation. Not only are the hymns written in Sumerian and the divine names normally given in their Sumerian form; even the organization of the collection with its general progression from the Sumerian south to the Akkadian north seems to reflect Sumerian, not Akkadian tradition.[4]

On the other hand, a curse formula found in two of Narām-Sin's inscriptions appears to contain a genuine Akkadian tradition:

<u>PBS</u> V, 36 rev. iv.	<u>UET</u> 1, 276, i-ii	<u>UET</u> 8, 2, 13, iii'
	^{d}EN.ZU	^{d}EN.ZU
	be-al	be-al
	DUL$_3$ su$_4$-a	DUL$_3$ su$_4$-a
	u$_3$	u$_3$
^{d}INANNA	^{d}INANNA	^{d}INANNA
an-nu-ni-tum	an-nu-ni-tum	an-nu-ni-tum
An	An	An

^{d}En-lil$_2$	^{d}En-lil$_2$	[^{d}E]n-lil$_2$
Il$_3$-a-[b]a$_4$	Il$_3$-a-ba$_4$	[Il$_3$]-a-ba$_4$
^{d}EN.ZU	^{d}[EN].ZU[5]	[^{d}EN.Z]U[5]
^{d}UTU	[^{d}]UTU	[^{d}UT]U
^{d}(E)n$_x$-iri$_{11}$-gal	^{d}(E)n$_x$-iri$_{11}$-gal	(The rest is broken.)
[^{d}]U-um	^{d}U-um	
[^{d}]Nin-kara	^{d}Nin-kara-ak	
i$_3$-lu	DINGIR	
ra-bi$_2$-u$_3$-tum	ra-bi$_2$-u$_3$-tum	
in ŠU.NIGIN-su-nu	in ŠU.NIGIN-su-nu	
ar-ra-tam$_2$	ar-ra-tam$_2$	
[l]i-mu-ut-tam$_2$	la-mu-tam$_2$	
[l]i-ru-ru-uš	li-ru-ru-uš	

It is significant that the PBS and UET texts list the same deities in the same order from ^{d}INANNA-an-nu-ni-tum on, but what is most interesting is that the UET formula mentions Su'en twice. This rather curious tautology must apparently be explained by the way in which the original scribe composed the formula. Since the UET inscription was originally inscribed on a statue of Su'en, the scribe began the curse formula by calling upon that deity as the one most vitally concerned with the statue, "May Su'en, the lord of this statue...." One god was not sufficient, however. The scribe wanted to strengthen the curse by including the other great gods in the curse formula as well, and to do this he merely attached a traditional list to his opening phrase with the copulative u, "and," even though that entailed repeating the name Su'en. Either he copied the list so mechanically that he did not notice this repetition, or the traditional order was too firmly fixed to be altered. In either case the fixed order of the list suggests that one is dealing with a partial canonical listing of the imperial pantheon, so it will pay to examine this list in more detail.

1. Eštar-annunītum

dINANNA-an-nu-ni-tum represents a compound name, since in other Old Akkadian inscriptions it is inflected as a unit.[6] The second part of the name appears to be a parrusīt formation from *anānum, "to skirmish,"[7] which would give the epithet, "She-Who-Continually-Skirmishes/The-Skirmisher."[8] If this is the correct analysis of the final element, the first element, though it is written with the Sumerian ideogram dINANNA,[9] should probably be read as Akkadian, since one does not expect an Akkadian epithet with a Sumerian deity. Thus the writer analyzes the name as Eštar-annunītum, "Eštar-The-Skirmisher."

This goddess, whose name is sometimes written simply as dINANNA,[10] is often paired with Il_3-a-ba_4,[11] the city god of Akkad,[12] so one should probably identify her with Eštar of E-Ulmaš, the city goddess of Akkad.[13] As the city goddess of the royal capital she was attributed the power of granting kingship,[14] so Sargon took the title MAŠKIM.GI_4 dINANNA, "deputy of Eštar,"[15] while Narām-Sîn, to whom she gave no enemy,[16] acted at her command.[17] Eštar also figures in stereotyped curse formulas of Sargon,[18] Maništušu,[19] Narām-Sîn,[20] Šar-kali-šarrī,[21] and the Gutian king La-'arab.[22] Narām-Sîn built a temple for her,[23] and he may have performed a hieros gamos in her honor, since one text seems to refer to him as the husband of Eštar-annunītum.[24]

The epithet annunītum could also be used independently as a designation for the deity, at least by the time of Šar-kali-šarrī.[25] After the Old Akkadian period this is the only way it does occur, which suggests that the epithet split off and became an independent deity. The new goddess, however, retained her former character as a war goddess. An Old Babylonian Narām-Sîn epic states that her standard along with that of Ši-laba was carried on military expeditions by the army of Akkad,[26] and a late Babylonian text designates her as Annunītum bēlet tāḫāzi nāšât qašti u išpati, "the mistress of battle who carries the bow and quiver."[27]

2. An

An is the personified heaven and chief god of the Sumerian pantheon.

Apparently the Akkadian monarchs inserted him and Enlil, who immediately follows, at this point in the royal pantheon out of deference to the ancient Sumerian tradition which regarded An and Enlil as the ultimate source of rule over Sumer.[28] It was a way of legitimatizing the incorporation of Sumer into the Sargonic empire.[29] Sargon took the title <u>pašīšum</u> of An,[30] and he invokes An in a Sumerian curse formula,[31] but, apart from these references and the Narām-Sîn text quoted above, An plays no important role in the Old Akkadian inscriptions.

3. Enlil

Enlil is the storm god who, as the executive power in the universe, ranked next to An in the Sumerian pantheon.[32] Like An he was adopted into the pantheon of the Sargonic empire to legitimate the Akkadian hegemony over Sumer. Sargon, Rīmuš, Maništušu, Narām-Sîn, and Šar-kali-šarrī all attribute their rule over Sumer to Enlil.[33] Sargon and Narām-Sîn both led their vanquished Sumerian opponents before Enlil in Nippur,[34] and they probably used those occasions to have their kingship officially confirmed by the human representatives of the deity.[35] As a result of his victory over Lugalzagesi Sargon claimed that title EN_x.SI of Enlil,[36] and in return for Enlil's favorable decision in the conflict he cleansed Nippur for the deity.[37] He also presented <u>satukku</u>-offerings to Enlil.[38] Both Narām-Sîn and Šar-kali-šarrī built temples for Enlil,[39] though the Sumerian tradition remembers Narām-Sîn in a different light.[40] Rīmuš gave him tribute from the booty of Elam,[41] and he, Maništušu, and Narām-Sîn all dedicated images to Enlil.[42] The god also occurs in numerous curse formulas of all the Sargonic rulers through Šar-kali-šarrī.[43]

4. Il-aba

During the Old Akkadian period Il_3-a-ba_4[44] was the city god of Akkad and probably the husband of Eštar-annunītum,[45] though the insertion of the Sumerian gods, An and Enlil, has obscured this connection in our list. Like his wife, Il-aba appears to have been primarily a god of war.[46] Rīmuš and Maništušu both invoke him along with Šamaš in oath formulas to assert the credibility of a statement,[47] but this is probably explained by his position as city god of the capital,[48] so these passages should not be used to make him into a Šamaš figure as a god of justice.[49] His position as god of the imperial capital may also explain his role as patron deity of the Sargonic dynasty,[50] or at least of Sargon and Narām-Sîn, who explicitly call him their personal god.[51] Šar-kali-šarrī laid the foundation for a temple to him in $\underline{KA_2}$.$\underline{DINGIR^{ki}}$,[52] and other texts mention a sangu[53] and a NIN.DINGIR of Il-aba,[54] as well as a canal named after him.[55]

5. Su'en[56]

Since the inscription on the statue to Su'en comes from Ur, one should identify Su'en as the Semitic equivalent to the Sumerian moon god, Nanna, the city god of Ur.[57] Su'en and Nanna appear to have been equated soon after Sargon's conquest of Sumer.[58] The daughters of both Sargon and Narām-Sîn served as Nanna-Su'en's en-priestess in Ur,[59] and Rīmuš[60] and Narām-Sîn[61] both dedicated offerings to him. Nanna-Su'en was worshipped throughout the empire, however, and was considered the city god of Gaeš[62] and Urum[63] as well as Ur. Narām-Sîn built a temple for him,[64] La-'arab, the Gutian, mentions him in a curse formula along with ^{d}Gutium and ^{d}INANNA,[65] and other texts mention a BALAG.DI,[66] a sangu,[67] and a PA_4.ŠEŠ of Su'en.[68]

6. Šamaš

It cannot be proven that ^{d}UTU in this list was read as an ideogram for Akkadian Šamaš,[69] but it seems probable. While Šamaš and Utu were identified,[70] there is no evidence that the Akkadians in Akkadian texts ever referred to the sun deity under its Sumerian name. Šamaš was probably included in this list because of his importance as the city god of Sippar and Larsa.[71] Maništušu[72] and Šar-kali-šarrī[73] dedicated offerings to him at the former site, and both Rīmuš[74] and Maništušu[75] invoke Šamaš in oaths to verify their statements, but otherwise the deity is largely limited to stereotyped curse formulas of Sargon,[76] Rīmuš,[77] Maništušu,[78] Narām-Sîn,[79] and Šar-kali-šarrī.[80]

7. Ner(i)gal

^{d}GIR$_{3}$.UNU.GAL is probably to be analyzed in Sumerian with van Dijk as ^{d}(E)n$_{x}$.irigal.(ak), "Lord-Of-The Underworld."[81] He was the Sumerian city god of Kutha whom the Akkadians identified with their own underworld deity Erra.[82] The Sumerian name became popular in Akkadian circles, however, and gradually pushed Erra into the background even in Akkadian texts. The beginning of this process may already be seen in the Sargonic period, where Erra is very popular in personal names, but absent from the inscriptions, being replaced by Ner(i)gal. Narām-Sîn credited Ner(i)gal with opening the way to his victory over Armanum and Ibla and with giving him Amanum, the cedar mountain, and the upper sea,[83] and Labaḫšum dedicated a hammerhead to Ner(i)gal for the life of Šu-Durul.[84]

8. Ūm

The name usually read ^{d}U.MES should probably be read as ^{d}U-um, and be interpreted as the Akkadian name for the deified day.[85] He is mentioned in a broken context in a Rīmuš inscription,[86] but otherwise does not occur in the royal inscriptions.

9. Ninkara(k)

The name ^{d}Nin.kar.ak, "Lady-Of-The-Quai (?)," is clearly Sumerian, but its attestation is almost totally limited to Akkadian contexts.[87] The Akkadians apparently adopted the name, if not the goddess, for one of their goddesses of healing.[88] Ninkarak was later identified with Nin'insina, "Lady-Of-Isin," the city goddess of Isin,[89] and perhaps it is already as this city goddess that she is included in this list.

10. Ilū rabiūtum in napḫarīšunu

Formally, the phrase, "the great gods in their totality," could be taken as appositional, but the parallels indicate it should be understood as a summary statement incorporating all the other great gods that the scribe has not mentioned by name.[90] This is, moreover, the most natural interpretation of the phrase, since a list of nine gods, two of whom seem rather insignificant, can hardly be called "the great gods in their totality." This is such an inclusive phrase that one may question whether, from the inscriptional evidence available, one could reconstruct a complete list of these "great gods" for the Sargonic empire. The other inscriptional evidence does enable one to fill out the list to some extent, however.

Dagan

All three texts in which the list discussed above is found come from the south, from Nippur or Ur, where the insertion of An and Enlil makes good political sense. If a similar curse formula were discovered beyond the Euphrates in the west, one might expect the insertion to contain the name Dagan instead. He occupied a position of authority in the Upper Country comparable to Eštar-annunītum in Akkad and Enlil in Sumer.[91] Sargon worshipped him in Tutul before his successful conquest of this region, which he attributes to Dagan,[92] and Narām-Sîn reconquered the same area with the weapons of Dagan.[93] Certain martial aspects appear in these inscriptions, but they should not be overly stressed in the analysis of Dagan's character, for they probably represent no more than the executive power by which Dagan enforced his legal right to give the land to whom he pleased. As with Enlil in Sumer,[94] it was the judicial decision of Dagan that really decided the issue.[95]

Nature Deities

The UET text which contains the Akkadian pantheon list also calls upon some nature deities to strengthen the curse by the exercise of their specific functions. Ninḫursanga and Nintu, two Sumerian mother goddesses, who also occur in Akkadian contexts along with genuine Akkadian deities,[96] are invoked not to give children to the man who tampers with Narām-Sîn's inscription.[97] ^{d}IM,[98] a storm god, and Nisaba, a Sumerian grain goddess who was adopted by the Akkadians,[99] are asked to prevent the man's sheaves of grain from ripening.[100] And, finally, Enki, a Sumerian god of the fresh water sources,[101] is asked to do something bad to the man's canals.[102] Each of these nature deities except for ^{d}IM is also attested in the Temple Hymns of Enḫeduanna as the city god or goddess of one or more cities.[103]

Other City Gods

The importance of the city gods as imperial deities is indicated by the fact that they are almost the only deities who occur in the royal inscriptions.[104] Their political implications are such that even Puzur-Inšušinak, the native Elamite iššiakkum of Susa,[105] includes many of them in his inscriptions along with his own Elamite deities,[106] and Narām-Sîn's treaty with Elam includes a couple.[107] Several others occur in isolated texts. Narām-Sîn dedicated offerings to Ištarān,[108] the city god of Der,[109] and he and his servant, Ištup-ilum, both made votive offerings to Nin-gubla,[110] the city god of Ki-abrig.[111] Finally, Lipit-ilī, a son whom Narām-Sîn appointed iššiakkum of Marad, built a temple for its patron deity, Lugal-marada(k).[112]

Summary

When one looks back over this list of gods occurring in the inscriptions of the kings of Akkad, two important facts emerge. (1) The gods which occur are primarily those who according to ancient Mesopotamian thought would be expected to play a part in the political life of the empire and whose support the monarch would thus need to assure the stability of his kingdom, i.e., the city gods. (2) There seems to have been a clear territorial principle which attributed the authority over the Upper Country to Dagan, Akkad to Eštar-annunītum, and Sumer to Enlil (with An standing in the background), though this scheme could sometimes be overlooked when a king was magnifying the deeds of a particular deity.

The Extent of Sumerian-Semitic Syncretism

At the same time this survey of the deities occurring in the royal inscriptions, since it includes a fair number of Sumerian gods, raises the problem of Sumerian-Semitic syncretism. How far and on what level had this syncretism developed before Ur III? It is not an easy question, for a careful analysis of the theophoric personal names and the material from the royal inscriptions indicates that the process of syncretism was quite complex, involving several stages and taking place on more than one level.

At the earliest stage, and on the most popular level, lies the indentification of the Akkadian sun god, Šamaš, with his Sumerian counterpart, Utu. This identification must be very old, for though it seems certain that the Semitic Šamaš was originally feminine,[113] very few traces of this original femininity are preserved in the Old Semitic personal names,[114] and none at all in the Old Akkadian inscriptions. Moreover, from the Presargonic period until the end of the Sargonic empire, the Akkadians wrote the name of their sun god with the Sumerian ideogram ^{d}UTU, not only where it occurred in inscriptions, but also, with only a couple of possible exceptions, in the personal names, which normally preserve a more popular phonetic orthography for the Semitic divine names.

Apparently the identification of the Semitic storm god, Addu, with Sumerian Iškur (^{d}IM) took place on the same level of popular piety, but somewhat later, if we may judge from the evidence of the personal names. By the Sargonic period, at any rate, the ideogram ^{d}IM was commonly used to designate this Semitic storm god, though other orthographies also remained in use in the personal names. One of these, An-da, seems to represent a "Western" orthography,[115] so one should probably assume that the Old Amorite form of this storm god shared in the identification with the Sumerian Iškur.

At Mari the identification of Semitic Eštar and Sumerian Inanna took place very early, in the Presargonic period, but whether this was the result of popular piety, or hinged on political considerations, is difficult to say. In Mesopotamia proper, however, the thorough-going identification of the two goddesses appears to have been the result of Sargon's attempt to lay a theological foundation for a united empire of Sumer and Akkad.[116] Thus it is not surprising to find that this equation, based, as it seems to be, on governmental authority, has had little impact on the popular piety reflected in the Old Semitic names, where, unlike Šamaš or Addu, Eštar continues to be written phonetically. The same is true of the equation, Su'en = Nanna, which leaves no traces in the Old Semitic personal names until after the Sargonic period.

The introduction of An and Enlil into the Semitic pantheon was also the result of Sargon's conquests, but here, in contrast to the preceding examples, it was not a question of identifying a Semitic god with a Sumerian one, but rather of introducing gods for which the Semites apparently had no exact equivalents. This could explain why both An and Enlil, though neither of them are very popular, do occur in the Old Semitic personal names of the Sargonic period; they did not have to compete with a corresponding Semitic deity.

Most of the other Sumerian deities encountered in the royal inscriptions, while they may have been identified with Semitic deities--Ner(i)gal seems to have been identified with Erra this early, and the equations Ninḫursanga/Nintu = Mamma and Enki = 'Ayya could not be much later--seem to have had little influence on popular piety, and probably reflect scholarly concerns for a syncretistic theology, perhaps for political reasons. A few Sumerian deities do occur in Semitic personal names, but they are largely a reflex of this scholarly activity, and occur too rarely to suggest any thorough-going syncretism on the popular level. The one exception is Baba, who occurs in Sargonic names under the orthography Ba-ba, which hardly derives from the scribal tradition, where the standard writing is ^{d}Ba-ba$_6$.[117]

Thus one sees that the movement that ended with the apparently seamless garment of "Mesopotamian religion" is in reality composed of several distinct strands. There is the popular piety which created indentifications between certain obviously similar deities, and there is the politically motivated theology which created new relationships, which were perhaps not so obvious, though they must have had a certain plausibility for the new theology to win acceptance. In some cases the new theology was accepted, and what began as politically motivated official theology ended, at a later period, in infiltrating the popular piety. The continuing symbiosis of Semites and Sumerians could only promote such a development. Nonetheless, it appears clear that the impetus for this process is largely dependent on the political ambitions of the Sargonides, before and even during whose time syncretism on the popular level was rather limited.

[1]Only a very few Semitic deities are attested in the Presargonic period outside of personal names. Mari provides the majority of them. Šamaš (CT 5, 2:8, n. 12146), Dagan (Edzard, CRRA XV, p. 53), Adad (ibid.), and Eštar all occur there, the latter under three different orthographies (cf. above, p. 100, n. 284). Eštar also occurs at Khafaje (OIP LIII, p. 147, 5). Su'en occurs in the Fara god list (SF, VAT 12626, i 5; 12644, obv. 1:5), in one text from Ur (UET 1, 11), and in two texts from his temple at Khafaje (OIP LVIII, 4-5). The god Zababa, whose origin is still difficult to determine (cf. the discussion above, pp. 55-56), also occurs in a text from Abū Ṣalābīkh and possibly in a Nippur text (R. D. Biggs, "The Abū Ṣalābīkh Tablets," JCS 20 [1966], p. 80; BE I, 108). One should also mention the dE-lum in the Fara god list (SF, VAT 12626, v 6), though one may question whether it is really Semitic.

From the Sargonic period there is also the god Ib(b)a'um (E. Douglas van Buren, "The God Ningizzida," Iraq I [1934], pl. IXb:1), which could possibly be interpreted as the earlier form of ibbû, "day of wrath" (CAD i, pp. 1-2).

[2]TCS III.

[3]Šulgi is obviously a later addition to the list.

[4]The linking of the cult centers of Akkad with those of Sumer, however, may reflect Sargon's attempt to lay a theological foundation for a united empire of Sumer and Akkad (cf. W. Hallo and J. van Dijk, The Exaltation of Inanna [New Haven: Yale University Press, 1968], pp. 9-10).

[5]Edmond Sollberger in his list of corrections to this text gives this name as da-zu and states that "the first two signs are damaged but certain" (UET VIII/2, p. 33). This reading, however, is suspect, since, if there is a god A-su (MDP 27, p. 54, nos. 153-154: il_3-a-su, il_3-il_3-su, il_3-su-x, cannot be taken as evidence for such a deity. These are to be read as personal names: Il-asû, Il-ilšu, and Ilšu-x. Cf. [I]l-su-ra-bi_2 [ibid., 152:1],

Il$_{3}$-SIPA, *^{d}UTU-SIPA*, and *^{d}UTU-il$_{3}$-ka* [*ibid.*, 155:1-3]), it is certainly a very minor deity and hardly seems appropriate in this list, whereas the pairing of Su'en and Šamaš is quite common in lists and is rather to be expected because of the parallel with the *PBS* text. At my request, therefore, Dr. Sollberger kindly recollated the passage. The preserved part of the second sign appears as , which I would complete so: ; cf. *UET* VIII/2, 13, iii' 5, for this form of the sign *EN*.

[6]This is very clear in one inscription which refers to the king as *mut ^{d}INANNA-an-nu-ni-tim*, "spouse of Eštar-annunītum" (F. Thureau-Dangin, "Rois de Kiš et rois d'Agadé," *RA* 9 [1912], p. 34, obv. ii). Here *^{d}INANNA-an-nu-ni-tim* must be a compound name because *annunītum* is inflected in the genitive case, showing that it is part of the construct chain governed by *mut*. Note also *AOF* 15, 95, n. 65: *a-[na] ^{d}INANNA-an-nu-ni-tim A.MU.RU*, "He dedicated to Eštar-annunītum."

[7]The verb is not attested as yet in Akkadian, but the root occurs in the nouns *anantum* and *anuntum*, "skirmish."

[8]Jean Bottéro explains this element as a Semiticized form of Sumerian *A.NUN.NA(K)*, "seed of the prince" (*ADS*, p. 55, n. 1), but such a derivation is difficult. When a Sumerian genitive construction of this sort passed over into Akkadian in the early period, the genitive element, though often not expressed in the Sumerian writing, almost always found expression in Akkadian as a double *k*. Thus on the analogy of *en$_{x}$.si.(ak)* > *iššiakkum* one would have expected *anunakkītum* (cf. Kramer, *CRRA* IX, p. 276, n. 19). There are also difficulties with the explanation which interprets the epithet as a feminine *nisbê* of *anuntum*, since the name is consistently written with the first *n* doubled, *an-nu-ni-tum*, through the Old Babylonian period.

[9]Gelb's reading of this Sumerian name as ^{d}Innin ("The Name of the Goddess Innin," *JNES* 19 [1960], pp. 72-79) is rejected by Jacobsen on the grounds that Gelb does not distinguish clearly enough between Sumerian and Akkadian material ("Ancient Mesopotamian Religion: The Central Concerns," *PAPS* 107/6 [1963], pp. 475-477, n. 6; = *Tammuz*, pp. 322-324, n. 6).

[10] This simple form hardly stands for another deity, since ^{d}*INANNA* occupies the same exalted position before An and Enlil in the titulary of Sargon as Eštar-annunītum does in Narām-Sîn's list (Hans Hirsch, "Die Inschriften der Könige von Agade," *AfO* [1965], p. 2), and both forms occur in *PBS* V, 36, without the slightest indication that two different goddesses are involved. This use of the Sumerian ideogram to write both the simple and compound form of the Akkadian name does imply the identification of Eštar (-annunītum) and Inanna, however. Cf. below, p. 153.

[11] *[Narām-Sîn] dannum šar Akkadê u kibrātim arba'im mut Eštar-annunītim muttarri ERIM.RI$_2$ (?) Il$_3$-a-ba$_4$*, "[Narām-Sîn], the strong one, the king of Akkad and the four regions, the man of Eštar-annunītum, the leader of the troops (?) of Il-aba" (F. Thureau-Dangin, "Rois de Kiš et rois d'Agadé," *RA* 9 [1912], p. 34, obv. ii); *Il$_3$-a-ba$_4$ u$_3$* ^{d}*INANNA* (*ibid*., rev. iii' 6-8); *[uššī bī]t Annunītim [u bī]t Il$_3$-a-ba$_4$ in KA$_2$.DINGIR^{ki} iškunu*, "(Year that Sar-kali-šarrī) laid [the foundations of the tem]ple of Annunītum [and of the tem]ple of Il-aba in *KA$_2$.DINGIR*" (*RTC* 118 rev.); *nūḫma* ^{d}*INANNA u Il$_3$-a-ba$_4$ lirāmāka*, "Calm down so that Eštar and Il-aba will love you" ("Keilschrift-texte nach Kopien von T. G. Pinches," *AfO* 13 [1939-41], p. 47, rev. ii 6, Old Babylonian Narām-Sîn legend).

[12] TH No. 41, *TCS* III.

[13] TH No. 40, *TCS* III. Ulmaš was apparently a district in Akkad (*CH* iv 45-52).

[14] *UET* 1, 276, ii 11-13.

[15] The term *MAŠKIM.GI$_4$* is just a variant writing for simple *MAŠKIM* according to Poebel (*PBS* IV, p. 180, n. 1). The *MAŠKIM* = *rābiṣum* (*ŠL* 295, 2) was originally a legally empowered agent of a court or of a high judicial or executive official, hence deputy or bailiff (Thorkild Jacobsen, "Sumerian Mythology: A Review Article," *JNES* 5 [1946], p. 130; = *Tammuz*, p. 108; Benno Landsberger, "Bücherbesprechungen," *ZA* nF 4 [1929], p. 276). If the *MAŠKIM.GI$_4$* is not identical with the *MAŠKIM*, it at least designates a related

official.

[16]*UET* 1, 274, ii 11-13.

[17]*in si-ip-ri$_2$ ^{d}INANNA* (*PBS* V, 36, rev. x + i?, ii, iii; duplicates given by Hans Hirsch in *AfO* 20, p. 20a; cf. *MAD* 3, p. 281). In each case the context is very difficult.

[18]*AfO* 20, p. 46, b9:49; *ibid*., p. 39, b2:46f., and b3:9-11, do not appear to be stereotyped formulas, but they are broken.

[19]*MDP* 14, II B, ii.

[20]*BE* I, 120 iii.

[21]*BE* I, 1:19.

[22]H. Winckler, "Eine neu veröffentlichte Inschrift eines unbekannten Königs," *ZA* 4 (1889), p. 406:19.

[23]*OIP* 14, 27:3.

[24]Cf. above, n. 11. The validity of this statement hinges on the interpretation of the word *mutum*, which this writer translated with the intentionally ambiguous "man" in footnote 11. The term normally means "husband," but it is also used in the sense of "warrior" (*AHw*, pp. 690-691), and one could argue for the translation "warrior of Eštar-annunītum" as a better parallel to "leader of the troops of Il-aba."

[25]*RTC* 118 rev.

[26]"Keilschrifttexte nach Kopien von T. G. Pinches," *AfO* 13 (1939-41), p. 46, obv. ii 6.

[27]*VAB* 4, p. 228:22.

[28]Thorkild Jacobsen, "Early Political Development in Mesopotamia," *ZA* nF 18 (1957), pp. 105-106 (= *Tammuz*, pp. 139-140).

[29]Sargon's (*AfO* 20, p. 38, b2:19-26) and *Narām-Sîn's* (*UET* 1, 275, i 30-ii 18) ascription of their conquest of the upper country to Dagan must be regarded in the same light.

[30]*PA$_4$(B).ŠEŠ AN* (*AfO* 20, p. 2). The variant orthography, *pa-šeš*, which occurs in the cruciform monument (F. Thureau-Dangin, "Notes assyriologiques,"

RA 7 [1910], p. 180, i 5), appears to confirm the reading pašīš(um) contrary to CAD a, I, p. 205a. Hallo and van Dijk interpret this title as meaning "older brother, brother-in-law of An" (The Exaltation of Inanna [New Haven: Yale University Press, 1968], pp. 7-8), but the older interpretation of the term as a priestly designation meaning "anointed one of An" seems much more solid. Cf. Johannes Renger, "Untersuchungen zum Priestertum der altbabylonischen Zeit," ZA nF 25 (1969), pp. 143-172.

[31]AfO 20, p. 38, b2:40-42; p. 39, b3:3-5.

[32]Thorkild Jacobsen in The Intellectual Adventure of Ancient Man, edited by Henri Frankfort (Chicago: University of Chicago Press, 1946), pp. 140-144. An inscription of Šar-kali-šarrī calls Enlil the king of the gods (Albrecht Goetze, "Akkad Dynasty Inscriptions From Nippur," JAOS 88 [1968], p. 55, 6N-T658, i 1-3, iii 8-10).

[33]Sargon attributes his victory over Uruk to Enlil's verdict (AfO 20, p. 44, b7:2-7). Sometimes he even credits Enlil with giving him the upper sea as well as the lower sea (AfO 20, p. 36, b1:1-12; p. 42, b6:48-58), but the title Sargon uses in these cases, LUGAL KALAM.MA^{ki}, "king of the land," is Sumerian and suggests that this version was for southern circulation. In the more expanded account of his northwestern conquests it is Dagan who gives him the upper country (AfO 20, p. 38, b2:17-26). Rīmuš also says that Enlil gave him the whole land including the upper sea and all the mountains (AfO, 20, p. 65-66, b9:1-16), but his area of operations appears to have been limited to Sumer (AfO 20, p. 52, b1:55-68) and Elam (AfO 20, p. 63, b7:36-48), so this may merely reflect his basically southern outlook. Maništušu says that Enlil made him grow great, named his name, and gave him the kingship (AfO 20, p. 71, b3:33-43), Narām-Sîn implied that the king holds the scepter for Enlil (UET 1, 276, ii 9-13), and Šar-kali-šarrī, the beloved son of Enlil (Albrecht Goetze, "Akkad Dynasty Inscriptions From Nippur," JAOS 88 [1968], p. 55, 6N-T658, i 5-ii 1), refers to himself as the king of the people of Enlil (BE I, 2:4-12; PBS XIII, 14:1-8; CTC 80:4-12).

[34]AfO 20, p. 41, b6:1-12; YOS 1, 10, Pl. L:15-18; F. Thureau-Dangin, "Notes assyriologiques," RA 11 (1914), p. 88:14-15.

[35]PBS IV, p. 219.

[36]Ibid.

[37]AfO 20, p. 44, b7:1-21.

[38]TMH V, 85ff.

[39]BE I, 1:7-11; 3:4-6.

[40]A. Falkenstein, "Fluch über Akkade," ZA nF 23 (1965), pp. 43-124.

[41]BE I, 5-6.

[42]AfO 20, p. 68, b12:1-14; F. Thureau-Dangin, "Notes assyriologiques," RA 8 (1911), p. 139; AfO 20, p. 71, b2:52-59; F. Thureau-Dangin, "Une inscription de Narām-Sîn," RA 8 (1911), p. 200, ii 5-9.

[43]AfO 20, p. 38, b2:43-45; passim.

[44]For this reading of the divine name see above, p. 34.

[45]See above, p. 147.

[46]Sargon attributed his victory over Uruk and the fifty governors to the weapon of Il-aba (PBS V, Pl xx, vii); and Old Babylonian Narām-Sîn legend also mentions him in the context of war ("Keilschrifttexte nach Kopien von T. G. Pinches," AfO 13 [1939-41], p. 47, rev. ii 6), and a kudurru from the time of Nabu-šum-iškun praises him as qar-du mug-da-aš-ru, "awesomely strong warrior" (VS 1, 36, i 17).

[47]AfO 20, p. 54, b1:59ff.; p. 63, b7:52ff.; p. 67, b11:11ff.; p. 70, b1:33ff.

[48]At Ešnunna one swore by the city god Tišpāk (MAD 3, p. 297).

[49]The only real support for this characterization is from the Old Babylonian period where the parties in a lawsuit are sent before Il-aba for judgment, and he is referred to as dayyān kittim, "judge of truth" (CT 29, 43:27; VAB 6, 218:27).

[50]Eštar was the personal goddess of the dynasty, or at least of Narām-Sîn, in si-ip-ri$_2$ ^{d}INANNA i?-li$_2$?-su, "by the command of Eštar, his personal

deity" (*AfO* 20, p. 20a, rev. 2:14-15).

[51] *PBS* V, Pl. xx, vi; *UET* 1, 275, ii 20f.

[52] *RTC* 118 rev.

[53] *MO* A 15:19.

[54] *ITT* I, 1246.

[55] *ITT* I, 1096.

[56] For this reading of *^{d}EN.ZU* see above, p. 50.

[57] TH No. 37, *TCS* III.

[58] See above, p. 112, n. 407.

[59] *UET* VIII, 12: *UET* 1, 23.

[60] *UET* 1, 10, Pl. D.

[61] *UET* 1, 275, iii-iv; 276, i 24.

[62] TH No. 12, *TCS* III.

[63] TH No. 37, *TCS* III.

[64] *PSBA* XXXI, p. 287.

[65] H. Winckler, "Eine new veröffentlichte Inschrift eines unbekannten Königs," *ZA* 4 (1889), p. 406:13ff.

[66] *CRAIB* (1899), p. 349.

[67] *OIP* LVIII, 4:2-3.

[68] *Ibid.*

[69] See above, p. 52.

[70] This identification is clear for the Sargonic period, as the writing *Be-li$_2$-^{d}UTU-si* for *Bēlī-šamšī* (cf. Ur III *^{d}Sul-gi-sa-am$_3$-si* = *^{d}Sul-gi-^{d}UTU-si*) indicates (*MAD* 3, p. 276).

[71] TH Nos. 13 and 38, *TCS* III.

[72] *CT* 32, 5b, 56631.

[73] *CT* 21, 1a.

[74] *AfO* 20, p. 54, bl:59, *passim*.

[75] *Ibid.*, p. 70, bl:33.

[76] *Ibid.*, p. 37, bl:37, *passim*.

[77] *Ibid.*, p. 54, bl:14, *passim*.

[78] *Ibid.*, p. 70, bl:44, *passim*.

[79] *UET* 1, 274, iii 19.

[80] *BE* I, 1:17, *passim*.

[81] *SGL* II, pp. 25-26.

[82] See above, p. 29.

[83] *UET* 1, 275, i 11-29.

[84] *EDSA*, Pl. 3, B.M. 114703.

[85] The two signs *MES* and *UM* cannot be distinguished in the Old Akkadian orthography, and there is a god *Ūm(um)* attested in the Old Akkadian period and later, see above, p. 55.

[86] *AfO* 20, p. 56, bl:1-6, *x E[N$_x$.SI] U[B.M]E^{ki} ^{d}U-um a$_2$-li$_2$-ik maḫ-ri$_2$-su*.

[87] Edzard, *WM*, p. 78.

[88] This was her character at least by the Old Babylonian period (*CH* R xxviii 50-69).

[89] TH No. 30, *TCS* III.

[90] E.g., *Aššur ilu ṣīru āšib Eḫursaĝkurkura Anu Enlil Ea u Ninmaḫ ilāni rabûti Igigu ša šamê Anunnaku ša erṣeti ina napḫarīšunu ezziš likkelmûšuma erreta marušta aggiš lirurūš*, "May Aššur, the exalted god who dwells in Eḫursaĝkurkura, Anu, Enlil, Ea, and Ninmaḫ, the great gods, the Igigu-gods of heaven (and) the Anunnaku-gods of earth, in their totality look upon him in anger and in wrath curse him with a grievous curse" (*AOB* 1, pp. 64-66:48-52); and *ilū rabûtum ša šamê u erṣetim Anunnaku ina napḫarīšunu šēd bītim libitti Ebabbara šuāti zērašu māssu ṣābīšu nišīšu u ummānšu erretam maruštam līrurū*, "May the great gods of heaven and earth, the Anunnaku in their totality, the protective deity of the temple (and) the brick-work of Ebabbara curse that man, his seed, his land, his troops, his people, and his army with a grievous curse" (*CH* R xxviii 70-84).

[91] He seems to have gained the title *šar mātim*, "king of the land" (*Syria* 12, pp. 164-168), from this role.

[92]*AfO* 20, p. 38, b2:17-35.

[93]*UET* 1, 275, i 30-iii 6.

[94]*AfO* 20, p. 44, b7:2-4.

[95]*UET* 1, 275, ii 29-iii 1.

[96]In the Atraḫasīs Epic Nintu and Mamma sometimes alternate (I 193, 198; cf. *CH* iii 28-35).

[97]*UET* 1, 276, ii 17-22.

[98]It is not clear whether the ideogram should be read in Akkadian as *Addu* or in Sumerian as *Iškur*. The other nature deities in the passage all occur under their Sumerian names, however.

[99]She has no genuine Akkadian counterpart as far as this writer knows.

[100]*^{d}IM u$_3$ ^{d}Nisaba [ku-]ru$_x$-ul!-su a [u]-si-si-ra* (*UET* 1, 276, ii 23-26; *AHw*, p. 513). What this curse appears to mean is that the rain will come and ruin the grain left in the field for drying before it can be gathered into the barns.

[101]Thorkild Jacobsen in *The Intellectual Adventure of Ancient Man*, edited by Henri Frankfort (Chicago: University of Chicago Press, 1946), pp. 146-148.

[102]Exactly what is not clear, *^{d}En-[ki] ID$_2$-su? A li-im-tu-ud* (*MAD* 2, p. 169; *AfO* 20, p. 78, 66:27-29; and note on p. 82).

[103]Ninḫursanga (Nintu) was the goddess of Keš (*TCS* III, TH No. 7), Adab (*TCS* III, TH No. 29), and ḪI.ZA (*TCS* III, TH No. 39); Nisaba was the goddess of Ereš (*TCS* III, TH No. 42); and Enki was god of Eridu (*TCS* III, TH No. 1).

[104]Maništušu did dedicate an offering to a rather obscure *^{d}Nin-a-a* (*CT* 21, 1, 91018).

[105]*HEI*, pp. 36-41.

[106]He mentions Šamaš, Enlil, Enki, Eštar, Su'en, and Ninḫursanga in the curse formula of one of his inscriptions (*MDP* IV, Pl. 2, iv 14-19) and Eštar and Ner(i)gal in another (*MDP* VI, 9, ii).

[107]The treaty mentions Il-aba (Walter Hinz, "Elams Vertrag mit Narām-Sîn von Akkade," *ZA* nF 24 [1967], p. 91, i 5) and Ninurta (i 18), one of the major

gods of Nippur (TCS III, TH No. 5), as well as an ^{d}Aš$_{3}$-ḫa-ra, who may be the same as Išḫara (ii 7).

[108]UET VIII, 11.

[109]TCS III, TH No. 33.

[110]UET 1, 274, iii 11; Edmond Sollberger, "Sur la chronologie des rois d'Ur et quelques problèmes connexes," AfO 17 (1954-56), p. 27.

[111]TCS III, TH No. 11.

[112]YOS 1, 10, Pl. 11:20-27.

[113]See above, pp. 52.

[114]*Ibid.*

[115]See above, p. 13, n. 23.

[116]W. W. Hallo and J. J. A. van Dijk, *The Exaltation of Inanna* (New Haven and London: Yale University Press, 1968), pp. 9-11.

[117]See above, p. 17, n. 77.

APPENDIX

OLD AMORITE ELEMENTS IN THE OLD SEMITIC PERSONAL NAMES

In the preceding discussion the writer has pointed to a number of elements in the personal names which can more easily be explained as Old Amorite than as Old Akkadian. These elements are listed here for the reader's convenience, but the detailed discussion of each element will be found under the first divine name with which it occurs. For the Old Amorite divine names see pp. 60-61.

1. Enpiq — This element occurs in the name Enpiq-Ḫanīš, and Buccellati explains it as a third person singular of the imperfect of the stem qatal from npq (AUP, p. 154). The Akkadian lexicon does not provide a reasonable alternative.

2. Īṣi (I-zi) — I-zi occurs as the verbal element in the names Īṣi-Anda, Īṣi-Dagan, Īṣi-Il, and Īṣi-ilum. It is a very popular element in Amorite names and is best explained as a G imperfect from *wḍʿ, "to go out" (APNMT, pp. 184-185).

3. Īmi (I-mi/me) — I-mi/me occurs as the verbal element in the names Īmi-Durul, Īmi-Erra, Īmi-Ilum, and Īmi-Šamaš. It cannot be explained from later Akkadian, and Goetze, at least, considers it Amorite ("Šakkanakkus of the Ur III Empire," JCS 17 [1963], p. 4, n. 34).

4. Išri — Iš-ri$_2$ occurs as the verbal element in the name Išri-DINGIR.

5. Izammar — I-za-mar occurs as the verbal element in the name Izammar-Tišpāk. The root would appear to be Amorite

*dmr, "to protect," since Akkadian zamāru, "to sing," does not seem as appropriate in the personal name.

6. Mēṣi — Me-ṣi, which occurs in the name Mēṣi-ilum, appears to be an Amorite causative participle from the root *wḍʿ.

7. Tarpa — Dar-pa occurs as the verbal element in the name Tarpa-iltum (DÍNGIR). It is either a third feminine singular or second masculine singular of the G imperfect from rpʾ, "to heal."

INDEX OF DIVINE NAMES

Ašar 16-17; 60.

Ašḫara 164, n. 107.

Ašratum 63, n. 6.

Aššur 28; 59; 78, n. 110; 162, n. 90.

ʿAštar-Kamos 39.

ʿAṯtar 39; 101, n. 285.

ʿAṯtart/ʿAštart 39-40; 101, n. 285; 102, n. 292.

Baal 75, n. 98; 117, n. 450.

Baal Z^{e}būb 119, n. 473.

Baba 17; 56-57; 133; 153.

Balīḫ 17; 58; 63, n. 9; 133.

Bēlet-ilī 44; 107, n. 355; 108, n. 358.

Bītum 17-18; 58.

Bunene 117, n. 461.

^{d}DA 13.

D/Ṭaban 18; 58; 73, n. 91.

Dagan 18-19; 43; 59-60; 106, nn. 342-343; 133; 151; 152; 155, n. 1.

Dibarra (see Erra).

Dingirmaḫ 44.

Durul 18-19; 58; 73, n. 91.

Ea (see 'Ay[y]a).

Ebiḫ (see Abiḫ).

'El 32-34; 95-96, nn. 230-234; 135.

'El-'eb 35.

^{d}E-lum 155, n. 1.

Enki 16; 21; 70, n. 57; 80, n. 119; 151; 153; 163, n. 106.

Enlil 15; 19; 21; 35; 41; 57; 75, nn. 98-99; 97; 246; 100, n. 279; 104, n. 319; 111, n. 393; 146; 148; 151-152; 153; 162, n. 90; 163, n. 106.

Enmešara 47.

^{d}EN.TI (see Abiḫ).

Era (see Erra).

Erra 15; 21-29; 40-41; 44; 53; 58; 60; 80, n. 117; 107, n. 355; 150; 153.

Erragal 22.

Eštar 5; 7; 10, n. 8; 26; 33; 35-36; 37-40; 41; 55-57; 60; 72, n. 77; 93, n. 218; 97, n. 246; 99, n. 269; 104, n. 319; 118, n. 465; 133-134; 137, n. 10; 147-148; 151-152; 153; 155, n. 1; 163, n. 106.

Eš$_4$-tar$_2$-BI-iš$_3$-ra-(a) 101, n. 284.

Eš$_4$-tar$_2$-ra-da-na 101, n. 284.

Eštar-Qa$_2$-ab-ra 101, n. 284.

Eštarat 100, n. 100.

Gazur 29; 58; 63, n. 9; 133.

^{d}GIR$_3$.RA 22; 29; 82, n. 140; 83, n. 149.

^{d}GIR$_3$.UNU.GAL (see Nergal).

Gir(r)a (see Erra).

Gula 17; 45; 108, n. 358.

^{d}Gutium 149.

Haddu/Hadad 14.

Ḫanīš 29-30; 59; 118, n. 465.

Ḫarīm 30, 58; 60; 133.

Ḫendursag̃a 41.

Ib(b)a'um 155, n. 1.

ID$_2$ (see Nāru).

Īda-il(um) 30-31; 60.

Igigu 162, n. 90.

Il 8; 31-34; 36; 60; 128; 133; 135.

Il-ab 34-35.

Il-aba 34-36; 60; 96, n. 233; 118, n. 465; 133-134; 146-149; 163, n. 107.

Ilbaba (see Zababa).

Illa 35; 59.

Illat 35; 59; 60.

Il-mār 35-36; 60.

Ilū 5; 134-135.

(Ilu)mer 36; 57; 59; 141, n. 43.

(Ilū)-Šibi 52-53; 60.

Ilū Sebettu 28; 37; 52-53.

dIM 151 (see Adad).

Inanna 12; 100, n. 281; 145-147; 149; 153.

dINANNA-ṣar$_x$-bat 100, n. 284.

dINANNA.UŠ 100, n. 284.

dINANNA.x.ZA.ZA 100, n. 284.

Innin (see Inanna).

Inin 5; 36; 60.

Ira (see Erra).

Išar 36-37; 60.

Išḫara 37; 57; 164, n. 107.

dIšḫuru 141, n. 43.

Iškur 153; 163, n. 98.

Ištar (see Estar).

Ištarān 40; 57; 60; 152.

Ištar-errakal 22.

Išum 24; 26; 40-41; 45; 60; 70, n. 63; 84, n. 157.

Ya/Ikrub-El 31.

Ya/Itūr-Mer 31; 106, n. 343.

dKA.DI (see Istarān).

Kar(r)um 41; 57.

Keš 41; 58; 63, n. 9.

Ki-ki 41; 57.

Kiti 41; 58; 63, n. 9.

Kittu 117, n. 461.

Kumarbi 75, n. 98; 76, n. 104.

Laba 42; 57.

Lā'im 42; 57.

Lamassum 42; 60.

Lubara (see Erra).

Lugal-du_6-ku_3-ga 47; 111, n. 393.

Lugal-marada(k) 152.

Malik 36; 42-43; 60; 133.

Māmētu 85, n. 159; 107, n. 355.

Mamma 8; 24; 36; 43-44; 60; 80, n. 117; 84-85, n. 159; 97, n. 246; 110, n. 388; 153.

Mammi (see Mamma).

Ma-na 45; 57.

Marduk 26; 54; 56; 73, n. 87; 75, n. 98; 111, n. 393.

Meme 41; 45; 60.

Mer (see [Ilu]mer).

Meslam 45; 58; 60.

Mot 117, n. 450.

Mummu 45; 57.

Nana 45, 110, n. 385.

Nanna 45-46; 60; 80, n. 117.

Nanna (moon god) 50; 112, n. 408; 153.

Nanše (see Nazi).

Nāru 46; 58; 60.

Nazi 46; 57.

Nergal 29; 41; 44; 45; 48; 81, n. 131; 85, n. 159; 87, n. 176; 98, n. 261; 105, nn.340, 342; 107, n. 355; 146; 150; 153; 163, n. 106.

Nikkal/Ningal 10, n. 9; 117, n. 461.

Nin-a-a 163, n. 104.

^{d}Nin-admu 14.

^{d}Nin-ag_2-ag_2 68, n. 42.

Ninazu 44; 54; 118, n. 462.

Ningirsu 14; 44, 56; 75, n. 98; 119, n. 477.

Ningubla 152.

Ninḫursaga 151; 153; 163, n. 106.

Nin'insina 17; 150.

Ninkarrak 45; 146; 150.

Ninlil 41; 47; 57; 75, n. 99; 104, n. 319.

Ninmaḫ 162, n. 90.

Ninmug 41; 45.

^{d}Nin-mul-si$_4$-a 68, n. 39.

^{d}Nin-š[um]? 47; 57.

^{d}Nin-TAG.TAG 47.

Nintu 44; 89, n. 207; 151; 153.

Nin-ul-šu-tag 68, n. 42.

Ninurta 54; 56; 83, n. 149; 119, n. 477; 163, n. 107.

Nisaba 47; 57; 151.

Nūnu 5; 47; 60.

Nūr-ilī 141, n. 43.

Padān 47-48; 58.

PI-li-ir 33; 48; 57.

Papsukkal 105, n. 336.

Rašap 48; 60.

Sataran (see Istarān).

Sebettu (see Ilū Sebettu).

Sin (see Su'en).

^{d}Sir/Sur-(ri)-ga$_2$-ga$_2$ 68, n. 39.

^{d}Sud-aga 68, n. 39.

Su'en 5-8; 35-36; 48-50; 57; 60; 70, n. 57; 73, n. 83; 78, n. 110; 97, n. 246; 117, n. 461; 133; 145-146; 149; 153; 155, n. 1; 156, n. 1; 163, n. 106.

Šadu 50; 57.

Šaḥr 51.

Šakan 50-51; 57.

Šala 19; 63, n. 6; 134.

Šalaš 19.

Šalim 51; 57.

Šalimtu 51.

Šamaš 5; 7; 14-15; 23; 33; 35; 51-52; 55; 57; 60; 63, n. 6; 79, n. 115; 91, n. 212; 94, n. 223; 104, n. 319; 117, n. 461; 118, n. 465; 146; 149; 153; 155, n. 1; 156, n. 5; 163, n. 106.

Šamuš 113-114, n. 421.

Šapš 52; 79, n. 115; 114, nn. 426, 429.

Šibi (see [Ilū]-Šibi).

Ši-laba 36; 147.

Šubula 41.

Šullat 30; 118, n. 465.

dTa-am-ba-a-a 117, n. 461.

Tešub 75, n. 98.

Tibar 5; 53; 58; 63, n. 9.

Tirum 53; 57.

Tišpāk 53-54; 59; 133; 160, n. 48.

Tutu 54; 57.

U_3 54-55; 57; 133.

dUB-na (see Nūnu).

Ulmaš 55; 58.

dU.MES (see Ūm[um])

Ūm(um) 55; 57; 133; 146; 150.

Uraš 75, n. 98

Ur(r)a (see Erra).

Date Due

APR 30 '86			
MAY 7 '86			